MANAGING VALUES

ETHICAL CHANGE IN ORGANISATIONS

Paul Griseri

First published 1998 by
MACMILLAN PRESS LTD
Houndmills, Basingstoke, Hampshire RG21 6XS
and London
Companies and representatives
throughout the world

ISBN 0–333–71106–8 hardcover
ISBN 0–333–71107–6 paperback

A catalogue record for this book is available
from the British Library.

This book is printed on paper suitable for recycling and
made from fully managed and sustained forest sources.

10 9 8 7 6 5 4 3 2 1
07 06 05 04 03 02 01 00 99 98

Editing and origination by
Aardvark Editorial, Mendham, Suffolk

Printed and bound in Great Britain by
Anthony Rowe Ltd
Chippenham, Wiltshire

Contents

Acknowledgements

I have been thinking about some of the subjects of this book for some years, and many people have unwittingly contributed to my ideas, sometimes through extended discussion, sometimes through stray comments made in desultory conversations which in one way or another have sparked something off. In one or two cases these go back decades rather than years. The list is probably endless, but I would like to mention in particular the following people: David Arbus, Tony Emerson, Maurice Green, David Langlois, Richard Pettinger, Tony Skillen, Norma Williams and Andrew Wright. Others have helped me in more formal ways. Most notable are Jon Groucutt, who read the manuscript in draft and made many helpful suggestions, and Chris Cherry, who was my doctoral supervisor at the University of Kent, now some ten years ago. I would like also to thank Sue Proudfoot who, as my line manager at London Guildhall University allowed me time to complete this book.

I am also grateful to a large number of individuals who have given up their time to be interviewed by me – as I have always guaranteed anonymity in all such interviews I can only here thank you all anonymously. In similar vein I would like to thank the very many participants of management programmes, most notably MBA (Master of Business Administration) students, who have discussed some of the ideas of this book in the course of their studies – sometimes quite inadvertently. You have all contributed to my thinking far more than you realise.

I am indebted to the editors of *Business Ethics: A European Review* for the permission to reproduce material originally published in that journal (October 1994) as part of Chapter 7.

My biggest thanks are to my partner Lyn Thompson, who has supported and encouraged me throughout the time I have been working on this, as indeed she always does. This is an immeasurable debt for which I am continually grateful.

Introduction

Business and values are inextricably linked. We have shared values, value driven, corporate values, professional ethics, managerial ethics, and other ideas, all pressing in their different ways on managers and organisations. A plethora of books and articles has been written on ethics and values in organisations. Most of these focus on the 'what' of value management. They look at what values should be adopted and implemented by organisations. They talk about honesty, integrity, equality and so on.

The great gap here is the 'how'? Managers talk about values and ethics – some practice these, many don't. Does this make the latter immoral? Given that we all have pretty good ideas about what we think is right or wrong, how is it that we don't all act ethically, every day, all day?

This book focuses on some of these 'how' questions. It is as much about behaviour in organisations as it is about ethics. It looks at the underlying issues surrounding changing the values and behaviour of individuals. By and large, the view outlined here is sceptical. The idea of managing values, in the sense of exercising a clear and planned influence over what people feel is right or wrong, is misplaced. I don't say you can't do it, but it is much more complex than would seem at first sight. Much of this book is devoted to showing the kinds of complexity. Each individual's value set is incredibly complicated, and idiosyncratic. Not only is it difficult to work out what someone really values, it is also difficult to make any sensible comparisons with other people's values. If we had vast reserves of time then we might be able to collect the information and make sense of it. But managing in organisations is a highly time-critical activity. So for all practical purposes the idea of managing values is not feasible. Most of the book explains and justifies this. A central part of the argument is that hearts and minds are impossible to disentangle. Values are a combination of cognitive and emotive factors.

So what can we do? Essentially the message here is that the most effective managerial strategy is to accept this practical limit to understanding values and treat it is a positive feature rather than as an absence of control. This has important implications. Many of the managerial presumptions relating to values need to be stood on their head. For example:

- unshared values are a vital resource to an organisation
- agreement is sometimes undesirable

- resistance to change should sometimes be encouraged
- often a person does not have a single stable value set at all
- we are mainly ignorant of the key elements of a person's values
- honesty is not always the best policy, sometimes it's not even a possible one
- we often don't really understand *our own* values
- rewarding good behaviour can undermine a person's values
- codes of ethics are often dead material, of questionable use for managing values
- 'business ethics' as a set of ideas is almost counterproductive.

These may seem challenging, but they all come out of a dispassionate analysis of values and motives. The key to the argument is that many ideas, such as eliminating resistance or sharing values, are mistakenly treated as paradigms, model solutions to organisational issues. In reality they all have limitations, based on context, information or other elements.

Very rarely here will you see statements that something is always or never appropriate. The vast amount of the text states that *sometimes* certain things may occur, or that other things *don't necessarily* happen. The approach I have adopted is to try to emphasise how varied the possibilities are, and hence how difficult it is for managers to make definitive choices on the narrow base of ideas which are proposed by organisational theorists. Of course, there are many situations in organisations where it is much better to do something, however poorly evidenced, than nothing. This point is recognised and accepted throughout the book. Nevertheless, it is important to acknowledge that it is acting without a firm footing. The worst error of all is to mistake a shot in the dark for a soundly based strategy.

A few words about the style of this book. The material comes from several sources. Much of it is derived from issues and incidents recounted to me by professional managers, in MBA or similar classes, in interviews, or in management development sessions. As a point of principle I always give complete confidentiality to material given to me, whether in writing, in an open discussion or in a private interview. So all cases and examples discussing individuals and organisations have been made into 'faction' – true in essence, and usually deriving from specific cases, but altered and amended to remove any trace of the real life source.

A large amount is also based on reflection and conceptualisation, relating to existing theoretical ideas but often going beyond these. Most of the book reflects a synthesis of material from these and other sources. Existing theories are mentioned and discussed, and novel ones are also introduced, but at all times the intention has been to keep a steady focus on the needs of practising managers.

I have tried to present ideas in terms as simple as is consistent with making a point clearly. This still can result in some difficult passages! But they are difficult because I have found it impossible to express them any more easily. Please bear in mind that the difficult material, as much as the easy, is there because it is important to the argument. There are no chapters or sections put there to fill the writing out. Everything in the main text is theory, argument, discussion, example. I have tried to pull specific material out into boxes. More extended explanations of the theories of other writers have been treated mainly in this way, as have some of the fuller cases and examples. This should help readers to follow the flow of the main text, and skip things they already know or move on when they feel they don't need further examples. As I hope this text will be useful on post-experience management programmes, such as the MBA, I have included questions at the end of each chapter for consideration and discussion.

A last point on style: values are heavily integrated into many other facets of people's personality and behaviour. The ideas in the book have to be laid out in a linear fashion, because that's how we read, but inevitably there are crossings over, and references forward and back. Some of these are flagged up, but some are implicit – indeed, readers might well see other connections that have not occurred to me.

The book is broken into three parts, each of which has four chapters. Part I, 'Understanding An Organisation's Values' presents the main elements of my scepticism over managing values. Chapter 1 argues that values are complex and so it's simply very difficult in practice to identify what values someone really holds. We begin to see the analysis of an individual's values as based on what they explicitly say *and* what may underlie this. Chapter 2 takes one example, that of honesty, and demonstrates how difficult it is to be sure what this really means for managerial action in concrete situations. Sometimes it is clear that all options for action may violate some of the concerns relating to honesty. Chapter 3 explores further the idea of under-standing values, this time from the point of view of how a manager can differentiate between recognising what other people value as opposed to evaluating their behaviour on his or her own values. How far can we set aside our own preconceptions and look afresh at other people's views? Chapter 4 looks more directly at the idea of shared values, and indicates the potential dangers with this.

Part II, 'Agreeing and Changing Values' focuses on some of the elements relevant to value change. Chapter 5, 'Personal Moral Skills' looks at the capabilities within an individual for change. In Chapter 6 'Value Rigidity' we examine in more detail the difference between what someone says they value and what underlies this. People's value sets start to look something like an iceberg, with a small visible set of explicit values and a large and gener-ally unexplored underlying complex. We also see the kinds of resistance

1 *Discovering People's Values*

1.1 Perceiving values – an example

Consider Case 1.1 below.

CASE 1.1   **The Unsympathetic Manager**

Jacqui Abilene works in the telephone banking division of a large retail bank. She is responsible for a group of twelve staff. There is an equal opportunities policy, which explicitly prohibits any form of sexual discrimination and identifies abuse, verbal or physical, as a potentially sackable offence. Despite this, the bank is very male-dominated in numbers, in general behaviour and in the distribution of managerial posts, so that except for Jacqui and her line manager, Jessica, all the other women in the department are in first-line positions. The environment is very hectic, and the general focus of staff on getting the job done quickly means that there is often not much time for courtesy and politeness – this is accepted generally as the culture of the bank. One day Jacqui got into a dispute with another of the telephone supervisors in the department. He proceeded to lose his temper and abused Jacqui verbally, calling her 'bitch' and 'stupid cow', and shouting so loudly that some customers on the other end of the phone complained. In particular he went on about how incompetent women were at the job and how it was better left to men to do the managing, and the women should stay as basic workers. 'They all go off and have babies at some point anyway.' Jacqui went to see Jessica, who was not at all sympathetic. 'Yes, of course it's outrageous, but this is a bank. What do you expect? You've been here long enough to know it doesn't make any difference complaining about it. If anything it makes it worse. I would put it behind you and get on with the job. I'll have a word with him but there's no point in starting a disciplinary action. Senior management wouldn't take any notice.'

Jacqui went back to her team, who asked what had happened. She simply said 'Nothing – Jessica doesn't give a damn for women, she's virtually an honorary man herself, attitudes and all.'

Clearly something odd is at work here – behaviour that is clearly at variance with the explicit policy of the bank is allowed to stand without any significant attempt to change it, at least by the line manager. The point I want to raise here, though, is that Jacqui assumes something about Jessica's *values*. She explains to herself and her team what happened by presuming that Jessica is not interested in gender equality. This of course *may* be the case. But equally, there may be other explanations. For example, Jessica may genuinely believe that any complaint is unlikely to succeed, or she may feel that the supervisor at fault is particularly powerful, or she may feel that Jacqui is not entirely blameless, and so on. There are many possible explanations – maybe only one is correct, but it is not clear in the circumstances which it is, and is unlikely to be so without a serious investigation.

This is the key issue of this chapter. Many management writers assume that, even though we might disagree about what is right or wrong, the issue of *what an individual believes* is reasonably straightforward – just look at their behaviour. It is then a quick step to conclude that the essential tasks of managing the values of an organisation are: (a) to discover what the values of the staff are; and then (b) to do what is necessary for the values of the staff to become more aligned with the values that management wish to promote.

Thus, Charles McCoy describes the central task of management as that of managing values and their environment, whilst in a similar vein Richard Pascale and Anthony Athos state 'An organisation's super-ordinate goals emerge, in part, from leadership which *instils values* through clarity and obsessive focus. A firms' history also contributes to its enduring value system.... New members are exposed to the common history and acquire insight into some of the subtler aspects of their company.' Interestingly, in a more recent article by R. and L. Lindsay, the same idea, of instilling values, figures as a crucial issue for effective management of behaviour.[1]

Put so simply, this seems unobjectionable. But it reflects a hugely optimistic assumption: that it is possible for a manager to get a clear view about the values and attitudes of the workforce. I am not going to say that this is impossible; I do want to suggest, however, that there are significant difficulties to overcome before anyone, manager or no, could be reasonably confident that they had an accurate estimate of the values of individuals or groups of people at work.

Consider the following example: The company has been through a difficult time. A recovery plan has been put into operation, based on a wide-sweeping restructuring exercise, which involved over 30 per cent redundancies, increased responsibilities for team leaders, loss of shift allowances for many staff and loss of promotion opportunities for many middle and junior managers. The company has survived but the perception amongst senior management is that morale is on the floor. So motivation consultants are brought in. They carry out a survey, using a custom-designed questionnaire and in-depth interviews (using only trained individuals) and conclude that the main difficulty is job insecurity. A programme of counselling and morale-building is put into place, with social awaydays, bonding exercises, increased contact between management and staff, and statements from the chief executive that 'all the bad times are behind us now'. Six months later the CEO reports to the board that morale has risen significantly, staff are more committed and more satisfied, and the consultancy exercise did the company a great deal of good.

While not based on any single example, this is not an uncommon scenario from the early 1990s. Clearly one could cite examples where such consultancy exercises did no good whatsoever. That is interesting (and a little disappointing for consultants!) but beside the point here. What I want to do is question how far the CEO really knows that morale had improved as a result of this measure.

There are at least three aspects of the case that can be questioned in this respect:

- perception of the situation by the CEO
- perception and response by the staff
- assumptions concerning the underlying intentions and beliefs of the staff.

One could also question the possible influence that the CEO may have had on the consultants. Did they feed back to the CEO the answer which s/he had already planted in their minds? We shall not go into this here, but it adds a further element of uncertainty to the situation.

Perception of the CEO
This is the most obvious way in which the CEO's view may be suspect. Senior managerial optimism is notorious. In interviews with professional staff, in classroom discussions with part-time MBA students (working as managers whilst they study), in meetings with professional consultants, and in discussion with other managers, the following story (or variants of it) has been recounted to me: senior management have brightly described the new corporate mission, or philosophy, or values statements; further down the line, middle managers have been consulted about these but expressed scepticism as to their importance; junior managers and team leaders have been simply aware of them, or been drilled to recite them by heart, and dismissed them as a fad, whilst front-line staff, the ones meeting the public, making the chocolate bars, fitting the doors or whatever, have been utterly unimpressed or totally ignorant. Moral: senior staff, and the strategic plans on which they often lavish so much attention, can easily be far more remote than they realise.

Perception and response by the staff

Another complicating factor is that staff will modify and adjust their responses, both to senior staff and to consultants and researchers, in the light of what they expect will result. The Hawthorne Effect is alive and with us[2] – if the workforce has been through a sequence of job losses, and is not directly informed of the further intentions of senior management, they may suspect that there are more job losses on the way. From this they may conclude that the best way to keep their job will be to appear knowledgeable and committed to the new deal. In other words, in the absence of a convincing and authoritative explanation about the current situation, people will supply their own, which may well be pessimistic, and act accordingly. So staff may well conceal their true views from senior management, or dam up the expression of their real feelings, to be released only in 'safe' collectivised situations such as trade union disputes (where an individual is unlikely to be victimised).

Assumptions about underlying beliefs

The two issues mentioned above are relatively straightforward. Although it may be difficult to know they have occurred, when they *are* identified certain kinds of remedial action can be applied that have a good chance of success. For example, if it becomes clear that people are withholding their true views because of fear of being selected for future redundancy, senior management can clarify the situation by releasing details about the state of the business. Alternatively, if senior management have become too remote then a process of breaking down the barriers can be adopted – adopting approaches such as single status facilities, or MBWA (management by walking about).

It is more difficult when management assume that their staff hold specific intentions or values. In the first two cases, discussed above, the issue has been that the management simply have the wrong beliefs about what staff think. In *this* case it is about having the wrong mindset. Box 1.1 outlines a classic model of leadership originally propounded some decades ago, by Douglas McGregor, which gives some flavour of this difficulty.[3]

BOX 1.1   **Theory X and Theory Y**

McGregor's model holds that managers' attitudes can be measured on a scale between two extreme views on staff –

Theory X, the ultra-autocratic view, that staff are lazy, solely motivated by financial gain, and take no interest or initiative in their work.

Theory Y, the ultra-liberal view, that staff are spontaneous, motivated people who are systematically drained of this by an inflexible work structure.

If a manager tends towards one of these extremes, s/he is going to interpret people's behaviour in those terms. So an autocratic manager who sees contented staff may well jump to the conclusion that they have somehow 'got one over' on the organisation. Equally, a more liberal manager might interpret the same behaviour as reflecting the 'true' underlying attitudes of the staff towards work.

So we don't interpret other people's values in a purely neutral way – our own beliefs and values prejudice us one way or another. Consider the individual relationships between a manager and an employee, for example. If there have been serious difficulties in the past, this is likely to create a certain mindset in the manager, an expectation that further problems will occur in the future. This then becomes a prejudice – a pre-judging of the employee's behaviour in the light of what has happened in the past. So if the employee becomes more motivated it is difficult for the manager to recognise this at all, and even when he does recognise it, he may well interpret the causes of this in terms of his own prejudice ('Oh Bob, yes he's obviously up to something, I haven't had a peep out of him for ages.'). Similarly, the history of employee relations in a particular organisation will tend to push individual managers to draw certain kinds of conclusion about the reactions of staff. So, where an organisation has enjoyed a relatively calm period of industrial relations, the manager is more likely to perceive the situation in terms of employee satisfaction than where there has been a significant level of strife, when an assumption may be made that apparent satisfaction conceals discontent.

1.2   Same act – different intentions

In Section 1.1, we saw three different ways in which a manager might fail to recognise what someone's true values are. This section will explore further the reasons why people's real values and intentions are rather harder to gauge than is often supposed. But first we need to look at motivation.

Many models of motivation at work operate on the assumption displayed in Figure 1.1 below.

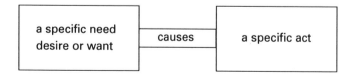

Figure 1.1   The causal model of motivation

some or most of the initial motives and needs. This is why I say that motivation is the process of finding a solution to the problem of satisfying diverse motives. Because of this interplay, motivation involves both heart and mind. Feelings and emotions are essentially bound to thoughts and beliefs in this process. *Values are both emotive and intellectual*. This is a central issue, which we shall revisit several times in later chapters.

We can now begin to see why the task of working out what members of an organisation actually value is more complex than one might suppose. We may well be aware that there will be a variety of different inclinations and needs underlying someone's behaviour, even though we may have only a faint idea about some of these. We are less likely to understand their own problem-solving resources – indeed, these are likely to fluctuate wildly in different circumstances. For example, in one situation someone may look at things in an equality-based way, and thus resolve a problem about what to do in the light of their own perception of what they see as fair for themselves. In another situation, though, they may consider all the possible consequences and make a judgement based on what value they give to all of these. In yet another situation, the person may feel such intensity of feeling that a particular feature of the situation assumes an overriding importance. And there are clearly other possibilities.

What this means is that a given item of behaviour evinced by two different people, even in apparently similar circumstances, will reflect their own idiosyncratic ways of blending their own personal motivational components. *The same behaviour may have entirely different roots*. Expressed thus it may seem quite obvious – unfortunately much management theory has had the destructive effect of replacing the complexity of real life with the oversimplicity of models; we need to rediscover that management is often about using our existing personal intuitions, flawed as they may be.

So the same act may arise from different needs, and may be arrived at by different thought processes. The line manager, let us call him/her W, faced with Mary's anger needs to be aware that it is a different animal from the angers of each of her colleagues, and whilst W may often be able to assuage most of these by one single response, s/he may not always be able to do so. Even when W does win over all members of the team, they may each, individually, be won over for quite different reasons.

So people's attitudes, values and motives are too complex for a manager to be very sure of why someone acted in a certain way at a certain time. Where we are talking about *values*, however, there is a particular kind of variance in motives and processes that needs to be emphasised. Two people may both express outrage at discovering that their line manager has acted immorally, say by purchasing textiles produced by child labour in a distant country. One, however, may do so from a *deontological* perspective – that one should never exploit child labour no matter what the circumstances. The other may condemn it from a *consequentialist* perspective – that on balance in these circumstances it was not necessary to do this. These terms are explained in Box 1.2. We shall return later to individual's personal moral codes – all I am doing here is pointing out how they can lead people to similar positions from quite different starting points.

BOX 1.2   **Two Kinds of Value**

Deontology – the idea that an action is good or bad in itself, irrespective of what the consequences of it may be. So someone might say 'Lying's wrong, always'.

Consequentialism – the idea that an action has to be judged in terms of what its effects are. Someone with this view might say 'It's OK to lie if it prevents some harm befalling someone'.

Philosophers often treat these as absolute positions, but in practice many people have deontological views about some things, and consequential views about others.

1.3   Evidence of people's values

Faced with all this, one might question how we can ever know much about other people's values. Clearly we can and we do. The point about the argument of the last section is really to emphasise how unsatisfactory the unidimensional approaches to motives and reasons are. In this and the next section we shall investigate how a manager might make use of diverse sources of information to improve his understanding of an individual's motives and values. This is a central issue for the question of how values might be managed. The perception of the manager is crucial at both the start and the end of any intervention on organisational values. At the start, it is a manager's estimate of the values of staff that initiates any activity relating to values. Equally, at the end, following any activity of this sort, it is the perception of the manager that determines whether it has achieved the desired result or not.

So the question arises concerning how good a manager might be at identifying the values of her staff. If we return to the example of Mary and her line manager, it is obvious that the line manager may be more or less competent at reading Mary's views. Four clusters of attitudes and qualities that assist the line manager in this can be identified:

attitude to self:
- ability to be distanced from own emotions
- recognition of own personal standpoints and perspectives

attitude to analysis:
- determination to look beyond the face value of the scenario
- determination not to rest on past experience as the prime model for present behaviour

recognition of alternatives:
- ability to imagine alternative perceptions
- ability to acknowledge alternative reactions, even when one cannot empathise with them

attitude to others:
- ability to empathise with others
- ability to balance perception of the team as a whole with their perceptions of those individuals who go to make it up.

We might try to treat the above as a set of measures of a manager's ability to understand other people. Ultimately, however, this would not be much use. Measuring means assessing quantifiable levels or degrees of ability, presented either in rough, quasi-quantitative terms such as 'much' or 'hardly at all', or more precisely as percentages, proportions or other numeric forms. But these obscure more than they illuminate, for what is relevant to this discussion is less a matter of *how far* an individual was able to, say, empathise with others, than it is a question of the *specific ways* in which they might, and how these might interact with other attitudes and qualities in the above list. We shall look later in this chapter at formalised methods of measuring values.

How might a manager's abilities and attitudes, as listed above, play a part in his perception of the motives and values of one of his team? At least three different overarching types of scenario can be distinguished:

(a) the manager may exhibit one of the four clusters outlined above to so great an extent that it overcomes any limitations in the others
(b) a distinctive capability in one or two of the areas may pull other attitudes along
(c) some or many of the above capabilities may combine to form the manager's views.

We shall examine in detail an example of (b) in Chapter 7 when we look at the effects of the ideas of consistency and sympathy on people's values. Two brief examples may help illustrate the way in which managers' attitudes, as identified above, will affect their overall perception of the values and motivation of their staff. First, consider an example of case (a): managers who adopt a highly analytical approach to their interactions with others. Even though they may not be particularly disposed to empathise with members of their team over an issue such as working unsocial hours, their drive to examine all aspects of a situation afresh, without relying on previous experience, may lead them to analyse and then recognise the perspectives of members of their team. Almost certainly at first this would be an intellectual recognition, but as time went on it is conceivable that this would result in a genuine empathy – a feeling, rather than merely a conceptual acceptance.

Consider now a second example, one that exemplifies case (c) above. A supervisor has worked with a particular team for some years, and he feels that he knows them fairly well – in doing so, he implicitly assumes that he would know what motivates them and what their underlying values are. As a result of the introduction of a 360 degree appraisal system, he receives feedback on himself from the team for the first time. Almost always this brings surprises about how one is privately perceived. The response of the manager, and how he will read his team in the future, will involve a process of him dealing with several factors – often he may have to dispel any resentment where the team members have disliked some of this acts (ability to distance oneself from emotions), then very likely he will need to re-evaluate how others might interpret his actions (ability to imagine alternative perceptions), finally leading to an increased understanding of the variety of responses made by different individual team members (ability to balance perception of the team and perception of its constituent members).

This analysis indicates how a manager's attitudes may function as resources for helping her recognise the values of her staff. It also demonstrates how the manager may make use of these resources in at least three overall ways, as illustrated by the last two examples. This fleshes out the point made earlier that understanding both values and motives of the workforce involves putting together evidence from various sources. As the above discussion indicates however, it can involve different *ways* of putting these together. But there is a down side to this – a manager's attitudes and perceptions are just as likely to take him away from the values of his staff.

I can hear someone balking at all this: 'This is all very well, but how does it help the practising manager with ethical change?' It helps in three ways. First, it underlines the point that the process of understanding people's values is no simple affair. Over and above straightforward factual issues about what someone may or may not say or do (which themselves on occasion can be difficult to establish) there are deeper problems relating to what a manager is to make of an individual's intentions. In this respect the image of a manager 'reading' or 'interpreting' someone's behaviour can be misleading, for that suggests a single line of evidence. In reality one is linking material from various sources, and in various ways. Hence it may be more appropriate to talk about a manager *constructing* a view of the values of their staff from their behaviour (and indeed the staff carrying out a parallel process of constructing the values of the manager).

Second, it can provide a basis, not so much for carrying out evaluation of ethical change processes, but more for developing an underpinning critique of methods of training and evaluation in this area. It is commonplace in the USA and the UK for organisations to carry out employee awareness programmes in areas such as customer care, or equal opportunities. Standard training practice is to develop a series of behavioural outcomes by which the awareness programme may be measured (one example that I came across recently: 'On successful completion of the programme, participants should be able to describe the key difficulties facing ethnic minorities in gaining employment commensurate with their qualifications and abilities'). As we have seen, the intention behind behaviour is critical. Describing difficulties of disadvantaged groups may be something that comes out of a variety of underlying values – not the least of which may be the desire not to be seen as racist, whatever the person's real views. One equal opportunities trainer said, in conversation with me, that he felt that he was getting through only when there was an increased level of conflict within the training group, because it was only then that people were revealing their true feelings. Overt agreement, whilst in general a highly desirable part of management and development, can be, in this type of issue, a significant barrier to progress.

Third, this analysis implies that a new kind of approach to management development is necessary. The direct expression of people's attitudes is always going to be a critical factor in the development of employee awareness, but an overlooked critical factor is the ability of a manager to *recognise* people's true values and abilities. In other words, there is a significant need to develop managers' faculties of perception, via the component attitudes mentioned earlier, such as distancing oneself from one's emotions, and so on. Whilst this has often been recognised as a feature of management development, it has usually been presented as an inner directed matter, that is one which will help a manager manage themselves.[8] What is being argued here is that it will also be critical in helping managers to understand, and therefore manage, others.

So values are themselves complex, but also there is the further degree of complexity and uncertainty – how able is the manager to interpret the values of a given employee accurately? As we see, there is a structure to this ability, which suggests that some managers will be better with some employees, and others will be better with different employees. So understanding the values of members of an organisation is intrinsically a two-way process – a dialogue as much as an observation.

1.4   Using evidence of others' values

Having outlined in the previous section some structural elements affecting how a manager may depict or interpret the values and motives of her staff, using primarily fictionalised examples,9 I shall discuss now an actual case related to me during a confidential interview, and indicate how the above material relates to it.

The individual concerned was a middle manager who agreed to participate in a research interview, during which we discussed certain ethical aspects of decision-making. She worked in a mid-sized organisation, with a responsibility both for a team and for certain strategic elements that crossed over departmental divisions. We discussed her change of attitude and ethical orientation as she had moved through several promotions. She acknowledged that she had, despite previous attitudes, become 'more management orientated' in her perceptions of events, more inclined to see senior management's point of view. She added, however, 'it's changed how I deal with some of my colleagues, particularly the ones who haven't been promoted as far as I have.' When questioned further about this she added 'I used to just react to them, like I would the comments of a friend – in fact some of them are my friends – but now I take a more detached approach. I'm always trying to explain it to myself, put it into context, like I'm trying to find an interpretation of what they're saying, as if I can't take it at face value any more.'

There are three elements of this case that I want to focus on:

- the detachment was a source of unease – as a kind of loss of intimacy
- the detachment was seen as a consequence of moving up the managerial ladder
- the resultant attitude was one she expressed as trying to find an interpretation.

The first point to be made about this is almost an incidental one, that detachment can have a negative as well as positive flavour. But, on the analysis given in the previous section, the explanation for this is that an intention to look beyond past experience, and an ability to acknowledge alternative points of view, had been undermined by a loss of *empathy* towards different perceptions. This would tend to look rather like case (a) from Section 1.3 – that is, where a single attitude had overcome others.

Second, managerial progression is often seen as a cause of attitude change. It is common to see the media talk of 'managerialism' as a set of beliefs and attitudes. This may lead individuals to associate such a set of attitudes with managerial roles, and therefore when they take up such a role they come to believe that the possession of 'managerial' attitudes is required of them. Sometimes this can be explained away as sheer self-orientation: someone may assume certain attitudes and behaviours because it is seen as appropriate for the role. Arguably, French managers will tend to vote Gaullist, and French workers tend to vote socialist or communist. Hence the newly promoted 'cadre' may feel a temptation to vote that way because it's the thing managers do. This is, however, probably less frequent than is often supposed by those who remain in the front line of production or service delivery. Often a newly promoted manager changes his attitude as a result of being in contact with a different range of organisational phenomena (note, *different* range, not necessarily a *greater* range; as indicated earlier, what is gained in terms of strategic knowledge and understanding is often at the expense of operational knowledge and personal empathy). With this change in experiences comes also a new range of potential inferences, beliefs and values.

The third point to make about the case is the most important – that the manager talked of 'trying to find' an interpretation for the behaviour of her staff. Why would someone feel that she has to *look* for an interpretation of people whom she already knows well? One aspect of this is simply that she has rejected her earlier views on their behaviour. Another is that she hasn't yet found a satisfactory replacement perspective. Look now at the contrast she expresses with the past – 'I used to just react to them.' One nuance here is that the present situation is no longer one of reaction but more a case of *intellection* – deliberated, conscious, interpretation. This is borne out by her comment about trying to explain things to herself.

But why shouldn't the manager just accept that because she was distanced from former colleagues, she no longer understood them as well as she used to? Perhaps to an extent she did, but clearly her response indicated that she was not completely satisfied to leave it at this. One aspect of this is probably a form of *cognitive dissonance*.[10] As we shall consider in Chapter 11, just as nature abhors a vacuum, so the human mind abhors the unexplained – if we don't have a good explanation, we will substitute a weaker, unusual or less justified one. In this case, the manager seemed to be seeking an explanation in terms of the past. Link this back to the sense that she had lost something, which for want of a better term we shall call empathy. I would suggest that the manager is seeking to recreate her understanding, not replace it with something entirely new. So it is less a case of reframing or remodelling, which implies that a fresh 'frame' or model is used, so much as recasting within an existing framework. The underlying paradigm for this is essentially *archaeological*. We shall look at this in detail in the following section.

One final point about this manager's views is important to note. It is commonly supposed that loss is undesirable. That is, other things being equal it is preferable not to feel that one has lost something. I want to suggest that there are times when this is not only acceptable but positively desirable.

Ellen Langer talks of the negative effects of taking things for granted, which she calls 'mindlessness'. [11] In contrast, she points out how creativity and greater understanding can often be stimulated by focusing on what one has always accepted and regarding it as no longer so certain. The manager who felt she had lost an empathy with her former colleagues may now have gained something: the opportunity to consider each of them afresh and treat them as new characters, to become re-acquainted with. Sometimes the past is not foreign enough – familiarity can be a barrier to understanding.

1.5   The manager as archaeologist

In the previous section we examined a single case of how a manager tried to understand the underlying attitudes and values of individuals. We are beginning to see that the task of identifying the values of organisation members is not one of simple observation – there is a two-way aspect to the process. Having looked at the capability of a manager to develop an appropriate interpretation of the values of a member of her staff, I want now to examine some more general aspects of this.

The key metaphors relevant to how managers understand – or misunderstand – the values of their staff are those of archaeology and anthropology. The archaeological one reflects the idea that some of the key building blocks of someone's values are buried deeply within an individual's consciousness. In other words, critically important aspects of someone's overall network of beliefs and attitudes lie beneath the explicit surface. These aspects may include:

- different experiences
- different personal patterns of logic (not all of which might be valid)
- certain characteristic expressions and behaviours that have become habitual [12]
- acts of self-interpretation and self-justification.

This accretion of attitudes does not proceed uniformly, however. The image of an orderly overlaying of one set of materials on top of another, sedimentary rock-style, oversimplifies human development. Even if one considers just one aspect of that development – adult learning in organisational settings – the pattern of change is not at all an orderly one. As Alan Mumford pointed out some years ago, learning is compulsive. [13] We learn things as they come along, not in a systematic way (unless of course we happen to be following a systematic programme of learning). So there is no simple set of levels of learning that come one after another. Certain other implications of this will be explored in Chapter 11.

The messiness of how we acquire attitudes and beliefs is reflected to an extent in the idea of an archaeological dig. Buried amongst a large amount of less significant material which comprise the mental state of an individual, there are key items such as memories of a forceful experience here, or of a penetrating thought there, an illuminating comment elsewhere. These fan out in their influence, and can often be conjoined in a pattern of elements. We may judge someone to be slightly discriminating against women on the basis of a relatively small number of incidents and comments. In making that judgement, we assemble these with our own beliefs, both about that person and about people in general. In other words, we *construct* a view. This squares with the analysis given in the previous section, of a manager trying to find a context for the views of her team.

This process is not solely 'archaeological', in the sense of trying to find and assemble parts of someone's overall value system. It also finds more literal parallels with anthropology. For the anthropologist is confronted with a set of practices displayed by a social group, be they adolescents in New York or elders in New Guinea, and has the problem of trying to give them some meaning. In essence this always includes an element of comparison, against norms of what is possible for human beings, and what kinds of connection are usual within social groups. The central role of the observer, and the question mark over whether they can ever be truly independent, has been long recognised in this field. But this is strongly paralleled in the area of understanding between individuals, even within the same social group. The variety of elements underlying individual values is often gravely under-recognised. For example, the following are a few of the factors that influence what values an individual holds:

- whether they perceive a certain issue in deontological or consequentialist terms
- what factual beliefs they hold, and what emotional tone those beliefs hold for them
- what they happen to remember at a particular time about past experiences
- what mood they happen to be in at the time, which would in turn reflect experiences they have had in the immediate past.

We will examine these and other elements of people's values in Chapters 6 and 8. One cannot say definitively *how important* a factor each of these is. The point is, however, that one cannot detach some aspects of someone's behaviour and say that these reflect what is basic, important and fundamental whilst other parts are more superficial and hence less important. People's value systems are complex, and are often surprisingly volatile – for

1.7   Moral realities and moral stories

The argument of this chapter has been essentially pessimistic – that the under-standing of an individual's values is far less straightforward than it might seem at first sight. In some respects the conclusions stretch further than this, for they imply that we should take a broader view, both of motivation in particular and of understanding personality in general. The last point to be made here – though there will be reference back to it several times in later chapters – is one about the idea of moral and ethical views as a form of reality.

Several times in earlier sections we have encountered the suggestion that individuals have actively to see someone's behaviour in a certain light. The case of the line manager, trying to see her staff in a certain way, exemplifies this particularly well. This could be seen as an attempt to present business ethics in a 'post-modern' light, as an attempt to portray ethical views as essentially *constructed*. Clearly, there is an upshot of this – why should we construct something one way rather than another? What is the status of conflicting ethical standpoints – are they equally valid? Are ethical judge-ments, in business as elsewhere, a kind of *story* we tell? If so, what founda-tion do they have? As one writer puts it 'No meaning exists beyond language. ... Knowledge... evaporates, to be reconstituted as constructed surfaces... .' [18]

To answer this properly would require a lengthy deviation into moral philosophy (beyond the excursus we have already made). I am not entirely unsympathetic to this approach, but there are three important qualifications I would wish to make. First, 'constructed' can admit of various interpreta-tions – people certainly do not choose their moral views in any obvious sense, nor do they 'just' tell a story about their feelings and opinions. Second, the main part of this chapter has been about the difficulties of establishing what someone's motives and views may be. This does not mean that no knowledge about values is to be trusted, any more than the diffi-culties over predicting the weather accurately should lead us to think that weather is a 'construction'. Third, even if there is any substance to the idea of ethics as having a constructed, story-like element, this should not lead people to dismiss ethical views or disagreements. It should lead people, front-line workers and managers alike, to take a more sensitive approach to those differences, and recognise that there may be more in someone's posi-tion than we had previously cared to think.

1.8 Summary

In this chapter we have primarily looked at the difficulties of understanding the moral views and motives of other people. This is a general issue, but we have kept the discussion focused for the most part on the issue of how far a manager can understand the views of her or his staff. Having looked critically at approaches to motivation, we have examined the problems of interpreting people's statements and behaviour. What comes out of this is that understanding values is a two-way process – the kind of manager doing the interpretation is as important as the kind of individual whose values are being considered. Along the way we have discussed critically the value of psychometrics and the use of non-directive interviewers as a means of discovering people's values.

At times some abstract stuff! In the following chapter we shall take a more specific look at one particular aspect of someone's ethics – their approach to honesty at work. This should put more flesh on the bones of this chapter. The reader is also advised to work through the following questions, as a way of gaining a further perspective on what has been discussed.

Questions

You may well find it useful to write down your answers to these, at least in brief, and then discuss them with someone else.

A Consider someone with whom you have worked over the last year or so. Try to identify what their deepest values might be. Now ask yourself what, in your experience of this person, your view is based on. How compatible is the latter with other value systems?

B Reflect on a critical incident in which you were involved recently at your workplace, one that somehow represented a conflict for you. Focus on one of your actions. Try to remember what motivational elements were in operation at the time. Were any inhibited or suppressed, or did they all (so far as you can recall) find some outlet in what you did? *How* did you resolve the conflict – by allowing one impulse to overcome the others, or by finding a way to accommodate several needs?

C Think of one of your own most cherished ethical beliefs. How far is this based on a feeling that this belief is absolutely valid in all situations, and how far is it based on your opinions about what kind of consequences there are of following or violating that belief? Now try to do the same for someone else – ask them.

Notes

1   McCoy (1985); Pascale and Athos (1981); Lindsay, Lindsay and Irvine (1996).

2   Any reader who is unfamiliar with the Hawthorne Effect is recommended to consult Pettinger (1996) pp. 113 ff. for a concise explanation.

3   McGregor (1960).

4   See Herzberg (1974) or Maslow (1987). Note that Maslow originally propounded his theory in 1943.

5   Vroom (1964).

6   Lawler (1973).

7   As Laurie Mullins sums it up (1996) 'There are many competing theories which attempt to explain motivation at work. These theories are not conclusive and all have their critics.'

8   Thus Jagdish Parikh, for example, outlines an approach to personal development for managers based on certain precepts from Hindu philosophy, but devoted to the mastery of oneself (1994).

9   By 'fictionalised' I do not mean to say that the examples are *fictitious*. Rather, they represent a collection of aspects from different real life situations that have been gathered together in one example to make the point clearer. They are not 'made up'.

10   The classical presentation of the theory is to be found in Festinger (1957).

11   See Langer (1993).

12   To paraphrase the French novelist Honoré de Balzac (1799–1850), habitual life creates physiognomy, and physiognomy creates the soul.

13   Mumford (1981).

14   Adams (1995) in discussing the work of M. Cook (1993).

15   Popper (1959). In the same vein, validation in the field of psychometrics has been criticised as a 'data dredge' for correlations (Johnson and Blinkhorn 1994).

16   Johnson and Blinkhorn (*ibid.*) and Scheider (1987) point out the difficulty of selecting appropriate criteria in this area.

17   Munro (1995).

18   Lyon (1994) p. 11.

2 *The Dishonest Manager*

In the first chapter we saw that the identification of people's values is less straightforward than is commonly supposed. The reader might be forgiven for thinking that this is an academic point, not directly relevant to managerial practice. But this is not so. The key issue is whether a manager can harness the values of the staff to help the organisation achieve its goals. To do this, it is essential that someone could say with confidence what the underlying values of the staff are – and the argument being advanced here is that they generally cannot. In this chapter we shall look in more detail at one issue – that of honesty. This will function as a characteristic example illustrating the argument of the previous chapter, but it will also extend the matter, for we shall see that conflicts between a person's values makes ethical understanding even more complex. Indeed, by the end of this chapter it may be less clear just what *is* honesty or dishonesty.

2.1   Honesty in managerial practice

If you ask someone what they mean by honesty, their answer will probably be something about telling the truth. They might include something about other ways of not deceiving others, or of being consistent between their words and their actions. Almost certainly they would regard honesty as ethically right, as the morally worthy course of action. I want to present some examples which can undermine the idea that this is always so.

This issue of managerial honesty is a good case in point of the extent to which business ethics is often viewed in black-and-white terms. In discussing honesty at work, Linda Trevino and Katherine Nelson, for example, are uncompromising: 'The caveat is: be completely honest about all aspects of your work, including your ability, the information you provide, and your ability to meet deadlines. Keep your promises.'[1] Similarly, in a highly influential collection of reprints, Fernando Bartolome sounds a more balanced note but ultimately at the same level of simplicity: 'Almost any organisation would operate more effectively with completely open and forthright employees, but absolute frankness is too much to hope for (and probably too much to bear).'[2]

Both of these approaches seem to ignore the distinction between deontological and consequentialist values, so that arguments are offered which seem to mix up issues of prudence, issues of cause and effect, and issues of principle. More worrying than this, there is no recognition of the essential inconsistency of most people where values are concerned – very few people have a clear and unvarying approach to honesty, for example. They will accept deceit in one kind of case and not in others. They will use sometimes convoluted principles to support one example of a 'white lie' and castigate another. Honesty is just one value, and it lives in a plural environment, where values conflict. This essential complexity seems to pass the above writers by. As we shall see in a few pages, there are very good reasons why complete honesty (if we can be sure that such a thing is always clearly identifiable) is inappropriate in organisations.

Amer Bhide and Howard Stevenson take a clearer, more overtly deontological line.[3] They enumerate case after case of behaviour where someone expresses falsehoods or is economical with the truth, stating moral disapproval (or assuming that the audience shares their condemnation) without once considering whether some dishonesty might be ethically valuable. Indeed, they end by suggesting 'Only our individual wills, our determination to do what is right whether or not it is profitable, save us from choosing between chaos or stagnation.'[4] Although it may be unfair to expect too much from what is merely a journalistic flourish at the end of an article, so stark a position is profoundly misleading. People rarely operate in a simple environment where there is a straight choice between something that will bring them an advantage and something that will not. Almost always there is uncertainty – judgement of risk is involved. People are also rarely in a simple position where they can unequivocally regard one possible course of action as 'the' right one, and condemn all others. Judgement is again necessary, about possible consequences, about the degree of significance of an action, or the extent to which there is a clear established truth, for example.

Consider the following case. You are in a meeting with a member of your team. He is extremely weak at his job, so much so that you have discussed with your divisional manager whether or not you can afford to keep him on. He is terribly depressed, and says to you 'I know I'm useless.' You may say a number of things in response to this, but one thing you would be quite unlikely to say is 'Yes, you are.'

Honesty – saying what you believe? Clearly if you do not explicitly agree with the weak employee's statement then you have not been completely honest. Of course, there may be good reasons why you say something else, but that does not mean you told the truth – *it means you were dishonest for a good reason*.

I have tried out this example with several groups of people. In almost all cases, people have been very uncomfortable with the idea that this is dishonest behaviour, though they have not been able to resolve the conflict between that feeling and their definitions of 'honesty' as involving the telling of truth and avoidance of deception. In most instances people have been keen, almost anxious, to say 'Yes, but that's because of...' or 'No, it's not lying, I'd say...' and then go on to give an example of a response which would avoid saying yes or no, but steer a mid-point between these. Obviously there *are* very good reasons why one would not say to an individual with low self-esteem – whatever their actual level of performance – that they were useless. And I do not want to insist that every ingenious way of getting out of this dilemma is really a form of dishonesty. Many responses are dishonest, though, but *that is not in itself the determining reason why we should not act in such a way*. I shall offer some reasons for this later on.

Consider another kind of example. The company makes popular consumer products, well liked by children. It is the sole large employer in a rural area, and uses a volatile process in manufacture. The plant suffers a serious accident, involving toxic air emissions, the inadvertent death of a whole flock of sheep and lambs, and significant injury to individuals. The press get hold of the story, and journalists descend asking awkward questions.

This is a familiar scenario – senior executives have attempted 'damage limitation' exercises in many disasters and ethically compromised situations of recent years. Some – including Union Carbide, the company responsible for the Bhopal disaster – resisted admitting liability for years on end. More overtly, tobacco executives have been careful to react in ways that resist admitting liability; in a number of somewhat farcical US enquiries managers have even denied ever having any suspicion that smoking might cause cancer.

Obviously, some exercises of this kind may be cynical attempts to cover up for past unethical behaviour, usually based on a belief that the risk of discovery or of unacceptable consequences was low (an assessment that often gets confounded). I am not going to suggest that all such behaviour ought to be considered as somehow morally acceptable – but I will ask the reader a question: in your heart of hearts, if you found yourself to be the manager on the spot when your organisation seemed to have been responsible for a major disaster, what would be your immediate *concerns*? (I emphasise concerns here, not the final decision as to what to do.) I would suggest that whilst most of us might well be horrified, and want to do what we could to rectify the damage, *we would not be unaware* of the longer-term implications for our employer and, derivatively from that, for ourselves. Many people faced with an aggressive journalist will try to deflect the worst aspect of the situation – at least until they gain a clearer idea of what actually happened. Crisis situations are, almost by definition, ones in which we cannot handle the information properly. There is usually too little, sometimes too much. But the picture needs clarifying. Emotions run high, and external people want to know what is going on. But we don't know ourselves. So we 'manage' the information. In doing so, maybe legitimately, maybe not, we are balancing truth against prudence. Whether that is dishonesty is a grey area, which we shall revisit shortly. My argument is that even when it is, the action in question could – in certain circumstances – still be ethically acceptable, owing to the balance of other factors.

In being aware of considerations other than just the immediate disaster, we are likely to adjust our behaviour. Recall the model of motivation discussed in the previous chapter – motivation is a solution to the problem of conflicting needs. A person's solution balances out those needs and gives them a weighting. One issue that might need to be considered is whether a certain response might, when publicised, give the public a misleading or maybe downright false belief about the safety of the company's products. Hence the whole business could be put at risk, with the potential knock-on threats to the local or regional economies within which the organisation operates. Similarly, it is not pure cynicism for insurance companies to tell people never to admit liability, for when one does so too readily one may well be throwing away money that otherwise could be used to compensate more deserving cases.

In case the reader should think that I am advocating a 'liars charter', I would emphasise simply that telling the truth, the whole truth, and nothing but the truth is not always either the prudent or even the right thing to do. Government financial ministers are always cautious about statements they make concerning possible devaluation of currency, because any suggestion that this might happen would lead to a run on that currency, more or less ensuring that the devaluation definitely will occur. So when asked 'Will the government devalue?' the stock answer – and the one which in consequentialist terms is the right one – is 'No'. Lying to produce the best ultimate outcome.

Clearly one will not be persuaded by this example if one holds a deonto-logical view that all attempts to divert from the pure unvarnished truth are to be avoided because they are immoral. In practical managerial terms, though, this is not the position of most of us. A senior manager may conceal an impending announcement of redundancies specifically to avoid people being distressed for too long – often a quite misguided thing to do, but not always an act done out of a simple desire to gain advantage. To take another example, most people in a professional environment are likely to conceal aspects of their career intentions from their managers at times. The person going for a new job may not want to advertise this fact, because it might be misinterpreted by their manager, or the manager might take offence. If you don't get the new job you are stuck with a resentful manager who may divert good work away from you to others who are perceived (possibly quite falsely) as more committed. Clearly there is a risk analysis here: if your deception is discovered things might be far worse than if you had come clean in the first place. But this is a consequentialist argument – it recognises that a value such as honesty has to take its place with other values, and be judged in the light of a variety of risks and potential conflicts. Being 'completely open and forthright, whatever the consequences' does not come into this approach.

One reply to all this might be: 'But surely, even though there might be times when we feel we have to be dishonest, it doesn't mean that lying isn't wrong, it's just the least wrong of the available courses of action. All things being equal, behaviour that involves deception is wrong because of that alone.' All things are rarely, if ever, equal, but I suspect the point of the reply goes further than that. I am happy to agree that lying and deception count against a particular course of action. As mentioned before, I am in no way suggesting that deception should be counted as a virtue. The points argued here are: (a) the consequentialist one, that this feature of a course of action may be outweighed by other considerations, such as sensitivity to people's feelings; and (b) the factual one, that most people do act this way depending on the circumstances.

2.2   Degrees of honesty

The point of the previous section was that for most of us lying is not necessarily the wrong thing to do. This does not mean that lying in the abstract is not wrong, but rather that for the vast majority of people there can be circumstances in which we would feel justified in lying or deceiving people. As we noticed in the previous chapter, this is another example of what might seem a common-sense point, were it not for the fact that much literature on business ethics waxes lyrical about honesty, neglecting the realities of day to day managerial practice.

In this section I want to examine more closely what honesty is. Given the examples discussed in the previous section, there seem to be at least three kinds of position that one could take:

(a) the concept of honesty has no place in managerial behaviour – whether or not we tell the truth is entirely down to the benefits we believe might come from this
(b) there are degrees of honesty – one might be more or less honest depending on circumstances
(c) honesty can be overridden by other factors at certain times.

Albert Carr supported the idea of (a) in his seminal article on honesty in business.5 He claimed that where, for example, sales negotiations were concerned, it simply was inappropriate behaviour to 'come clean' directly, that the practices in this area – the rules of the game, if you like – were such that it was assumed that each side was bluffing. Other treatments of negotiation behaviour support this view – almost any textbook on industrial relations will present an analogous account to Carr's in the collective bargaining arena.[6]

There are two ways that Carr's argument can be taken – as a *description* of the practice of business, or as a *recommendation* of how people should operate in business. If it is meant as the latter, then it is subject to the kind of argument put forward by the great German philosopher, Immanuel Kant, that lying erodes the whole idea of communication, and hence is self-defeating.[7] One might well think that nowadays we *have* arrived at an erosion of communication in business and public affairs. When the politician today says 'We shall not raise taxes' the common reaction amongst many people may be 'They would say that wouldn't they?' In other words the politician is perceived as speaking from a self-interested viewpoint and hence is not to be trusted. Nevertheless, the situation has not degenerated to one where all dialogue has lost a connection with truth.

BOX 2.1   Kant

The great 18th-century philosopher, Immanuel Kant, discussed similar positions to those propounded by Carr. His argument was that if everyone acted that way, no-one would be able to trust anything anyone said, and hence language and communication would eventually lose their meaning. In his terms, the practice of lying for advantage was not *universalisable*. Kant's argument is very clearly aimed as a recommendation – he was arguing a strong deontological view that all lying is wrong, irrespective of the consequences.

Whilst Carr's argument seems to reflect the views of many people concerning how business is actually conducted, few are prepared to condone it completely . Individuals and groups with whom I have discussed the argument have tended to accept that this is what often (note, not universally) happens, but they tend to add that it is to be deplored – a view expressed even by those who agree that they themselves do act in this way. So it seems to be partially true as a description, but not acceptable as a recommendation. What this implies, though, is that whilst the *practice* of honesty is partial, the *concept* of honesty as a virtue still applies – if we condemn something, that reinforces the fact that we have an ethical belief. If business were *just* a game, played by different rules from that of, say, social intercourse, condemnation would not apply. It wouldn't make sense to complain of dishonesty in business. The stock answer, which would cancel out all discussion, would be 'Well, that's business.' Some people do feel and say that, but many don't. Hence it doesn't give us a clear idea about why people are dishonest, and it certainly doesn't help us to predict when someone might be dishonest and when not. So we can reject (a), not because it might be thought immoral, but because it is not a clear explanation for departures from total honesty (remember that we are here not trying to establish what is right or wrong, but what underlies the examples considered in the previous section – what makes them possible, if you like).

The second and third positions are easily confused with each other. Position (b) states that one can be highly honest, fairly honest, not very, or not at all. Position (c) states that I am either honest or not, but whether I am will depend on various circumstances. Part of the reason they can get confused is that people are likely to vary the depth of their honesty depending on the circumstances of the moment (that is, they combine the two). But the two views are nevertheless separate.

An explicit expression of (b) in recent years was the admission by John Armstrong, during the so-called 'Spycatcher' trial, that for political purposes one might be 'economical' with the truth. This implies that at times one may provide the full truth, at other times, less than the full truth. One clearly could go further, and say that at other times one might lie a little bit, and at still others tell whopping big lies.

How far does this explain the examples given in Section 2.1? Consider again the depressed poor performer. If the manager said to that individual 'Oh, no, you're not useless at all' that could be counted a significant (albeit maybe justified) lie. On the other hand, if they said 'I wouldn't say useless, but I would agree that we haven't seen the best of you in this job' then that might be less of a lie, perhaps more a case of being economical with the truth. Similar points could be made about different public statements in the example of damage limitation after a major accident.

This does not, though, take away from people's expectations of how far they are being told the truth, or indeed the feeling of discomfort individuals have of not telling the whole truth. This is the point at which we need to revisit the definition of honesty. One dictionary definition[8] gives the following for 'honest': 'fair and sincere in character or behaviour, free of deceit or untruthfulness' and if one looks up 'sincere' one gets 'free from pretence or deceit'. Finally, if in turn one looks up 'deceit' and 'deceive', one gets (deceit) 'concealing of truth in order to mislead' and (deceive) 'make (person) believe what is false, mislead purposely...'.

What these dictionary definitions indicate is that honesty is an absolute – free from deceit. Deceit is the relative term – one might mislead someone a lot or a little. As a primitive analysis of the concepts involved, this supports the view I expressed earlier, that one may be dishonest, but this does not imply that an action was thereby unethical. It also makes clear that being 'economical with the truth' is very likely to be a form of dishonesty, for it is usually done with a view to misleading people. So position (c) is supported by this, whilst position (b) is undermined. It seems, then, that the best way of viewing the incompleteness of our honesty-behaviour is to acknowledge that honesty is one value or virtue, which can be overridden by other values, depending upon the circumstances.

What have we achieved by coming to this? What it shows is that if we are to make sense of how and why people do not tell the pure, unvarnished truth as they see it at a particular moment, we need to look at their behaviour in terms of the multiple factors affecting them at that moment, some of which might be relevant to the impulse to be honest, others of which might lead someone away from being honest. We need to see how honesty gets prioritised – or de-prioritised – against other considerations. It is not excluded from business behaviour, nor is it a matter of degrees (though what underlies it may be). It simply competes with other requirements. In the next section we shall link this more explicitly with the account of motivation given in Chapter 1.

2.3   The motive to be dishonest

The previous section showed that whilst the issue of honesty is always a consideration when a manager is called upon to act, that does not mean that every time a manager is dishonest they are wrong to be so. Recall the model of motivation discussed in the previous chapter – a decision to do something is a solution to the problem of satisfying conflicting needs. In the cases we looked at earlier in this chapter the manager clearly has needs other than merely telling the pure unvarnished truth. In one case it is avoidance of unnecessary bad publicity to the organisation. In another it is a desire not to hurt someone's feelings. In the light of a particular situation, a choice is made that not hurting feelings is more important than whether or not someone is deceived.

As in Chapter 1, we have spent time reaching a fairly common-sense position. And again, this may be a reminder that theory can often lead us away from the obvious. This is not necessarily something to despair of – it is important to gain an understanding of which parts of our everyday beliefs and responses (which we tend not to analyse too closely) are well founded, and which do not stand up to scrutiny. The idea that ethical considerations can conflict, and may be de-prioritised in favour of other factors, is one of those positions that does seem to stand up when considered in more depth.

Returning to this issue of dishonesty as a (sometimes) legitimate course of action, two questions suggest themselves:

- when is someone likely to value honesty less highly than other considerations?
- when is someone justified in doing so?

We shall consider the first of these now, and the second in the following section. The first question, then, might seem to be a 'straightforward' matter for investigation by a behavioural scientist. Thus one could imagine someone trying to devise a questionnaire, or carrying out a series of interviews, to discover when people are dishonest and why. Unfortunately there are some specific difficulties in this area.

'Are you dishonest?' is an intrusive question – it challenges someone's self-image. There is a built-in belief in most people that dishonesty is wrong, so most of us when asked are likely to immediately *want* to answer 'Good Lord no!' – and sometimes we may give in to this want. We then try to interpret our behaviour in ways that project us in the best light. This is a cornerstone of *attribution theory*.[9] The idea behind this model is that the interpretations people give of their own and others' behaviour, reflects, amongst other things, a view about what was the cause of the behaviour. This cause is located either within the individual themselves, or in external events. If the *locus of control* is placed within the individual, then the causal explanation is given in terms of character traits, personal effort, determination, and so on. If it is placed outside the individual, then the explanation of someone's behaviour is couched in terms of luck, constraints, external forces, and so on. The internal locus of control, then, says 'it's down to me', whilst the external says 'it's down to the outside world'.

Some research has suggested that people tend to interpret behaviour along the lines depicted in Figure 2.1:

	moral behaviour	immoral behaviour
self	internal	external
others	external	internal

Figure 2.1   Internal and external causes of behaviour

In other words, when I feel that I have acted in an ethically worthy way I see my behaviour as a product of my own strengths of character, whilst I dismiss that of others as being a response to the external environment; and when I feel my behaviour is (later, presumably) unacceptable, then I try to explain it away ('I had no choice' or 'I was under a lot of pressure') whilst that of others is castigated ('She's just a nasty piece of work, stress or no stress').[10]

In a different kind of discussion (about learning in organisations) Chris Argyris illustrates this point well.[11] He describes how almost everyone who read a transcribed conversation between a manager and a subordinate recognised the shortcomings of the approach of that manager, yet were unable to realise that the way they described this situation revealed the same shortcomings (judgementalism, failing to listen/explore and so on). They were able to attribute the weaknesses to the manager they observed, but failed to acknowledge the same weaknesses in themselves.

Clearly, whilst there may be evidence supporting this tendency, it is not universal, and one could easily find cases in which someone deployed the opposite explanation. For example, the hero who says 'It was nothing, anyone would have done the same in those circumstances' and so on. What is important is the *pattern* of explanation – where the locus of control is depicted internally, then along with it goes acceptance or attribution of responsibility, with consequent praise and blame. Where the locus of control is depicted internally, then responsibility is deflected or mitigated, with consequent dismissal of praise or blame.[12]

How does this affect our attempt to find out who is honest or not, and when? Well, where any research is based on personal testimony, there will be a significant danger that what the researcher hears reflects, not actual behaviour but simply an *expression* of a location of control, whether it's a self-report or an evaluation of someone else.

Face-to-face research has the particular difficulty of the relationship between researcher and the researched. As Bill Bain[13] has pointed out, standard survey techniques are not really appropriate in this context. He offers a solution in the use of 'vignettes' – mini-cases and examples – which may have an advantage over naive interviewing, but it is doubtful whether this can eradicate the effects of attribution theory once one is looking at people's own acts.

None of this is to suggest that people are totally self-deceived, or totally insensitive to others' motives. But it does imply that we cannot easily separate out one kind of explanation from another. It means that the search for the (honestly) dishonest manager is fraught with difficulty. One approach I have taken in a small sample (ten subjects) was to interview managers without referring to the question of honesty or dishonesty, discussing issues such as decision-making.[14] Interviews tended to reach a 'switching' point, when someone articulated for themselves what I was inquiring after: 'Oh, you mean have I been dishonest?' What was interesting was that the switch seemed to *fix* the locus of control, which then stayed firmly in one or another place. In some cases this was to externalise ('I was dishonest because of the pressures of the job', 'You can't be too principled round here', and so on) whilst in a few the refocusing was internal ('Yes I have been dishonest, and I really feel bad about it'). Generally, once the locus of control had been firmly located it stayed that way, and the material of the interviews tended to become less valuable.

So it is unclear how we can identify someone's level of honesty by question and answer methods. A more interesting hypothesis (at the time of writing untested) is to adopt a form of repertory grid analysis, to discover individuals' personal constructs in this area. A summary of this method is given in Box 2.2.

BOX 2.2   Repertory Grid Analysis

Originated by G. Kelly, as a means of discovering individuals' personal constructs, or ways of interpreting experience, repertory grid analysis combines the intensity and potential depth of one-to-one interviews with the independence of structured questionnaires. The method is intended to allow an individual to present their own way of thinking about a certain field, rather than respond to the ideas presented by the researcher.

The core activity in the method is to present three objects – say three well known people – and ask the subject how one of them differs from the other two. This can be carried out for all three of these objects, with the subject considering how each in turn differs from the other two. In explaining how one differs from the others, the subject of the analysis is presenting a rudimentary *construct* – a way in which they structure and comprehend the world.

The method can be used iteratively with a variety of different threesomes, or the threesomes may be mixed. Similarly, a subject might be asked to think of three (or more) examples relevant to the field being researched. Repetition of the activity can establish a set of constructs that are individually distinct and together cover the main areas of the field in question – computer analysis can also be used to assist in the process. Once a set of constructs has been identified it can then be used as a means of ranking all examples that have been identified, or extended to new cases.

The method is not foolproof, in the sense that some degree of researcher bias may still be present in the initial narrowing down of the field. It also assumes that each individual has a clear stable set of constructs that are only waiting to be discovered. Nevertheless it is a powerful method for understanding people's attitudes and values in a variety of different areas.

For further reading, see Stewart and Stewart (1982).

Methods such as repertory grid analysis may well prove a fruitful source of material concerning people's attitudes towards ethics in general and honesty in particular. It certainly may help people to take a more detached approach to their own attitudes, and to be less likely to fall into the trap of taking a fixed, and partial, approach to the locus of control when attributing causes to behaviour. In the deeper senses that we have been considering in this and the previous chapter, however, there may be certain limits on how far such methods can go. These reflect the profound complexity that investigation of people's motives can reveal.

Recall the 'manager-as-archaeologist' concept, a useful if one-sided way of recognising the difficulty of getting to the bottom of someone's attitudes. What it indicates is that individuals' values continue to evolve, continue to be affected by events and experiences, and continue to be readjusted against other concepts and against other values. The origins of someone's explicit behaviour and expressed views may lie deeply, and may well be deeply distorted by a variety of different phenomena. As mentioned in Box 2.2 one assumption is that an individual's conceptual framework is a stable and well organised structure. In practice this is unlikely to be the case. New experiences create new perspectives on values, so the idea of stability is highly restricted, at best. More importantly, individuals do not always think logically. People often have inconsistent views, and rarely notice this. Granted, the theory of cognitive dissonance suggests that when a contradiction or incongruity in our expressed beliefs swims into our view, we try to resolve it, but it is misleading to depict this as a rearrangement or re-interpretation of existing values. Self-justification and self-deception are just two reasons why the results may be less a restructuring of what is already there and more a case of something new being expressed. Also, people's values are made fluid by the colour of their memories and perceptions of events. When Charles Foster Kane, the newspaper proprietor in *Citizen Kane*, says that people will believe '... what I tell them to believe'[15] he is misdescribing what happens; in reality people do not often believe what they are told to believe, but they are likely to believe what they are repeatedly made to *feel*. The newspaper that tries to influence policies does not do so by presenting concise, complex and well argued analyses, but by simple highly emotive 'human interest' stories, where some individual or other has suffered grave loss as a result of this or that. The degree of appeal – the colour – of the story can strongly incline people's opinions and beliefs (both ethical and factual). This is another case of irrationality, but one to which we all are highly susceptible day in day out. So there are several reasons why even a sophisticated methodology such as repertory grid analysis cannot easily establish what someone's values are.

So what about observation? Why not simply *look* at what people do, and how far their behaviour could be described as honest or not? This falls foul of arguments presented in the previous chapter, and in the earlier part of this one. We can *see* people's explicit behaviour, but we often can only *infer* their intention. Obviously there will be many times when, in practical terms, it is crystal clear that someone has been dishonest – when to suggest otherwise would be to fly in the face of ordinary experience of life. But that does not exhaust the range of cases in which dishonesty might have occurred. Many times an allegation of dishonesty may be made when there are plausible alternative explanations. For example, someone may be told something one day and deny it to someone else the next. Dishonesty? Possibly, but just as often it might be forgetfulness, or misunderstanding. Observation *per se* cannot resolve this, and once an individual tries to introduce an element of triangulation by asking people (in one way or another) what was in their mind when they did something, the problems of self-justification and self-deception can easily recur.

Obviously there are mixed methods, such as 'critical incident analysis' where an individual describes a certain highly charged event, and then outlines their feelings and intellectual responses to the situation. But this is not in principle any better than testimony-based material, for the same effects of attribution theory will be operating, and there will also be a further complicating factor that people tend to describe events in terms of their own analysis of them. Someone who felt that they had acted dubiously will emphasise the influence of external events, the force of other people, the great constraints on them, their lack of information, and so on. Recall that people feel uncomfortable with admitting dishonesty. Attribution theory suggests that there would be no easy separation of someone's account of what happened, in a critical incident analysis, from their feelings toward their behaviour.

One might look to external evidence – for example what *other people* say about whether so-and-so is generally, or has on specific occasions been, honest. But again there are complicating factors. Individuals are themselves affected by the colour of their experiences. A friendly, but almost openly deceptive, supervisor, may well be able to charm their team sufficiently so that they would not want to see her/him as immoral – so they say s/he's honest. An autocratic, abrasive manager is less empathised with, and hence people find it easier to see them as dishonest – when in fact their regular abrasiveness may mean that they have no scruples about telling the truth whether it hurts or not.

One could multiply the examples, but the argument is established well enough from the above. Social research methods encounter severe problems in the area of dishonesty. None of the above rules out such methods as offering no possible insight into people's behaviour, but it does cast doubt on the idea that any one method might a satisfactory measure of a person's honesty. This amplifies the argument of Chapter 1, that deeper probing makes it very difficult to determine with much confidence what someone's underlying motives really are.

2.4   Honesty right or wrong

We are left with a question about when we might count it right to be honest or dishonest. Although the prime purpose of this book is to understand how ethical change in an organisation is possible, this question illustrates well certain other contextual issues relating to ethics in business.

Recall the argument earlier in this chapter and the previous one. People's underlying values are difficult to fathom. They possess a variety of different needs, values and wants, and most situations where they are called upon to do something require a choice between conflicting motivational elements. Sometimes it is impossible to avoid violating one value or other, hence we are forced to make some kind of prioritisation between values (and other elements).

'When should we be honest?', therefore, becomes a question about the relationship between that virtue and others. We might think we could resolve this by replacing it by the question 'Which virtues are more or less important than honesty?' But this is still too simple. A situation often does not present a straight choice. I may be confronted by several possible courses of action, for each of which there is a motivational profit-and-loss account, as is illustrated below in Box 2.3.

Not all the considerations outlined in the case are themselves ethically worthy, but they are all ethically relevant. The most striking thing is that for the most part *they are all possible*. Risk analysis is important in all decisions, and central to ethical ones. The implication of this is that the ethical worthiness of a certain course of action is in part determined by how accurate someone's estimate of the situation is. Morality is not immune from chance.[16] Furthermore, the manner in which the issues in the example might be combined to lead the person concerned into a certain course of action is, as noted before, a highly idiosyncratic process, for which generalisations are not really appropriate. So we have two different aspects of honesty for which it is difficult to make a clear ethical evaluation, except in hindsight. Hindsight is useful, but (a) it is notoriously easy to be right after the full facts have come out, and therefore no estimation of risk is necessary, and (b) it is irrelevant to the dilemma the person faced in that situation (though obviously useful for future situations).

So, is honesty the best policy in the case below? Clearly the answer to this depends partially on the weighting someone might give to the plus and minus points given there (in that respect the material in the table is more like a business scorecard than a profit-and-loss account). But also it turns on *how events turn out*.

BOX 2.3   **Case: The Missing Millions**

Employee A worked for a large retail bank. One day she discovered a significant discrepancy in some accounts managed by her section head. The
section head was on holiday, so she had to deal with this herself. She felt
that there were four possibilities: (a) there was financial impropriety of
which her section head was at least aware, if not a willing participant; (b)
the impropriety was apparent rather than real, and when the section head
returned all would be explained; (c) there was no impropriety, only an error,
which again the section head could resolve when they returned; (d) there
was something beyond her knowledge or understanding which would
explain everything. As a result she felt there were two main courses of
action (although each had important sub-branches): 1. reveal the discrepancy to the section head's line manager; 2. wait until her section head
returned. The 'ethical profit-and-loss account' that she saw in the situation
is summarised below.

Ethical plus points	**Ethical minus points**
Reveal action:	
Personal reputation for probity.	May be no fraud.
Possible loss to the bank averted.	Possible reputation as a 'grass'.
Own job protected against trading loss.	Poor future relations with manager.
Will not be identified with the problem.	May reveal own misunderstandings.
Good example/precedent.	May stir up a hornets' nest.
Conceal action:	
Won't be accused of meddling.	May be identified with the problem.
Reputation as loyal to section head.	May fail to avert major losses.
Reputation as shrewd.	Problem may be a harmless mistake.
Section head owes her a favour.	Poor example/precedent.
	Subsequent action may be too late.

One last example may seal the approach adopted in the preceding sections.
In Box 2.4 we have a case where someone can choose between lying and
allowing people to be seriously and detrimentally deceived. Of course, as in
most cases, it turns on the specific circumstances of the situation, which are
not transferable to all situations. The circumstances are not in themselves that
rare, however. So they represent a typical kind of difficulty about *telling* the
truth and its relationship with *helping others access* the truth. The rhetorical
question I leave the reader with here is – we can see which action is direct
dishonesty, but which option is *not* likely to lead to deception? Probably each
reader will have their own view. The point is that no option could be seen as

an unblemished approach. Each could involve the employee in deliberately allowing others to be deceived.

BOX 2.4   **Case: Privileged Information**

Employee X is taken into confidence by his line manager, who tells him that there are some redundancies to be made, although they are not within their own department. X is sworn to secrecy. Later X is approached by some of his colleagues, one of whom, Y, asks him whether he knows anything about redundancies. X knows Y well. In particular he knows that Y is neither rational nor discreet. Even the slightest indication of redundancy will send Y into a spiral of speculation, of the 'we're all doomed' version.

X has the following options:

(a) *Confirm that there are redundancies, but not affecting their department.* Clearly this breaks the promise to the line manager, but more importantly it is highly likely, given what X knows about Y, that it will lead to Y spreading false rumours around the department, worrying people groundlessly.

(b) *Deny any knowledge of anything; this is a straight lie.*

(c) *Try to palm Y off by saying that it won't affect them;* this runs the risk that Y will say 'Ah, so you do know something. As if it won't affect us! Of course it will, and you know how many of us are going to get the chop...' (and so on). So again X's action will result in people being misled about what is really likely to happen to them.

2.5   Self-deception

The other side to honesty is how far one understands one's own beliefs and feelings accurately. In a recent work, Daniel Goleman has argued strongly that we have to lie to ourselves, as much as to others, as a defence mechanism.[17] The reality of life is just too fraught with potential trauma for us to be able to tolerate it all directly. We deceive ourselves as a way of diverting our attention from painful or uncomfortable experiences.

One consequence of this is that someone may, on occasion, make statements to others that they superficially believe to be true, but which conceal an awkward fact from themselves, even though this may be plain to others to see. A manager whose job is under threat may avoid recognition of this, as it is frightening and possibly a cause of personal disappointment. They 'officially' believe that all is well. So they discuss plans with their team, they talk about what will happen when they recruit a new administrator, and so on. 'Why is she lying to us? We all know she's on her way out. She must know that herself.' She knows and she doesn't know, that's the key issue here. Some dishonesty involving others stems from dishonesty relating to ourselves.

Much of what gives rise to this will be explored in Part II, where we look at people's values and what supports these. One aspect may be mentioned here – as Simon has pointed out, false beliefs about our own values can grow up because they may go unchallenged.[18] An individual may start their managerial career with a high degree of concern for the welfare of their staff. As time goes on, however, they may grow less concerned and act insensitively, even bullying team members. But they explain away such actions – to themselves at least, if not to any other audience – by face savers such as 'Well, Jack's far too *laissez faire* about his work' or 'She's got to learn somehow.' The lack of an appropriate challenge (and confrontation is rarely the right kind of challenge) allows this process to continue to a point where the manager's self-perception is completely at variance with how others see them. When asked, 'What are your values?' they may answer, with some degree of sincerity, 'Respect other people, look after your staff' without recognising how little truth remains in this. A concern and commitment in the past has become a hollow wish in the present.

We shall see a model relating to self-deception in Chapter 7, but the key point here is that self-deception exists, and in many ways it is extremely difficult to identify, especially for the individual who deceives themself.

In this chapter we have taken the issue of honesty, and its close relative, deception, and looked at them as an example and extension of the general argument given in Chapter 1. What comes out of this is that not only is it difficult to see what people's motives and values really are, at times it is also difficult to establish precisely what kind of action is to be counted dishonest or not. Along the way, I hope that the examples we have looked at demonstrate that in real life (from which they are all taken, suitably anonymised) ethical issues are muddy, involving guessing outcomes, choosing which of several motives one will satisfy and which must be frustrated, and trying to make fine judgements about relative merits. Perhaps it's not surprising that, despite our best intentions, we fall down pretty often. In the next chapter we shall see that the question of what counts as 'falling down' is itself highly variable between individuals, groups and cultures.

Questions

A   Recall a situation in which you had to relay some personally sensitive information or opinion to someone else at work. Not counting the way you did in fact make the communication, think of at least three different ways you could have done so – different setting, different wording, different medium, or combinations of all of these. What would have been the pros and cons of each?

B   Consider a situation in which you withheld some item of information from someone. Try to recall your reasons for this. Each of these, in effect specifies a particular concern. Now try to imagine ways in which you could have satisfied those concerns but still delivered the information.

C   Think of a situation in which you will have to decide whether and how to present some sensitive information in the near future. Consider at least four different ways of doing this, and for each of these identify the main possible outcomes. Try to estimate how likely these outcomes are.

Notes

1. Trevino and Nelson (1995) p. 132.
2. Bartolome (1991) p. 15.
3. Bhide and Stevenson (1991) pp. 45–53.
4. *Ibid*. p. 53.
5. Carr (1968).
6. For example, see Salamon (1987).
7. Kant (ed. Paton 1948).
8. Taken from the *Pocket Oxford English Dictionary* (OED).
9. A clear account of attribution theory is given in Mullins (1996) pp. 154–6.
10. As the great chess writer and former world title contender David Bronstein says (whilst discussing and analysing past chess games) 'It is difficult to be objective when annotating one's own games. Variations favouring the annotator always appear interesting – one talks about them willingly and in detail... One usually looks for (and usually finds) justification for one's mistakes, but those of the opponent seem natural and therefore require no explanation' (Bronstein 1980 p. 10).
11. Argyris (1993) pp. 12–23.
12. P. F. Strawson gives an illuminating philosophical account of this phenomenon (1962)
13. Bain (1993).
14. Using an interview methodology not dissimilar to that of McLagen and Snell, I started with open questions around the idea of 'my most difficult decision', omitting reference to any overtly ethical term (McLagen and Snell 1994).
15. Welles and Mankiewich (1941).
16. An interesting debate of how luck can play a significant role in ethics was conducted some years ago by two moral philosophers, Nagel (1979) and Williams (1985).
17. Goleman (1997).
18. S. Simon (1974).

3 My Values – Other People's Values

In the previous chapter we saw that once we explore an issue such as honesty in depth, it tends to become ever more problematic. The sureness we have about the idea dissolves when we subject it to a searching analysis. Honesty started off as a clear moral value, then we saw situations in which it could be right not to be honest, and eventually we had cases in which it was no longer clear what was the honest course of action – where all possible options would result in someone being deceived.

In this chapter I want to generalise the argument. We shall focus on one or two commonly supported values, but the key question affects all values and purported virtues – how far does *my own* understanding of ethics prejudice my understanding of *other people's* values? This is, in a way, a return to the issues dealt with in Chapter 1, but now from a different perspective. There we were looking at the depth and complexity of an individual's motivational frameworks, here we are looking at some of the factors that get in the way of my understanding those frameworks. With the growing globalisation of business activities, this is becoming an ever more acute problem – how do I square my own values with the behaviour of others that seems to reflect very different values? Not that it is solely a matter of cultural differences – all situations in which one person assesses another's values involve this kind of difficulty.

3.1 A dialogue

In the following dialogue, A is the line manager in a retail organisation, B is a counter assistant.

A Thanks for coming to see me, B, I'd just like to chat to you about a couple of things.
B Okay.
A How are things going generally at the moment?
B How are things going? Well, they seem to be alright.

A No problems?

B Not from my point of view. Do *you* think there's a problem?

A No, not a problem exactly, but there is something that is causing me – well, not just me, a couple of the team as well, really – er, shall we say that there's something not quite right about the way you handle customers.

B Not quite right? What do you mean? Can you give me an example?

A Well, it's not that you do anything wrong exactly, more that...

B Look, can you please stop beating about the bush. What's the matter? Am I doing something wrong?

A Well... Let me put it like this. A retail organisation lives off trust. Customers come here, I know they moan about us, but they come here because they trust us. They feel that we won't sell them shoddy goods, that we'll give them a good price, and so on.

B Sure. So what's that got to do with me?

A Some of us have noticed that you have a somewhat... well, you don't always inspire confidence.

B What – you don't have confidence in me?

A No, you don't inspire the confidence of the *customer*.

B What, have people been complaining about me then?

A No, not exactly, but one or two of us have watched you at the counter and you don't really show the seriousness that people expect from a place such as ours.

B Seriousness? Do you mean the incident with Mrs Y yesterday?

A Well, that's one of them.

B I know her, our families have been friends for donkeys years. I can't act like she's a stranger. I banter with her when she and her husband come round and I treat her the same here.

A Well, you could be a bit more formal without treating her as a stranger, couldn't you? And remember, it's not just her, there are other people in the queue who are watching it all.

B Okay. But is that it?

A Well, it's a general pattern. You joke around with other customers, and you're not going to tell me they're all old friends.

B Shouldn't we make them feel a bit at home? Isn't there something in the corporate code about treating the customer as your friend?

A Yes, but is that the same as being familiar with them?

B Isn't it, in a way? I mean, maybe not taking liberties but talking to them like a person, not just a customer.

A Well, for us they are first and foremost a customer.

B But from their point of view they're first and foremost a person. They have to buy food and things, but it's just a pain really. I mean, you wouldn't go shopping if you didn't have to.

A Look, this isn't getting anywhere. The point is, you don't seem to be sufficiently respectful to the customers. Generally the staff here are warm but polite. You're over-friendly and not polite enough. All this jocularity and so on may go down well with some people but at some point you'll get someone who really objects. Then *you'll* be in trouble, *we'll* probably lose a sale, and doubtless there'll be a letter to head office. Joking around is a risky business.

B Look, you can get nutters going over the top whatever you do or say.

A People aren't nutters just because they don't like one of your jokes. I mean, I heard you say the other day... something like 'That'll warm your toes'. I mean, that's really quite intrusive.

B Well I can't remember saying that, but it's the sort of thing I might say. They must have been buying some socks or something.

A A hot water bottle actually.

B Well there you go.

A It's too familiar. People don't want you to refer to what they might feel like in bed. It's... it's... well, somewhere along the line someone will strongly resent that sort of comment, and you'll end up regretting it, believe me.

Clearly there are some aspects about this dialogue which, though interesting from a Human Resource Management (HRM) perspective, are not at first sight so relevant here, such as the way in which the manager finds it difficult to come to the point, and the general tone of the interview – judgmental, lacking in evidence of listening, few open-ended questions, and so on. I do not want to evaluate the management style here, or who was right or wrong. The issue I want to discuss is the question of terminology, and what this implies about the interpretation of values. In practice this will end up with a discussion of the manager's style – but also of the employee's as well.

The first point to be made is about the literal content of the disagreement. Clearly, A and B are not disputing *specific* actual facts. B *has* been joking with customers, *does* make personal comments, *did* (or at least does not disagree that they might) talk about something warming someone's toes. Within the dispute, though, there are *general* factual questions raised. A talks of the likelihood of someone complaining. B responds by predicting that there are always people who complain (dismissing them as 'nutters'). These are characteristic moves in a disagreement of this kind. But are they *driving* the dispute? Is the argument resting on those probabilities?

In terms of *logic*, possibly the factual issues might underpin the argument, depending upon the precise way the conversation was re-constructed. In terms of the *experience* of the protagonists, I would venture to say not.[1] People are often convinced that a certain course of action is right or wrong, and they are likely to grasp at possibilities to substantiate their view. What is grasped at may have little actual evidential value one way or another. The difference of view that A and B have about complaints illustrates this. At heart this particular part of the discussion seems to be about the risk that is being run by B. One suspects that in a literal sense it is true that every counter assistant eventually gets complained about for something or another. It is also true to say that there is always some degree of likelihood that someone may be offended by just about anything one might say – although it must surely be a very small likelihood. Part of the argument, then, must be a conflict of beliefs about how likely this is, but I would suggest that *the difference in beliefs about risk reflects the protagonists' different underlying values, rather than the values being based on different beliefs about risk*. Factual elements may be *involved* in a disagreement such as that between A and B, but it is rare that these are what the disagreement is *about*.

The main area of disagreement in the dialogue above centres around certain key terms and phrases. Table 3.1 indicates some of the important parts of the discussion (given in the order in which they appear in the dialogue).

Table 3.1   Key term analysis of dialogue

Manager	Assistant
something not right	
	something the matter
trust	
confidence	
	complaining
seriousness	
	banter
be formal	
	make the customer feel at home
	you are their friend
being familiar	
	treat them as aperson
respectful	
warm but polite	
	nutters
intrusive	

Most of these are, or contain, words that philosophers of ethics would describe as 'thick' moral concepts – that is, they carry both descriptive and evaluative elements.[2] Thus, for a word like 'respectful' the descriptive element would probably revolve around the idea of someone being polite in their behaviour and taking special account of the wishes and needs of certain individuals, and the evaluative element would involve the idea that this is appropriate or indeed required for certain people in certain contexts (for example, elders, customers and so on).

For much of the discussion, A and B are less concerned to refute directly or reject the other's suggestion as they are to *redescribe* what had happened. That is, the to and fro is less to do with trying to establish an agreed set of bases (from which they might come to a common set of conclusions) but is more an attempt by each to establish an alternative interpretation. This is unsurprising so far as the descriptive aspect of the terms used is concerned, for as we have seen there was little direct dispute about what had actually happened. What is more interesting is that there was no argument about the evaluative elements – hence there was no discussion of whether joking with a customer counted as respectful or as disrespectful behaviour. The only point at which there seemed to be the beginning of a dispute about a particular term was when A disagreed about B's use of the term 'nutters'. Having disagreed, and having appeared to offer some evidence in the form of the comment on 'warming toes', A moved on to talking about intrusion, again a case of offering an alternative interpretation rather than arguing the merits or demerits of the view of the other person. So a second feature of this disagreement is that it is *less a matter of the application of commonly agreed terms as a conflict of interpretations*, issuing in a different vocabulary.

Obviously this is an illustrative example, and one could not draw universal conclusions from it. I would suggest, though, that it is a typical kind of discussion, and hence there is a degree of generalisability about the above analysis. What seems to be most striking is that the dialogue involves *very little deep listening*. The protagonists do not attempt to deal very much with what the other has actually said, but try instead to replace it with another approach. What is also both interesting and in a way disturbing is that the disagreement turns on the use of words and phrases that are not entirely determinable by external evidence. The precise amount to which ethical terms include a subjective element is controversial – nevertheless some element there is. The dialogue given above can be resolved only via something being agreed by both parties. But the logic of the argument does not seem to allow that possibility, nor is there any opportunity for reference to an external standard of what a word or phrase really means (indeed, as we have seen, the disputants seem to go out of their way to *avoid* such a means to clinch the issue one way or another). An agreement in these circumstances is not well represented as something that is determined by the logic of the dispute. It is better construed as involving an element of choice, for example about whether one particular act of B's constituted respect or not. The *choice* might be affected by various factors –

A's desire for consistency, comparisons with other people's behaviour, B's own interpretation of his acts, and so on.

What is clear from the dialogue, though, is that in this typical case of a workplace disagreement – not on the face of it an especially ethical disagreement, even – there is significant difficulty in being able to establish a systematic framework for resolving disputes. Logical argument is not neglected, but is not a core feature of the dispute. Factual questions seem to follow in the wake of the disagreement, rather than lead them (one might question whether they could or should lead them, but we do not need to consider that issue in detail here). Elements of choice seem to have a prominent role. The resolution of a disagreement of this kind, then, is not explained very well by a model of discussion as a form of joint investigation. It seems to be better represented as a kind of negotiation.

We have not even started on matters such as the values of people from different cultures, or the various sources of people's individual personal value systems, and yet we have already encountered significant difficulties. The above analysis, however, certainly does not demonstrate that agreement is impossible. It is intended to present some of the key practical difficulties that can stand in the way of agreement. We can and do come to agreements over ethical issues, inside and outside organisations – in the light of this section it is worth reflecting how significant an event this must be.

3.2   Mindsetting

In the last section we saw how a common or garden disagreement presents serious difficulties for any attempt to take a structured, universal framework as the sole model of disputes or how we can settle them. In this section we shall explore some underlying factors of such disagreements. Why does one person not see events in the way the other does?

Part of it is down to *mindsetting*. I use the word 'mindsetting' rather than the more common 'mindset' for two reasons:

- a setting is something that is more amenable to deliberate change, is more dynamic
- a setting is more appropriate for a given relevant range, and may be altered – or even thrown out – by extreme circumstances.

The idea of a structure or framework for processing information has been discussed by several writers in recent years. Goleman talks of schema, whilst Ellen Langer talks of 'premature cognitive commitment' as a phenomenon that can often stifle understanding by substituting for it.[3] We referred to this earlier under her term 'mindlessness'. What she means by this is that we all adopt frameworks and make assumptions about reality, from which we then switch off. They function as an autopilot – sometimes very usefully allowing us to do two or more things at once. But we end up becoming unaware of them, and hence unaware of whether they are appropriate or not. Something develops as a technique to help us handle a particular kind of context. But later, although the technique is still in operation, we have lost sight of whether the context is the same.

The key issue here is that although dynamic in potential, mindsettings have a tendency to develop their own inertia. They arise from a context in which they help resolve a certain type of problem. 'I wouldn't trust anyone at work, they're all out for themselves.' This originates in experiences that someone has had – probably some unfortunate situation where the individual trusted someone at work and subsequently felt let down. It is unlikely that someone saying this would seriously believe that it was literally true of all their colleagues. But it becomes their standard framework, in their minds intended to avoid repetition of the worst aspects of what they suffered in the original experience. Later, however, this becomes static and acquires a hold over the individual. So when the organisation changes, or the old colleagues leave, or the individual moves to a more open and trusting organisation they find themselves out of step. Their attitude grew up in one context, but is no longer appropriate in the new context. Unless they come to a recognition that the value is out of its appropriate context they will find continuing difficulties with the kind of behaviour of their new colleagues. This reveals a further aspect of the complexity of values. They have complex origins and underlying components, and once these are severed from their original rationale they are an encumbrance, a limitation on performance and personal opportunity.

The point is that we have forgotten that we are using a certain idea, much as we lose any direct awareness of whether we have socks on when we are driving down the highway. This can be the source of many tricks and games. It can also be a great barrier to creativity, for we labour on making assumptions that flow out of one of these cognitive commitments without realising that we don't have to. Sometimes the best way to break them is by adopting a 'child at play' attitude, hence the plethora of play-style activities to assist managerial decision-making.

Cognitive commitment gives values and moral terms their permanence. But it takes our attention from what the origin of the values may be, and hence whether they should remain with us or need to be amended. Values that arose in one context, and as a result of one kind of range of experiences and beliefs, persist long after the originating events have faded from view. Often what sustains them is an image of that past context, almost a kind of nostalgia. Depending on a whole variety of factors this may become more or less rigid. We shall look in more detail at the rigidity of values in Chapter 6.

But it is important to recognise that this rigidity is in one sense apparent only – it rests on a failure to compare an idea or mental framework with its current context. This obviously offers a range of potential solutions for dissolving rigidity when necessary (though we shall see some good reasons in Chapter 6 for not doing so).

This kind of apparent rigidity is visible in the dialogue analysed earlier. The manager has built up a view about familiarity based on prior experiences. He has developed approaches and rules of thumb to help him evaluate relationships with customers. The new assistant's behaviour challenges these views, and the underlying mindsetting, but the manager fails to rise to this, because he is unaware of where his values in this situation have come from. He has forgotten what led to this view. He no longer knows what problems it has developed to solve. Having forgotten, he is in thrall to one of his own values. Similarly, the assistant has a mindsetting based on earlier relationships, and may be having the same kind of trouble adjusting these to the new context.

It is important to emphasise that however rigidly someone holds an idea it is not necessarily permanent. Underlying not just the practice but also the principle of most methods of assessing personality is the idea that an individual represents a blend of a variety of factors, roles, types and so on. We shall not re-enter the arguments outlined in Chapters 1 and 2 concerning the application of these. Assume (just for this paragraph) that such measures are capable of yielding a reliable, valid assessment of someone's personality. Take a crude oversimplification of such a personality assessment – a person comes out as 5 per cent factor x, 65 per cent factor y, and 30 per cent factor z. Clearly most of the time someone will exhibit y-appropriate behaviour. But there will be times – admittedly not many – when even x-appropriate behaviour may be evinced without any contradiction of the results of the assessment instrument. We are not, therefore, set – fixed – in a specific form of behaviour. We can move between different mental orderings as appropriate. What this implies is that even when someone appears 'set' in a rigid, dogmatic view, they may well act more flexibly in certain situations. If a setting proves inappropriate because the situation is outside its relevant range, then we *can* change to another. This may not always be freely chosen. But it does not have to be a static condition. This also helps us to see why some people may seem hypocritical. They hold a value in one situation, and do not realise that they are comfortable with some other, incompatible value, in another situation, where some other aspect of their personality is finding full expression.

In this section we are focusing on the intellectual side of personality, and how that relates to our perception of, and response to, other people's values. Not that the emotional side is any the less relevant. In Chapter 7 we shall look at how the intellectual demand of consistency in action can combine with the emotional one of sympathy to assist the process of ethical change.

Amongst the many models that are relevant to this discussion I want to focus on three – two are the very well known models of Peter Honey (learning styles) and Meredith Belbin (team roles).[4] The third is a model specifically relating to ethical decision-making. The speculative results we establish from each can then conjointly suggest some reasons why ethical disagreements can so easily occur, and why these can actively prevent us understanding what another person really values.

The Honey model of learning styles presents four overall personality types as these relate to learning:

- pragmatist – flexible between general concepts and specific situations
- activist – mainly interested in getting on with things
- reflector – interested in exploring the deeper significance of concrete situations
- theorist – comfortable with generalisations and overall patterns.

These in turn arise out of the well known model of the experiential learning cycle developed by David Kolb from some ideas of Kurt Lewin:[5] experience–reflection–generalisation–experiment. The relationship is depicted in Figure 3.1 below.

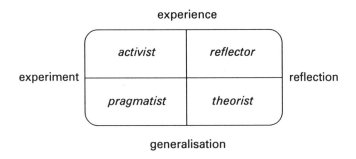

Figure 3.1   Mapping learning styles against experiential learning

Consider now how the protagonists in our earlier example, A and B, would fit on to this model. I would suggest that A, in his aversion to coming directly to the point, and in his avoidance of discussing specific examples unless pushed, displays a relatively low level of the activist style. He is less concerned to tie his views down to concrete evidence, and to an extent is risk-averse. B, on the other hand, seems to be relatively lower on the theorist sector. He is happy to take risks, and relate more directly to the concrete than to the general. Unsurprisingly, then, the two have a difficulty communicating and agreeing values, for they have a difference in intellectual *setting* – their schemas conflict.

Now consider the points that arise from application of the Belbin model of team styles. Meredith Belbin outlines a nine-fold model of team roles that individuals can take, each of us again being a specific blend of these. This model is summarised in Table 3.2 below.

Table 3.2   The Belbin model of team roles

Plant	Interested in ideas. Impractical and often inattentive. Highly creative.
Shaper	Interested in getting their own view pushed. Not averse to conflict.
Resource investigator	Networker. Likes finding solutions before problems. Easily bored.
Coordinator	Ensures balance and fairness, and keeps the team to the point.
Monitor–evaluator	Logical, realistic and conservative.
Complete finisher	Good at dealing with details, can become over fussy.
Implementer	Practical person who gets on with the job.
Team worker	Concerned that social needs of the team are addressed.
Specialist	Mainly interested in their own particular area of expertise.

In contrast with the Honey analysis, in this case it is probably the similarity between the two that has contributed to the problem. For both A and B would seem to display a certain amount of shaper behaviour – not content to submit their own view to that of the other. Of course there are aspects that are different – B seems to show some signs of a resource investigator (sociability), whilst A shows some degree of a monitor–evaluator (judgementalism, albeit somewhat incomplete). Nevertheless, the striking aspect here is that the two of them were both operating within a common but entrenched perspective.

'So what use are these models? One says they are too different, the other they are too much the same.'

The benefit of the models is precisely *because* they present things differently. It is not at all inconsistent that they yield different kinds of result – they are looking at different aspects of the personalities involved. Despite all the critical comments made earlier concerning formalised methods of measuring personality, what these two models indicate is that a certain amount of illumination may come, not so much from the tightly controlled use of the measures to provide a high level of probability, but as a means of suggesting possibilities, and thus generating further questions and possible courses of action. The value, then, is not in what is *established* but in what is *uncovered*.

The third model I want to look at is much less common, and relates specifically with ethical mindsetting. Forsyth identifies four kinds of what he calls 'ethical decision ideologies',[6] as indicated in Figure 3.2.

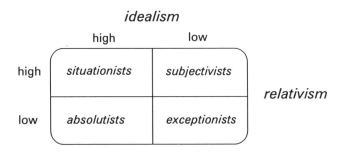

Figure 3.2   Ethical decision ideologies (after D.R. Forsyth)

Summarising very briefly, situationists are most likely to analyse each situation to arrive at a specific moral evaluation of it, without necessarily drawing much on precedent; absolutists will work from a set of strongly held ethical principles, which they will then use to evaluate each circumstance (this group is most likely to adopt a deontological approach to values); subjectivists are prone to take a personal stance to each situation; finally, exceptionists operate from general principles but treat these flexibly.

What can we say about A and B in relation to this model? Well, there is some evidence that B operates from a low relativist position – the references to the company code and treating customers as friends, for example. There is no obvious evidence that B might feel that different circumstances require different approaches, so his position may be more of an absolutist one than exceptionist. A on the other hand, seems, to be equally as idealistic as B, in that he is concerned about impressing his evaluation on others, but is more of a relativist, in the sense of recognising that different situations require different approaches. Hence A probably tends towards the situationist type.

The three models might be summarised thus:

A: Determined to get their own way (Shaper); inclined to generalisations (Reflector/Theorist); idealistic but not uniform (Situationist).

B: Determined to get their own way (Shaper); inclined more to concrete action (Activist/Pragmatist); uniformly idealistic (Absolutist).

Perhaps it now becomes clearer how the points of similarity and of difference help to suggest explanations of the dialogue analysed above. Clearly there are emotional aspects – both parties are determined individuals. But they also have a fairly strongly held sense of ethics, the difference being that one of them sees this is general terms whilst the other sees it in more concrete terms. Unfortunately, the one with the more concrete ethics tends to be less concrete in his thinking, being more of a reflector/theorist, whilst the one with a more universalist ethics tends to be more concrete and action-orientated.

Clearly this is only an illustration. As has been argued earlier, these do not represent *the truth* about either of these individuals or of the dialogue that they entered into. As an illustration, it may, however, give a flavour for some of the reasons why an understanding of someone else's values can be hindered by one's own mindsetting.

Part of the conflict between A and B is that they approach the issue differently, but not too differently. Clearly, there is an assumed agreement that this is a significant issue – and recall that each has a strong sense of ethics. But each assumes that they also approach ethics in the same way. A avoids factual questions because in his view this will not determine a specific ethical conclusion (given his situationist approach). B asks for factual examples precisely because he *does* see ethical principles as determining the right course of action given a specific set of circumstances. Both see the question of facts as a matter for dispute, as if they can see what the other is going to do with (or without) the facts. But in truth their needs are different. Facts will help one person get a better idea, and not help the other at all. Far more appropriate would be to see a dialogue of this kind as a sort of trade that might help each come to a better understanding of the situation.

Moral relativism has both a common-sense, everyday, following, and an academic following. But the argument for it often turns on two questions: (a) whether we can ever be justified in questioning someone else's ethics; and (b) whether it even makes sense to compare ethical values derived from widely differing cultures. So far as (a) is concerned, the above analysis is not intended to suggest that we cannot ever question other people's views. But it does indicate that we are likely to encounter grave difficulties in *resolving* such questions. Some of the implications of this will be drawn out in the next chapter. For the moment, it is worth noting that the argument assumes both that we can have a meaningful discourse on ethics and that it is often very difficult to bring this to a creative resolution. The issue reflected in

(b) – the idea that different cultures have incomparable systems of ethics – is considered in the following sections.

3.3   Cultures and values

The issue concerning the values of people of different cultures has become a central question for business management over the last half-century. The growth in international trade, the increase in international corporations, the acceleration in international labour mobility and migration, have all meant that it is far more common today for an organisation to have significant representation of several different cultures. With each different culture comes a fresh set of values. With each fresh set of values comes the question of how these may be integrated within an organisation, or how far their differentiation is to be tolerated or even welcomed. I am going to suggest that the differentiation may be more valuable than is commonly considered.

Hopefully we have seen enough, in Chapters 1 and 2, as well as in the earlier part of this chapter, to acknowledge that the idea of 'the' values associated with even a single organisation, let alone a societal culture, is a fiction – apparently similar behaviour can conceal potentially huge differences in attitude and intention. It is worth noting, nevertheless, that such a view is not shared by all writers on business ethics. Thus Richard de George[7] talks of the basic moral norms to be encountered in all societies – he identifies truthfulness, not arbitrarily killing other people and respect for property. His arguments for these are curiously varied, however. The defence of truthfulness is very much in the Kantian mould – we couldn't carry on communicating if we didn't presume truthfulness. On the other hand, his argument regarding not arbitrarily killing seems to rest on the belief that all societies should engage in intersocietal commerce: 'If a society is not to exist in isolation it must attempt to guarantee the safety of others who visit it... Otherwise these interactions can not take place... If lives are threatened... commerce tapers off or comes to an end'.[8] There seems to be a confusion here between economic prudence and morality, between what is necessary to ensure that international trade runs efficiently and what society feels is right. Certainly the state in general provides only a limited degree of safety for visitors and foreign nationals. The USA, the homeland of de George's addressed audience, does not always guarantee the safety of those who live in it, let alone visit – as anyone who has visited the poorer parts of its inner cities can testify. I suspect that de George might feel that this is missing the point. But once one talks of what *society* wishes, then one falls into the unitarist trap of presuming that similar behaviour reflects similar beliefs. One is also faced with significant terminological differences, and different interpretations of what counts as 'arbitrary'. The killing of street children, as reportedly has happened in Brazil in recent years, is presumably what de George would regard as arbitrary, but clearly Brazilian citizens have not reacted to it with sufficient a consensus of public outrage as to force politicians to stamp it out.

Tellingly, in an earlier section, de George tries to argue that there are certain things that should be resisted, despite the possibility that they are accepted in other countries '...slavery is ethically wrong not because Americans believe it to be wrong, but because the practice fails to recognise human beings as human beings. It makes them chattels... .'[9] I am not sure whether there are any longer societies where slavery as such is openly tolerated (as opposed to covertly – some cases of the treatment of immigrant chambermaids in the UK and USA has been identified as covert near-slavery). Nevertheless, if there were, de George is stuck with the difficulty of non-universal values, which might push him into having to say simply that it's wrong, and despite his protestations, justifying this on American, liberal values.

Perhaps the example of slavery may seem a little remote today. Take the issue of the equality of women and men. This is generally acknowledged as a value in many countries, and is supported by legislation. de George would seem to have to say that it is either a universal moral norm or is culture-specific. But if it is a universal norm, then there are major variations in the way this translates into values in different societies. First, actual practices seem to vary tremendously from espoused ethical values, so that despite equal opportunity and pay legislation across the whole of the European Union, women seem still to be faced with the notorious 'glass ceiling', and men seem still to take less than an equal share in domestic and child-rearing duties. Second, what is meant by 'equality of opportunity' is interpreted differently, so that in one country it may be construed in terms of a legislative framework, in others it may be seen in terms of social action. Third, there are some Islamic countries where relationships between the two genders are not conceived on the US model of legal identity of opportunity. Concepts such as the value of family life, the preservation of traditional roles are regarded as governing the lifestyles and opportunities of women in such societies. It is easy enough for a Westerner to dismiss these as discriminatory societies (though there is wide variation between different Islamic countries in the treatment of women, so they cannot be too easily stereotyped on the one model) but all this does is register a difference in values. It does not explain what the status of each of these two kinds of value system is. The idea of gender equality is, then, difficult to establish in any simple universal form. Perhaps it might therefore be a culturally specific value? But then de George is left again with the difficulty of trying to justify it in cross-cultural terms.

The reader may well ask: doesn't this simply mean that gender equality isn't a basic moral norm? It doesn't say anything about the other concepts that de George has mentioned. Accepted, it deals only with equality. But then one needs to ask what point is being made about 'basic' universal ethical norms. If they are meant to be a *foundation* then why are some there and others not? If they just happen to be ones that are commonly shared, isn't the whole argument a bit circular?

Where are we in this discussion? The main question was how one might integrate values from different cultures. We have been critically discussing the views of Richard de George, who holds that some values are basic to all societies. The argument has been that: (a) it's not clear how far de George's own examples *are* common; (b) it's not clear what 'common' really means; and (c) it's unclear what implications there are for values that may not be common.

Part of the difficulty here has been the taking of a *judgement*-orientated approach, whereby arguments are put up that are supposed to demonstrate that something just *is* either a common value or culturally specific. Following the trend of argument of Chapter 1, however, I want to suggest a different focus. The key issue seems to be – what kinds of difference are there between cultures in moral terms, and what impact does this have for ethical communication and behaviour? In taking this approach, we shall see that the differences between different ethical views is a dynamic element, and that the existence of such differences is a *resource* to an organisation, not a problem.

3.4   The value of ethical differences

Linda Trevino and Katherine Nelson[10] identify four different levels of comparison between values of different cultures (and along the way make the important point that no culture is completely deterministic – people can and do make up their own minds):

- universal standards
- comparable values
- values in tension
- incompatible values.

These can be seen as a scale from complete unequivocal acceptance at the top to complete rejection at the bottom. Unlike de George's view, this ranking is not presented in normative terms, but as a descriptive model of how people from different cultures might relate their respective values systems. I will argue that there are opportunities for ethical growth in all four cases. But before that is possible it is necessary to gain a clearer idea of the significance of a particular value within a culture. It may be that a specific value in culture A is in tension (to use Trevino and Nelson's term) with the nearest equivalent in culture B, but this does not fully make sense until the *grip* of that value within the culture is understood. Is it a central, core value, the denial of which would undermine many other things? Or is it relatively peripheral, open to revision without a great deal of further reconstruction?

Discussion of national culture in relation to business immediately conjures up two kinds of model. First there are models of the cultures internal to organisations, of which the best known are the Harrison/Handy and Deal/Kennedy models. These are summarised in Box 3.1. Second there are models relating to national cultures, of which the most influential in management education are those of Geert Hofstede and Fons Trompenaars, which are outlined in Box 3.2.

BOX 3.1   **Organisational Culture Models**

Both the models outlined below identify organisational cultures as approximating to one of four types, or as containing elements of these extremes.

Deal/Kennedy[11]

macho	high risk, quick feedback
work hard play hard	low risk, quick feedback
bet your company	high risk, slow feedback
process culture	low risk, quick feedback

Harrison/Handy[12]

role	emphasis on rules, order, structure
power	emphasis on personalities and internal politics
task	emphasis on the direct requirements of work
people	emphasis on individuals as members of the organisation

---

It might seem that the Hofstede and Trompenaars models are the ones relevant to our current discussion, but I would suggest that there are at least two reasons why organisational culture models are also relevant. First, the content of the organisational models, though couched in business terms, is not necessarily restricted solely to organisations, and hence there is a degree of applicability to national cultures. After all, it is the ethical issues affecting business that is the subject of this book, so this application is not inappropriate in this context. Second, the models are descriptive in nature – they

---

BOX 3.2 **Models of National Culture**

Both of these models measure national culture along a range of dimensions. These are not extreme types but attributes or qualities which cultures will demonstrate to a greater or lesser degree.

Geert Hofstede[13]

power distance	how far equality is valued
uncertainty avoidance	how prone to taking risks or avoiding them
masculinity/femininity	how far ambition and achievement is preferred over collaboration and relationships
individualism	as opposed to collectivism
long-term	as opposed to short-term

Fons Trompenaars[14]

achieved *v.* ascribed status	how far importance is placed on what you do/or what you are
sequential *v.* synchronous time	how much importance is placed on now, the present, or on the relationship with the past
individual *v.* collective	similar to Hofstede
neutral *v.* emotional	how much importance is placed on emotional expression as opposed to keeping a 'stiff upper lip'
universal *v.* particular	rules and generalities as opposed to flexibility
diffuse *v.* specific	how far relationships in organisations are based on the whole person or on limited contractual bases
individual *v.* environment	are people masters of their fate, or is the external world more powerful?

---

provide a framework for describing and understanding organisations. They are not predictive (unlike the Hofstede and Trompenaars models, which do make substantive predictions about different national cultures). Hence there is no empirical harm done by making the connection. Although the focus will therefore be on Hofstede's model of national cultures, organisational cultures will also enter the following discussion. I shall not discuss in detail Hofstede's own conclusions. The more important question is the extent to which his model can help us get a fix on the importance of certain values in a given culture, and from that how much of a creative dynamic is afforded by a conflict of values between one culture and another.

Let us take a well-worn issue from international business ethics: the question of tips, bribes, 'lubricating' payments and other examples of making an unauthorised or unofficial payment to an individual for the sake of achieving a certain business outcome. Clearly there are several kinds of phenomenon here. We could distinguish, for example, between payments that are offered spontaneously, as a means of suborning someone, as opposed to those that are demanded, as a form of ransom. We might also want to identify differences in degree, where a relatively small payment might be seen as less serious than one involving a multiple of the average wage.

It is commonly assumed that the practice of making such payments has a differential ethical dimension depending on whether or not the action happens in a 'sweetener' or a 'non-sweetener' culture (my term, for want of any better). Thus if a citizen of the UK goes to the USA and offers a 'lubricating' payment, it might be considered that this is less ethically justifiable than if they went to, say, Pakistan, because in the latter case gifts and payments are more acceptable. Equally, if a citizen of Pakistan makes such an offer in their own country it might be regarded as more acceptable than if they do the same in the UK.

The issue to explore is not whether this provides a framework for deciding the ethical soundness or otherwise of such an action. Rather, the key question is what it means to say that the practice is a part of the culture? Are all practices equally important to a culture? What lies behind such a practice? Is it something that can be handled in a different way? The answers to these questions might, incidentally, help people to resolve such dilemmas, but from our point of view they may help to understand the limits and possibilities of ethical understanding and agreement.

Clearly, the same practice may have different significance in different cultures within which it is practised. In one case it may be a means of showing respect to a client or supplier, in another it may be a component of the price of a product or service. Now take a culture that on the Hofstede model comes out as high on uncertainty avoidance. That is, people in that culture are prone to want a high level of certainty before committing themselves to action. Does this on its own give a hint on what role the practice of making such facilitating payments might have in that culture? One possibility might be that it is in virtue of their aversion to risk that people in that culture try to seal agreements and increase their chances of success in sales negotiations. Payments would then, in this kind of culture, represent a form of contractual binding, an extra, invisible part of the transaction. On the other hand, a culture high on power distance might also support payments, but on the different basis that these might be seen as a mark of acknowledgement or of deference. In this case, there would presumably be rules around what could be given by a lower status person to a higher, and vice versa. High power distance suggests organisations with power cultures (in the Harrison/Handy sense of the term). In these one might expect to see payments and gifts made internally as a means of creating the personally based favour and influence that is the base currency of a power culture. So the cultures of societies and of the organisations that exist within them may provide a framework for understanding the colour that a practice such a 'sweetening' payments and/or gifts has for such a society.

Obviously this is speculative, and is vastly oversimplified. A culture would need to be measured along all the Hofstede dimensions before even a start could be made on a detailed understanding of the role of non-contractual payments and gifts. But the points above illustrate that some idea of the significance of a practice, and the values associated with it, can be made as a result of a general view of the culture within which it exists.

Now, what does this say about the *conflicts* between individuals from different societies that have different views of 'sweetening'? Clearly, if there can be extreme misunderstanding at the individual level between individuals from the same society, as we saw in Sections 3.1 and 3.2, there is going to be at least as much, if not more and of a greater order of complexity, where individuals from different national cultures are concerned. This does not rule out the possibility of agreement, but it makes clear how great a challenge it might be.

Consider an individual from a culture with a high degree of what Trompenaars call *achieved* (as opposed to ascribed) *status*. That is, it is a culture in which status is accorded to people on the basis of their own behaviour, rather than, say, on a class basis. For an individual from such a culture the idea of a gift would be more likely to be perceived in instrumental terms. That is, it would not be seen as a gesture of deference, for that concept relies on a certain level of ascribed status, but would be perceived as part of the process of achieving the desired end. Hence if they were offered a gift this would be seen as a means of securing a contract, or create some kind of expectation or sense of obligation – in other words, it might be seen as no different from a bribe. Suppose they come into contact with someone from a culture with a high level of long-term focus (admittedly we are mixing models here, but not dangerously so). Such a culture is likely to perceive a gift or sweetener as a means toward developing long-term relationships. Hence it is less an attempt to create an obligation for a specific contract as it is a means of trying to pave the way for future friendly relations.

So a direct misunderstanding can come about as a result of the cultural frameworks within which the individuals concerned operate. But this is not a purely negative result, for the seeds of a way forward are contained within the differing approaches. Clearly it is possible for the individual from the high achieved status culture to discuss what is intended by the offer of the gift. They might explain that they see this as an attempt to secure a specific outcome. In so doing, they present a view that the individual from the high long-term focus can process in their own terms, that is as a step towards or away from a long-term end. Hence a dialogue can begin. The conflict itself, and its underpinning context, can be the resource for its own resolution, for it can jolt individuals out of their mindsettings as often as it will entrench them.

Obviously a dialogue might not begin – the first person might simply say 'That's a bribe' and the second might therefore think that in the long term they can't do business with such a person. And, as mentioned above, there are many diverse factors to add into this highly schematised outline of what could go on between individuals from different cultures. One reason why I have avoided making categorical assertions about specific countries in this discussion is precisely because each of these represents so particular a blend of different factors that the transferability of the argument might be obscured.

There are other issues to consider in the light of this discussion. One of these is what needs to be in place for the process outlined above to be possible at all. For it requires that individuals be able to reflect on their own practices, understand what the underlying values and concerns of these are, then present them in a manner comprehensible to an 'outsider', and enter into a dialogue with their counterpart concerning theirs. A tall order. Unfortunately, certain cultures may be intrinsically structured in a way that makes this difficult to achieve – for example, a culture with a high level of collectivism may find it harder to encourage independent critical enquiry, because this often involves individuals asking awkward questions of established collective practices and assumptions. A highly masculine culture, in Hofstede's sense of the term, may inhibit the development of skills such as active listening, open questioning and so on, which are essential for a dialogue that might move people towards mutual understanding. We shall come back to the question of what capabilities are important for ethical change in a later chapter. For the moment, the point is that ethical change does require certain generic skills and abilities.

Ethical agreement between cultures, then, is possible if each side has materials that can be used to build the appropriate kind of bridge. Not all such attempts work, just as not every throw of a rope across a stream gets to the other side. But if contact is to be established it is on that basis – that elements exist which afford points of contact between the cultures involved. That is why we have examined the potential role of models such as Hofstede's in helping to contextualise particular expressed values and practices. Once they are contextualised, one can begin to see what can or cannot be easily changed in that context. It also becomes possible to see which points in the contexts of the different cultures may afford points of contact. The mindsettings that these reflect can be straitjackets, or they can be resources.

What is also important is that in building a bridge one cannot help but change the terrain on one's *own* side – for at the very least there exists a track where there was none previously. And in practice, the changes that may result go beyond this analogy, for they can often involve the reconstruction of one culture's beliefs and values as a response to the challenge of meeting another. This is an important source of *internal* pressure for change, which we shall consider later.

Overall, then, in this section we have been looking at the question of the possibility of a meaningful dialogue between people who come from very different cultures. We have seen that the elements of communication and agreement can be present, but the precise significance of these requires an analysis of the culture in question – for which we sketched some ideas using the models of Hofstede and Trompenaars. Such communication also requires certain generic skills.

To summarise this whole chapter, the key question has been how far one person can make sense of the values of someone else. We considered this on a mono-cultural basis in the earlier part of the chapter. The answer seems to be that there are many factors involved, hence whilst agreement is possible it is easy to miss. Much of our discursive behaviour inhibits agreement due to the structure of discussions and arguments, certainly in a manager-to-employee context. In this last part we have seen how the international aspect lends a further series of dimensions, rendering the issue of value agreement challenging but ultimately quite elusive. In the next chapter we shall look at organisational cultures again from a different perspective, and consider one practical implication of this strand of argument.

Questions

A   How does your own organisation deal with the issue of facilitating payments? Is there a blanket ban, are exceptions allowed and if so, on what basis?

B   Analyse your own organisation using all the culture models outlined in this chapter (the national ones as well as the organisational ones). Try to interpret them as a totality – what overall does this tell you about the business and how it influences people's values?

C   Try to think of your most cherished belief. Where did it come from? What does it rest on now? What kind of context is it suitable for? Most telling of all, are you hidebound by it – is it an ossified or a dynamic mindset? (You may well find this easier in discussion with a close colleague or friend.)

Notes

1. We shall look at the contrast between the logical and psychological structure of people's arguments and beliefs in Chapter 5.
2. For a discussion of 'thick' and 'thin' ethical concepts, see Williams (1985).
3. See Langer (1993) Chapters 1 and 2 and Goleman (1997) Part Two.

4. Meredith Belbin's original presentation of his model can be found in his 1981 text. Honey's work on learning styles can be found in Honey and Mumford (1986).
5. See Kolb (1985).
6. Forsyth (1980).
7. de George (1993).
8. *Ibid.* p. 19.
9. *Ibid.* p. 12.
10. Trevino and Nelson (1995) p. 277.
11. Deal and Kennedy (1982).
12. Handy (1993).
13. Hofstede (1991).
14. Trompenaars (1993). It is worth noting that he uses a modified form of this model in another work (Hampden-Turner and Trompenaars 1993).

4 The Myth of Shared Values – Organisational Totalitarianism

In the previous three chapters we have seen some of the difficulties surrounding the idea that a manager can and should get a clear understanding of people's values. In this chapter, which concludes the first part of this book, I want to apply some of the ideas presented earlier to a key arena of modern management thinking and practice – the suggestion that managers should be trying to create a sense of *shared value* in their organisations. What we shall see is that, whilst the promotion of shared values can assist in creating an openness that contributes to corporate success, it can all too easily degenerate. Thus are created mechanisms for imposing totalitarian cultures in organisations – mechanisms that are harmful to corporate success. In contrast, we shall see that celebrating diversity, in values no less than in other areas, is a more solid foundation for managing an organisation's workforce.

4.1 Shared behaviour *versus* agreed values

In a number of small-scale classroom experiments I asked about 30 postgraduate management students, all practising managers, to identify (in writing) the clearest examples of shared values at work. I also asked them to identify their *evidence* for saying that the group had a common or shared set of values. Perhaps the latter was a somewhat abstract question for professional managers, who by their very work are more accustomed to activist-orientated behaviour. At any rate, the first question was easily and eagerly answered – for the majority of respondents the idea of shared values seemed to be almost synonymous with effective teamworking – very 'Japanese management' style. The second question was either ignored or met with puzzlement, and produced responses that tended to repeat the first answer. Afterwards we had a brief discussion of the point of the exercise and what I was looking for. I recall one person who said 'I don't see how we can give a separate answer for number two. If we're talking about shared values all we can do is describe what we saw or heard. Isn't that the evidence?' In effect this participant's view crystallises one of the key themes of this chapter. What are values inferred from? In the broadest sense, which includes what people say as well as what they do, the answer is – people's *behaviour*. But if we try to establish someone's values from their behaviour, we must recognise that there are many different values that could be the spring for that individual's acts. So a principal issue is the severe under-determination of people's values by their behaviour. We have already touched on this in earlier chapters. The key twist, illustrated by the quote above, is that in the practical day-to-day situation, most of us fail to see the under-determination. We fail to spot the distinction between what we think so-and-so's values are and what our evidence is for thinking this.

I shall not go over the role of intention in behaviour, although clearly the arguments of earlier chapters imply that it is difficult for a manager even to recognise what values people have. The first question we need to address is what it really means to *share* values. Management literature seems to slither past this question. Tom Peters and Robert Waterman, in the most celebrated source of the idea of shared values in a management context,[1] seem to presume that an organisation with shared values is one in which the work-force as a whole – or a sufficient majority – simply hold the same values. In a similar but more detailed vein, Andrew Campbell and Kiran Tawadey identify shared values as conformance of the values of employees to those of senior management. They explicitly identify 'company values' as 'what senior management believes in', and a little later state that 'Employees who have personal values similar to the organisation's values find a sense of fulfilment and meaning in their work and behaviour standards.'[2] The language here seems to suggest that the issue is one of whether or not an individual's values *correspond* to some external set of 'organisational' values. There are two additional nuances worth noting here – first, that employees' values should be identical with organisational ones; and second, that the employee must fit in with the organisation's values, rather than the other way around. We shall come back to this idea of correspondence in Section 4.2.

Obviously there is more than that. The influence of prevailing organisa-tional behaviours on an individual – the way that being in an organisation tends to shape and develop our attitudes and values – is one reason why the phenomenon of shared values is more than mere correspondence (a point that I suspect Campbell and Tawadey would happily acknowledge). Under-lying this view, however, are several concepts that need further explanation, in particular the following three:

- the 'existence' of a single value within an individual's overall framework

- the idea of 'an organisation's values' and the associated question of how uniform is the culture of the organisation
- the manner in which value conformance is expressed or interpreted in an organisation.

4.1.1 The existence of values

Many writers on business ethics see an important part of their task as identifying a list of key values or virtues that are relevant to the world of business. They then go on to infer that a key task of business ethics is to establish whether an organisation possesses or holds these, and how far individuals can be influenced to hold the same values. So Laura Nash talks about the common denominators of ethics – honesty, reliability, fairness and pragmatism – whilst at a more abstract level Ronald Green presents an overall framework of objectivity in decisions, which he terms 'NORM'.[3] The bases for these two examples illustrate the main alternative routes to such proposals: Nash claims to have arrived at her set via an extensive poll (her term) of managers in the US; Green is proposing his as the result of his own analysis – though he acknowledges a debt to two philosophers, the contemporary John Rawls and the 18th-century Immanuel Kant (see Box 4.1 for a brief indication of the relevant ideas of these two philosophers). In both Nash's and Green's cases, though, the overall strategy remains the same – given a set of recommended values or value structures, the key issues are: (a) whether organisations display or support these; and (b) how does a manager increase the degree to which individuals within those organisations also support them?

BOX 4.1   **Two Philosophers**

Kant   The test of whether something is a moral statement is: could I consistently accept it as a universal law, applicable to all?

Rawls   The test of a just society is: could I accept the lowest place in it?

See Kant (ed. Paton, 1948) and Rawls (1971).

Let us leave for the moment the idea that organisations themselves have moral standards (we shall consider this in Section 4.1.2). How do we decide that an individual 'has' a particular value? What would be our evidence for this? In these questions we have returned to the issue of Chapters 1 and 2, and the conclusions reached in those chapters still applies. People's values and motives exist in a complicated and ever shifting nexus, often with conflicting and competing elements. When someone acts in a certain way, this is best understood as being a solution – and possibly a transient one at that – to the problem of reconciling different influences. Doubtless there are regularities and patterns in how someone acts. But if an individual happens consistently not to act in ways that I, as an observer, would describe as, for example, *fair*, this might be explicable in at least seven different ways:

- That individual does not believe in fairness as a value.
- The individual believes in fairness, but this tends to be overridden by other factors that are seen as more important.
- The individual believes in fairness at least as much as other values, but he/she holds certain factual beliefs which make it unlikely that they choose courses of action that the observer would deem fair.
- The observer and the individual treat the value in question in different ways; for example, one sees it in deontological (that is, absolute) terms, the other in consequential (that is, relative) terms.
- The observer is biased either with regard to the individual or with regard to the idea of fairness.
- The observer does not hold the same factual beliefs as the individual.
- The observer interprets the idea of fairness in a different way to the individual.

Where there are differences as indicated above, it must be doubted whether someone can justifiably assess the others' values. Only where there is a relative existing concurrence of values *and* factual beliefs between an observer and the individual can the former infer with any confidence whether someone does or does not 'share' with them a particular value. We shall see later that it is more difficult even than that!

4.1.2 The organisation's values

There are two related areas that need to be considered where the question of 'organisational values' is concerned. One is the idea that an organisation can itself be said to 'have' values at all; and the other is the extent of homogeneity of values within an organisation's culture.

Can an organisation legitimately be ascribed values at all? Legally, an organisation is treated like a person – for example, where issues of liability are concerned. That is to say, an organisation may be held responsible for debts, liable to give or receive compensation, and so on. However, even in the legal sphere there are constraints on this. Certainly, in UK law, organisations are 'personalities' only in a civil sense. They cannot be tried in a criminal court. Where criminal proceedings are involved, it is the directors or employees who are tried. So the legal analogy breaks down just at the most relevant point to our discussion. If an organisation cannot be said to act criminally, what sense is there in ascribing to it moral responsibility, and hence moral attitudes?

At the heart of this is really the question of what kind of thing is an organisation? Is it a singularity to which values, learning attitudes and so on can be ascribed? Or is it described so obliquely, only metaphorically?4 When a question of this kind is put thus, there is a temptation to push the issue further than the terminology can really bear. Certainly it seems possible to give extreme answers either way to this question. So one answer would be that an organisation is a social unit which takes on personal characteristics by virtue of being composed of human beings as members – an investment bank might be seen as aggressive because the vast majority of its brokers are. Equally, an answer at the other extreme would be that the ideas of corporate culture and organisational values are entirely metaphorical, conveniences to help simplify the complex reality of a large group of people.

In practice neither answer is really satisfactory. Some organisations, partially because of their structure, partially because of other factors such as the nature of their business, degree of competitiveness, and so on, are culturally simple. Wherever you go in the organisation you will find similar responses from the staff, similar approaches to non-standard problems and tasks, and so on. By comparison, other organisations are much more complex. Subcultures abound. The same task presented to different groups might elicit quite different responses. I call this difference the *degree of cultural saturation*.

Figure 4.1 portrays this on two dimensions – degree of conformity and number of key cultures – leading to nine different organisation types. This model indicates that organisations vary widely in the extent to which they can be regarded as a unified whole, and hence it demonstrates that they cannot all be conveniently identified as possessing one set of values.

As much as anything this model emphasises that the whole project of trying to manage culture and values is more appropriate for some organisations and less for others. However, the main point I wish to draw from it is that the idea of an organisation as the bearer of attitudes and values has greater sense the further to the top left an organisation is placed. Equally, it has less sense the further to the bottom right the organisation might be. A minimalist organisation is not one in which it is particularly useful to talk about sharing values at all, for there is little if any central core of values that define the organisation. On the other hand, a highly conformist monoculture (which I have labelled 'totalitarian' with deliberate bias – (see later in this chapter) is one where there does seem to be some sense in talking about 'the organisation's values'.

Degree of conformity within workforce	Number of cultures represented in organisation		
	Monoculture	Few subcultures	Many subcultures
high	totalitarianism	imperatorial power bases	team culture
medium	influential role model	party/faction based	departmentalism
low	tolerant	loose confederation	minimalist

Figure 4.1   A model of cultural saturation

So the issue about 'the organisation' gives limited support to the idea of shared values, but only for those organisations in which values are already shared! Whilst in some circumstances it is quite possible to pull an organisation from one side of the above diagram to another, one might doubt whether it is *always* possible. Perhaps more importantly, it may be questioned whether it is *desirable* to try to turn an organisation with, say, an effective departmental cultural format into one dominated by a single set of norms and ideals. What kind of problem is solved by doing this? And what kinds of problems are created by this 'solution'?

The other issue arising from this model is the question of 'whose' values represent those of the organisation. As mentioned earlier, Campbell and Tawadey see this specifically in terms of 'senior management'. Similarly, Peters has identified early senior managers – often but not always the founders of companies – as the key sources of the organisation's culture and values. This view in itself tends towards what I have called totalitarian or role model-based cultures. In contrast, it becomes less and less clear what the source of 'the values of the organisation' might be as we move across and down the diagram, but it also becomes less and less important.

4.1.3   The expression of conformity

The third point to be made concerning shared values is the theme of internal intention *versus* external behaviour. This returns to the question of what it means to say that someone holds a particular value or virtue.

BOX 4.1   **Scenario – The Sales Discussion**

Stephanie Jellison is the marketing director for APP Ltd, a packaging company. APP have a long-standing contract with an ice-cream producer to supply cartons for multiple ice-cream and lolly packs. One day she discovered that the paper used for these packs had been treated with a highly toxic bleach. Stephanie discussed the situation with John Hugnet, the sales representative for the ice-cream account.

She said: 'Obviously we'll have to change the packaging. I know the suppliers say it's actually quite safe, but we can't be seen to be wrapping kids' lollies in something that might be toxic, whatever they say. Might as well sell them frozen yoghurt dioxin flavour!'

John replied, 'Yes, the issue of what we've been telling the company all this time could really do us in with them. You're right, we must change the card base for the packages as soon as possible.'

'Yes, but it's not the client I'm thinking of, it's all those little children. It would be terrible'.

'Of course, yes, you're quite right.'

Box 4.1 illustrates a characteristic dialogue relating to the idea of agreement in values. Micro-events of this kind are the very soul of organisational life, and they tend to pass by almost unnoticed. The statement made at the end is the central point. A good case can be made that these two are talking about quite different things. Granted, John agrees with the proposal, but as Stephanie is his boss, he is quite likely to do so for reasons unconnected with the issue itself. His own spontaneously delivered comment emphasises a different issue, not one directly of safety but of the commercial consequences of violation. The great temptation is for Stephanie to conclude that she and John agreed about the issue. The existence of several agreement phrases in John's language (two uses of 'yes', two 'you're right', one 'of course' in a matter of a couple of sentences) might naturally lead her to this, but a difference has been subtly expressed, in a way that a John-type character could easily exploit later if things went wrong, for example, by saying 'Well, although I went along with the decision to change the product, I did say at the time that the PR issue could be important.'

The lesson from this example is the complexity that underlies apparent agreement in ethical judgements. It is clear that John agrees to a proposal at least partially for a different reason to Stephanie's. Verbal agreements are the cornerstone evidence of whether or not people share the same values.[5]

Unfortunately, they are not infallible guides. Figure 4.2 indicates the key factors underlying verbal agreements regarding values.

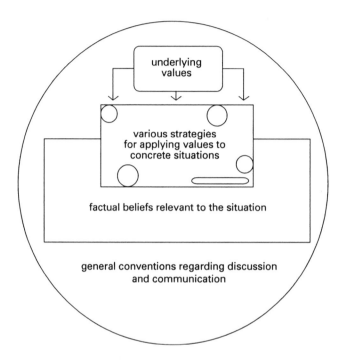

underlying
values

various strategies
for applying values to
concrete situations

factual beliefs relevant to the situation

general conventions regarding discussion
and communication

Figure 4.2   The context and content of value judgements

As the diagram illustrates, multiple factors underpin and contribute to someone's verbal judgements of values. But it is not the case that the kind of superficial 'agreement' exemplified above exists solely when all factors 'pull' in the same direction. Different elements may conflict, and in doing so cancel each other out. Consider the following range of possible sources of superficial verbal agreement, which almost certainly are not exhaustive. Two people engaging in a discussion about ethics may:

● share exactly the same values, apply these in the same way to the situation at hand, and share the same factual beliefs relevant to the situation
● have the same basic beliefs, differing in how these should be applied to situations, but this difference is itself cancelled out by their differing factual beliefs

- have different basic ethical values, but different factual beliefs leads them to agree in a particular situation
- come to an agreement for social, or power-based reasons, with one or both choosing not to make open their true feelings
- attribute different meanings to key words or phrases
- fail to ask the right questions to elicit the key elements of the other person's views
- fail to hear clearly the verbal subtleties that mark separate values.

Take an example of the second of these, relating to attitudes towards risks to health. Two people may both hold that organisations should minimise health risks to their employees and their customers. One, however, views this as a near absolute, that is as virtually a deontological value with few if any conceivable exceptions. The other sees this in more relative terms, depending on other factors such as the degree of risk, commercial importance of the operations involved, and so on. So a difference in approach is built in. However, in a particular situation, for example the question of the strength of a safety harness used by construction workers, the second individual may believe that the harnesses are not strong enough to bear the loads placed on them over a period of time. Hence she perceives that there is a very high risk of injury to the health of employees. In this situation, she might well agree with the first person. The difference is cancelled out by other factors.

Similar examples could be given for the other cases outlined above. Of course, often these things do not happen, and misunderstandings get discovered and usually ironed out. What is important is not the specific frequency of such misconstructions, but the difficulty of building in ways to avoid them. Only a very astute individual would be likely to avoid the pitfall that Stephanie falls into by assuming that John agrees with her. Of course, he *does* agree, but only in one sense. He may disagree with her about basic values, about the likelihood of certain things happening, about how values should be applied to situations, and so on. *Verbal conformance in concrete cases is not definitive of underlying agreement in values.*

Chris Argyris talks about mixed messages – contradictory statements – that are a characteristic, if somewhat paradoxical, way in which senior managers avoid directly confronting difficult issues.6 He characterises these as defence routines. That is, they are mechanisms to enable organisational life to go on. Although they are not exactly functional within the business, for they contribute towards deep-rooted problems inhibiting communication and learning in the organisation, they do serve a purpose. They are inherent in organisational processes, not in any shallow sense a haphazardly occurring fault.

Argyris uses the example of autonomy *versus* control in organisations.[7] Senior managers want their middle-ranking staff to have a degree of freedom, and reinforce this in both actions and words in non-critical situations. But in critical situations — which, as Argyris points out, are just the ones in which a delegated middle manager will want to show their capability — the senior manager feels she needs to come in and give her support: that is, take over the reins. The message is 'clearly' put over in an ambiguous fashion — 'you are in charge, but ultimately I need to have the final word.' Obviously this is paradoxical, and Argyris goes on to explain how such a paradox can exist in an organisation. For example, one important mechanism for sustaining such paradoxes is to refuse to acknowledge that they exist, or that anything needs discussing about such utterances. R.D. Laing, in the admittedly different context of family relationships, has illustrated how such falsehoods contribute to the stability that family members seek in their different ways.[8] This does also underline the points made in Chapter 2 about self-deception — if you can't discuss it, you can't challenge it — so how does someone break out of the spell?

It underlines, though: (a) how *indirect* language and communication can be; and (b) that these processes contain a built-in tendency to be problematic. Here is further support for the view presented above, that the idea of gaining a clear and truthful agreement in values is less straightforward than first sight might suggest.

4.2   Diversity

The previous section indicated some of the problems associated with the idea of trying to create a sense of shared values in an organisation. It indicated that in the strong sense of shared *attitudes,* rather than just behaviour, the ideal of sharing is less feasible than is generally supposed. In this section we shall consider whether it is even desirable.

4.2.1 Totalitarian organisations

In Section 4.1.2 we considered the range of levels of cultural saturation, and in particular I labelled the high conformant monoculture as 'totalitarian'. This is a strong term to use. Are all such organisations really as oppressive as the term suggests? And does this mean that shared values are such a bad thing? The answer to these questions is, in order, no and not necessarily. Remember, though, that a high conformant monoculture is the prime kind of organisation for which it makes sense to talk about 'the values of the organisation'. There are tendencies within such organisations that can easily degenerate into oppression. This both undermines and undervalues the diversity of modern workforces, which are becoming increasingly multi-ethnic as the world becomes a more convergent global economy.

The idea of sharing values may be made clearer if we adopt a schematic approach to the issue. The question of an individual sharing values with the organisation might be symbolised thus:

For any V, $V(o) \rightarrow V(i)$

where V is a value, o is the organisation, and i represents a member of the organisation. The above formula is thus a shorthand for saying that all organisational values are also values of the individual. In other words, that an individual's values *correspond* to those of the organisation. Obviously this is grossly oversimplified. We are leaving aside, for example, the issue of how 'the' organisation's values have been arrived at, or whether it really makes sense to talk about identifying all of someone's values. We are also ignoring, for the moment, the issue about the relationship between holding or having a value and putting it into practice. Furthermore, we are also overlooking attendant issues relating to application and how one decides between competing values, and how far someone's value set may be structured or may be just a jumble of ideas and feelings. Nevertheless, we shall try to press on with the analysis.

What happens when some $V(i)$ does not equal a $V(o)$? Does this mean that the individual does not share the organisation's values? Not necessarily, for the individual may hold values over and above those of the organisation, for example values relating to family life. So the issue must be the other way around. Not sharing the organisation's values is presumably indicated when there is a $V(o)$ not equal to any $V(i)$. The key managerial task is now clearly defined – find some appropriate method to ensure that a $V(i)$ is created that does equal the $V(o)$ in question.

This then is the formal expression of what was referred to earlier as the correspondence approach to sharing organisational values. It is an influential idea that underlies many managerial approaches to ethical change. Francis Aguilar quotes, with approval, William Adams (CEO of Armstrong World Industries): 'One of my primary functions is to promote the company's values and culture. I am particularly concerned in getting new employees to understand these things.'[9] In the context in which this appears it is difficult not to read 'understand' as meaning 'accept'. Later Aguilar comments: 'The overall business ethics process at Armstrong World Industries is characterised by senior management's personal involvement in defining and encouraging ethical behaviour on the one hand and detecting and punishing ethical misconduct on the other.'[10] Note again that by 'ethical' he means ethically right, morally correct. Obviously, when the examples are all ones of bribery, theft and profiteering, this approach may seem unexceptionable, but Aguilar does not seem even to notice that this might not always be the case. What we have here – despite all the well intentioned backdrop – are the foundations for totalitarian organisational culture. I would venture to suggest that this is a specific consequence of the oversimplified approach exemplified in the formulae given above. For they abstract the discussion from the very issues that we have seen give ethical issues their bite and their great difficulty. The Armstrong method seems so simple – respect dignity, maintain high moral standards, show good taste and common courtesy and keep all stakeholders' interests in balance.[11] In reality these principles will be only as strong as the individuals who make use of them, and in particular only as strong as the perception of those individuals – their ability to identify and recognise the diversity of values even one person may hold. When values conflict, or when a novel kind of situation comes along, then the schoolroom style of the Armstrong approach is exposed as inadequate.

4.2.2 An example

In the preceding section we considered the correspondence approach to the idea of shared values. In this section we shall look in detail at just one kind of example that presents serious difficulties for such an approach. Consider Box 4.2.

BOX 4.2   **Living in Two Worlds**

Bernard Atti is a successful entrepreneur, running a flourishing division of a major retail conglomerate. He started his own business importing craft goods from central Asia to the USA and western Europe, and was recently bought out by one of the largest retail store chains in the world. He has a Harvard MBA, a seat on the board, lives in New York's most fashionable area, and is regarded as an honest and fair operator.

Bernard was born in the steppes of central Asia, in one of the regions from which he now exports goods to the West. His mother was a Frenchwoman, an archaeologist interested in the region, who met, fell in love with, and married the son of a tribal chieftain. Bernard's father died when he was young and, despite some opposition from the tribe, his mother brought him up in France and the USA. He does, though, retain close ties with his father's tribe, of which he is regarded as an honorary leader (the tribe's king, Bernard's cousin, is very supportive of his relationship with them).

BOX 2.2 (cont'd)

Bernard has been a strong supporter of equal opportunities in the USA, working particularly to help newly arrived migrants from Afghanistan, Mongolia and other former Soviet states, Pakistan, northern India and Tibet. He is especially well respected for his establishment of cooperatives to help recent immigrants to the USA set themselves up in employment or open their own businesses.

Bernard's dilemma is that the values of the USA are not those of his father's tribe, which he sees as an important part of his heritage. The tribe lives a semi-nomadic life in a sparsely inhabited region. They and other tribes in the area live an austere but sustainable lifestyle – no-one need starve, though all must work hard. The benefits of the 20th century are present in the form of medical supplies, radios, and more recently TV, but not in any technological development of the primary lifestyle, which is based on hunting, rearing live-stock and trading small domestic items and clothing. Bernard's business was originally built upon the goods that he imports from the tribe, though he now also trades in other remote areas in Brazil and Zaire. To his credit he has done a great deal to improve the living standards of all with whom he deals.

In the tribe there are very strongly held views about gender differences – women are completely responsible for all domestic decisions, men make all the external choices, such as where the family will live and what they will do for work (which the women may well be involved in under the direction of their husbands). Children work, often from a very young age. Honour and courage are seen as crucial male values, and whilst there is little inter-tribal conflict, there is intense individual competition amongst young men within a tribe and with other tribes, which on occasion can become bloody and even fatal. Disability is not tolerated – an individual who cannot ride is not supported except by their own immediate nuclear family, sometimes not even then.

The tribes are themselves extended families. In this region, the needs and demands of one's family and tribe take precedence over any other social group. So Bernard has found that although his tribe are happy that he should import and export goods from other parts of the globe, they will not tolerate him trading with their neighbours except through them. This they happily do, taking a very large cut. This is not unfair by the standards of the region. As the area lies on one of the great trading routes of the past, this practice has often been an element in the movement of products across the country. But one consequence is that neighbouring tribes are considerably less well-off in terms of medical supplies and other modern imports.

The problem Bernard faces is that the key social building blocks of the lifestyle of his family are in direct conflict with recognised standards in his chosen home country of the USA. In the USA state welfare is supplemented by a large private system to support the ill and the disabled, whereas his father's tribe would see this as wasteful of precious resources. US legislation strictly enforces gender equality, whilst the tribe would regard this as wilfully undermining the fabric of their way of life, and of the different dignities of each sex. The code of conduct of the organisation for which Bernard works talks of 'not profiting unfairly from our suppliers, and always giving a fair price for goods and services', which sits uneasily with the tariff that Bernard's tribe imposes on his trading with other local tribes. Child labour on the scale operating within Bernard's tribe is completely rejected in the USA. Violence on an individual basis is accepted by the tribe as a mechanism for men to maintain their self-respect and manhood, whereas in the USA it would simply be treated as assault.

Clearly a person in Bernard's position would easily feel torn between these two contrasting sets of values. He would seem to have four options:

● Take the US value set as fundamental, thus denying the claims of his ancestry.
● Take his tribe's value set as fundamental, becoming an ethical tourist in the US.
● Try to find points of contact and compromise between the two systems, risking the chance that both will see him as having sold out.
● Ignore the conflict, and live two lives (thus running the risk of being seen as a hypocrite).

It is inappropriate to make a generalisation about what Bernard ought to do in this situation; it is neither the purpose of the example nor the intention of this book as a whole to make such judgements. Nevertheless, there are several important points to note about this example:

● Which of Bernard's value sets are relevant to the question of whether or not he shares the values of his organisation? Each is instrumental in his business activity, each has a claim on his personality. In truth one would have to say both or neither. This, then, is an acute personal dilemma for him.
● On the formal version of the correspondence approach (as constructed earlier in this section) Bernard might indeed share the organisation's values – presuming that it has a relatively typical set of US corporate values, all these would be held by him. Of course it's what else he holds that presents the difficulty.
● Whichever option Bernard espouses will involve him in ethical loss. He can reject one or other or both of the value sets, or try to resolve them at a smaller violation of each. Of course, there may be important business

consequences of his response to the dilemma. If the western market, or indeed Bernard's co-directors, discover the conditions in which his tribe produce the textiles and ornaments that he imports, they may insist on changes. After all, where child labour is concerned, people might point to the example of Levis, who have worked to improve the lot of children in developing countries by supporting educational programmes. Why not with Bernard's people? Bernard, however, is acutely aware that if he attempts a similar kind of social change, one which required that the children be educated rather than go to work for example, the tribe as a whole might simply decide to stop producing the goods and revert to an all-subsistence economy. Whilst this would not be good for Bernard, in western terms it would also not be good for the tribe, for they would lose the opportunity to acquire modern medicines and other benefits deriving from contact with the West.

- The models of value proposed by writers such as Aguilar or Trevino and Nelson lack sufficient capacity to deal with this dilemma in the way in which it is experienced. Trevino and Nelson are realistic in recognising that individuals are not always consistent in their behaviour, talking of 'our multiple selves', in particular the divergence between our 'office' self and our 'family' or 'religious' selves.[12] But their examples are mono-cultural, which tends to lead to an underestimation of the scale of this kind of divergence in ethics. Furthermore, their recommendations to help managers deal with this dilemma, and develop more integrity, are naive in the extreme: 'Begin by analysing yourself. Get to know your own office ethical self. Is it consistent with your personal ethical self?' then later, when talking about other people '...be realistic. Make no assumption about ethics at work... You can learn a great deal simply by keeping your eyes and ears open. But the best way to find out how your people think is to ask them... .'[13] As methods of analysing either self or others, these suggestions woefully underestimate the difficulty and the fragility of the exercise of understanding people's values.

  Francis Aguilar seems also to miss some of the complexities here. In discussing ethical dilemmas he seems to give no indication of what might be a way through such difficulties. Indeed his language suggests a strong deontological element that renders resolution almost impossible. In discussing a case where a company had illegally boosted profits, he says 'Restitution of the money is morally correct. Avoiding harm to innocent individuals is also morally correct. It is not clear [in this particular case] how the company can honor both principles.'[14] Perhaps the terminology of moral correctness is part of the problem here.

- Attempts at bridging the gulf between the two value sets may undermine both in Bernard's mind without providing a resolution. A forced compromise is likely to lead to some degree of ethical loss to each value set, which is probably at least as bad as outright rejection of one or other of them. To take the least problematic area, a requirement by Bernard that he be allowed to trade more freely with other tribes, so long as they continued to make some payment to his tribe, could easily be seen by the tribe as straightforward interference in what is regarded as a legitimate trading practice, and may still contravene the company requirement on unnecessary profiting.

An attempt to identify points of contact that might afford the basis for accommodating the two sets is certainly an attractive proposition. One problem with it, though, is that there is no guarantee that any points of contact which are identified will be substantial enough to support a rapprochement. Another, potentially more serious, is that such an attempt requires a deep analysis of the ethical concepts involved. But, as the contemporary philosopher Bernard Williams puts it, reflection can destroy knowledge. Some moral codes are built on an element of unquestioning acceptance, which analysis erodes.[15]

It is also difficult to see how, in the case of Bernard's tribe, the socially approved tolerance of individual violence may be appropriately supplanted by something more acceptable to US citizens, such as an extended focus on sporting activity. This does not seem to square with the idea that manhood is demonstrated via a confrontation with danger. The analysis of ideas such as courage and danger involve a necessary reference to the reality of danger inherent in the activity in question. Sanitised, safe, versions are not the same thing at all. The value is not satisfied by an alternative practice, it is *replaced* by it. And it is quite feasable that members of the tribe will perceive the subtext of such a replacement, and as a result reject it out of hand. This has important implications for approaches to moral development (as we shall see in Part II of this book).

- The final point to note is that this kind of tension is becoming more and more frequent as the world becomes one global economy. Ever more individuals are experiencing the incongruities of different social frameworks, including the embedded value systems of parent and expatriate cultures. Whilst this may have the beneficial effect of creating greater points of similarity and contact between different cultures, it also creates along the way an enormous degree of ethical conflict – internal as well as external, as individuals try to reconcile ideas coming from different religions, class structures, and economic histories.

We have discussed this hypothetical case in detail because it raises some of the most critical points for the 'correspondence' approach to sharing values, an approach that finds its fullest expression in high conformant mono-cultures. Recall that the 'correspondence' approach presents the issue of shared values in an organisation as a two-fold task – first, define a set of corporate values; second, devise methods for bringing around the values of the staff to being identical with the corporate values. But, first, Bernard's difficulties stem from the incompatibility of two value sets, to both of which he has a strong allegiance. He already *shares* the organisation's values. That doesn't help to resolve his conflict. Second, the implicit assumption that getting people to understand a set of values is instrumental in getting them to accept those values is in this case, not exactly disconfirmed, but certainly undermined. Third, a highly conformant monoculture is likely to find Bernard a difficult nut to crack – he is successful precisely because of his ability to straddle two worlds. If it is perceived by the organisation as a problem it is one that they rely on for their business.

Such cases as Bernard's present key difficulties not only with the 'correspondence' approach to shared values, but more widely to the idea that organisational strategy is best served by conformance at all. As Gareth Morgan puts it 'Creativity thrives on the tension created by diversity, and it is essential that steps be taken to ensure that organisations build enough tension and variety into processes where involvement is required.'[16] Diversity is to be celebrated as a key driving force in organisational regeneration.

These last two sections have been concerned with conformance and the stresses that this places on monocultures. In itself the argument has not justified the label 'totalitarian' for such organisations, but the reader will remember that at the outset of this discussion I said that highly conformant monocultures do not *have* to be so. What I have tried to do here is present one kind of case that presents difficulties for such organisations, and indeed for any attempt at creating a strong form of shared organisational values (as opposed to shared behaviour). There are other kinds of example that could have been discussed in detail. Two such cases are: (a) people who, despite the best efforts of those concerned with selecting the kind of person most amenable to the organisation's values, slip through the net, and are opposed, even antagonistic, to the corporate values system; and (b) people whose values change over time through their experiences. What all of these create is a challenge for an organisation that tries to develop a high level of consensus towards a single set of values. The label 'totalitarian' does become appropriate where differences and conflicts are refused expression, which is often the unfortunate function of corporate statements of ethics. An organisation that has a statement in its code of values saying 'We will respect each other'[17] obviously has a problem if it needs to express such ideas in so directive a manner, but equally the pseudo-predictive nature of the sentence suggests an inability to acknowledge or accommodate alternative approaches (of course one might doubt whether it is really so scrupulously observed, but that is a different question). In the final section we shall consider a more positive aspect – the vitality of alternative points of view.

4.2.3 Diversity in values

Consider the average multinational organisation. It generally has a specific national core, reflecting the cultural origin and preconceptions of the key figures of its early development (usually the founder or a very early chief executive) which in one way or another is expected to provide an influence beyond the home country's boundaries to a variety of different corporate outposts abroad. At those outposts there are many potential points of divergence from 'home' behaviour, including routine operational decisions as well as non-routine situations (which are likely to have wide ranging strategic implications). There are various approaches that such an organisation can adopt to help solve the dilemma of dispersed operation against central planning, which can all loosely fit into one of the following five types:

- **A system-wide solution**: all activities across the organisation are controlled by reference to a single methodology, often expressed in a series of rules covering all eventualities.
- **An HR solution**: staff in the dispersed part of the organisation are selected on the criterion that their attitudes and opinions display a high level of conformity with corporate models.
- **An executive solution**: create an overall framework within which local outposts can customise decisions to the situation 'on the ground'.
- **The leadership-driven solution**: the leader of the organisation maintains a control over decisions by placing him or herself in the critical non-routine situations, necessarily therefore journeying physically around the various outposts.
- **The output-driven solution**: it doesn't matter precisely what internal processes are used to achieve desired results, so long as those results are achieved (but bear in mind that some of these outcomes might themselves require a considerable degree of conformity in operation).

Examples of these solutions can be found both in modern commercial multinationals, as well as in historical early multinationals (most of which were military or religious empires). Thus Genghis Khan adopted a leadership-driven solution by being at the front of his conquering forces, as much as the UK-based newspaper magnate Robert Maxwell did by taking key decisions himself. The Romans adopted a combined executive/HR solution by selecting the commanders who were most loyal to the state, by training everyone, down to the meanest footsoldier, in established practices, but also by allowing each commander a degree of flexibility in how they dealt with citizens of conquered countries (perhaps an early example of 'think global, act local'). Equally, a company such as Nissan, whilst maintaining the close attention to staffing and values adopted in their home country, have taken steps to customise the 'Japanese' approach in their operation in Sunderland in the north of England.

Central to all these attempts at solving the problems of dispersed operation is the question of values. The personal conflict discussed in the Bernard Atti example is now replicated at the corporate level. The organisation has a 'home' from which a clear set of values has been developed, but now sends its representatives into a situation where such values may be less widely accepted, or even directly opposed by the host country's own social norms. It is clearly inappropriate to try to provide a formula for solving such problems at a stroke – different responses are more or less appropriate for given types of organisation. Senior managers need to take into account the organisation's existing structure, its culture(s) and climate, communication technology and systems, the types of industry they are in, the complexity of their core business, the nature of their competition, as well as some of the specific features of the countries in which they intend to operate, before deciding how to solve this dilemma. Such multinational operations provide particularly good examples of diverse values, for there is both the national/regional cultural dimension as well as the individual one. Each of these may contribute to an ethical diversity.

The solutions to this problem of balancing local values with 'home' values are in part to be evaluated in terms of how value diversity is treated by them, and what kind of benefit may be expected or risk run by each. For example, the leadership-driven solution entrenches an ethical monolith. Likely as not it derives from an organisation that is totalitarian or nearly so. The benefits of simplicity of decision-making are clearly at the costs of difference being sublimated, local understanding being overridden by central requirements, and opposition to central authority not being resolved openly. The single-system approach, whilst still mono-cultural in tone, creates the opportunity, via the detail of an organisation-wide system of rules, for localised values to influence additions or amendments to the system. By contrast, the executive or the outcome-driven approaches allow a considerable degree of flexibility and tolerance, but without any drive to bring local values into the centre of the organisation. All of these, therefore, in their different ways, have the major shortcoming of limiting diversity, and thus of depriving the corporate body of the benefits to be gained from diverse values.

How might diversity be a benefit to an organisation? First, it is worth noticing that a national diversity brings other benefits which, though not superficially related to ethics may be so at a deeper level. For example, styles of thinking diverge across the globe – Indians, for example, tend to be vastly more adept at mental arithmetic than Europeans. Native Australians, living in their traditional environment, have an enormous capacity for recollecting geographical experiences, such as following a trail, compared to, say, their fellow non-original citizens who derive (mostly) from British immigrants.[18]

As we have seen, some features of ethical agreement and disagreement involve factual beliefs and approaches to analysis and application. Hence the cognitive difference is itself a means of providing fresh examples of what Peter Senge calls mental models.[19] These can thus provide an important resource for an organisation to develop new value structures.

More crucially, a diversity of cultures and nationalities provides a wide range of alternative clusters of feelings and emotions relating to issues. One simple advantage of recognising and celebrating this is that it helps an organisation to understand its external stakeholders (such as customers) if their values find some form of expression internally via some staff members. It also creates the opportunity for a particular kind of 'double loop' learning, in that an organisation may come to learn at the 'single loop' level about how individuals from a particular country respond to the corporation's activities, but at the 'double loop' there is the wider benefit that the organisation may build up the capability to meet new value challenges in the future, either from operating in further countries or where fresh values come along. It creates a new kind of strategic competence in the organisation. One aspect of this is where exposure to difference provides a springboard for self-reflection. This might include an evaluation of the level of cultural saturation (along the lines indicated earlier), which itself carries implications about how important value management may be for an organisation. Equally the reflection may involve developing general strategies for shaking out mindlessness, making mindsetting the flexible tools they should be, rather than the dead weights of prejudice.

Diversity is a key resource for organisations. We have discussed mainly the diversity that comes from international difference, though the issue is far broader than that – class/caste and religion are two further important differentiators. The argument has been strongly in favour of maintaining and recognising the importance of diversity in values, and highly critical of the more extreme approaches to the idea of shared values. It is worth noting, though, as a final point in this discussion, that sharing values is not intrinsically wrong – far from it. Part of the mistake that can easily be made is to confuse sharing-as-communicating with sharing-as-accepting. The latter is dangerous, the former highly desirable. This confusion arises from the idea that a simple set of organisationally defined values can be imposed on a group of employees. The key lesson from all of this, as indeed from the whole of the first part of this work, is that values are not simple objects that can be uncovered and where necessary amended or replaced. They are part of a complex dynamic, reaching from the heart of an individual's personal identity into their external behaviour and activities, and in some ways beyond, to the dialogue which they have with others. As such they require the closest and most careful attention if they are to be brought to the disposal of organisations as a means of helping create and drive greater effectiveness. In Part II we shall begin to see how this might happen.

Questions

A   Look back at Box 4.1. Do the two protagonists agree or not? Do they share the same values?

B   Compare your own organisation in relation to the model of cultural saturation. Having identified a likely place for it on the model, consider what kinds of process might shift it to another place on the matrix. To what extent can management control these processes?

C   How does diversity influence the breadth of values in organisations with which you are familiar? To what extent does difference loosen the grip of mindsettings – or does it at all?

Notes

1.   Peters and Waterman (1982) pp. 10 ff.
2.   Campbell and Tawadey (1990) pp. 2 and 5.
3.   Nash (1990) pp. 32–4; Green (1994) pp. 86 ff.
4.   In this area it would be impossible to ignore the enormous influence of Gareth Morgan (1986), who has provided a powerful, and as yet unchallenged, critique against the idea that there is one overarching way to perceive an organisation.
5.   Which is not to decry the importance of actions. These, however, as the argument of earlier chapters has indicated, are only comprehensible via the intention with which they are done. Verbal evidence is essential for a full understanding of intention. Contrary to popular belief, actions don't speak, but they do powerfully illustrate.
6.   Argyris (1993) pp. 40 ff.
7.   Which Argyris rightly acknowledges to be a perennial problem. 'The point is not how to get rid of the dilemma. That will never occur; it is built into the concept of decentralisation. the point is how to deal with it.' (*ibid*. p. 41).
8.   Laing (1970).
9.   Aguilar (1994) p. 75.
10.   *Ibid*. p. 79.
11.   *Ibid*. p. 74.
12.   Trevino and Nelson (1995) pp. 144–6. This idea of 'different selves' is also explored by E. Gergen, who describes it as 'multiphrenia' (1985, 1991).
13.   Trevino and Nelson, *ibid*.
14.   Aguilar, *op. cit*., p. 34.
15.   Bernard Williams discusses the whole issue of the relationship between different sets of moral values in great detail (1985 Chapters 8 and 9).
16.   Morgan (1988) p. 77.
17.   This is a real example, though for obvious reasons the organisations involved shall remain nameless.
18.   Though sadly much of that traditional lifestyle has disappeared. The conceptual framework which underpins that lifestyle has been very ably outlined by Bruce Chatwin (1987).
19.   Senge (1992).

Conclusion to Part I

We have seen in the preceding chapters that values are intrinsically complex, and therefore very difficult to get a clear fix on. This raises an important issue for anyone intent on trying to manage values in an organisation – how are they going to get clear where they are starting from with any individual, and how are they going to know whether they have got anywhere? We have also seen that the monochromatic approach to ethics, where things are just plain right or wrong, seems to miss or ignore the muddiness of ordinary dilemmas, where it is less a question of doing what is right and more one of taking a risk on what is likely to turn out least wrong.

One could easily fall into a state of over-doubt, of being suspicious of everything that anyone says to you. What value underlies that comment? Why did they do that? This borders on paranoia, if one is not careful. The point is not to make one feel deeply unconfident about the day-to-day interactions and judgements one makes with and about other people at work; rather it is to focus on the fact that most of the time we are working on assumptions. We guess, sometimes rightly, sometimes not, about the values of people we work with. This is an extremely important feature of the·management of values – it is founded on assumptions, not sure facts. This aspect will continue to be a key theme in Part II of this book.

PART II

Agreeing and Changing Values

In the first part of this book we looked at the difficulties of understanding other people's values, and thereby the difficulty of managing these effectively. The argument was primarily critical of the optimism that many writers on business ethics display. In this second part we look in more detail at the process of value change. What we shall see is that it is much more than just trying to change values.

5 *Personal Moral Skills*

In this chapter we shall look at some of the factors on which values are built. As the previous chapter began to suggest, much of this is less to do directly with the particular judgements that people hold as it is with the *platform* on which judgements rest. Factors such as reasoning, imagination, and communication skills are also highly important.

5.1 Logical and psychological arguments

Expressions of value are characteristically expressed either as a statement of what is right or wrong or as an injunction to someone to act in a certain way, that is in 'ought' form. 'The government ought to compensate victims of crime' or, similarly, 'It is right for the government to compensate victims of crime'. Similarly, 'XYZCo was wrong to carry out a dirty tricks campaign' or 'XYZCo ought not to have operated a dirty tricks campaign' and so on. This kind of form is particularly important for philosophers trying to elucidate the basic values and forms of ethical reasoning people use. It is not so helpful if we are trying to understand the process involved when people come to the values they have and what can be done about them. One reason for this is to do with the relation between the *formal* expression of the structure of someone's ethical position and what particular part of their position is dear to them. To take an example we have already discussed, someone may have very strong views on the practice of making personal payments to representatives of other companies as an inducement to trade. The *logical* structure of their argument might run thus:

1. All business decisions ought to be made impartially.
2. If one knows one will derive a personal gain from a particular business decision one cannot be impartial.
3. Bribery involves the offer and acceptance of personal gain as a return for taking a particular business decision.
4. X has offered me a personal gift of £10,000 if I decide to do z.

Therefore:

5. X has tried to bribe me, which is wrong.

In this form the argument seems very clear cut, and difficult to argue with. But the trouble with this is that if doubt is cast over one of 1–4, then this model of reasoning would suggest that the same level of doubt must attach to 5, the conclusion. In practice, this does not happen, for there is a *psychological* structure of the individual's position, which may well be quite different. For example, the individual might feel thus:

1. Bribery is wrong.
2. X has offered me £10,000 if I take decision z.
3. My knowledge of the possibility of personal gain if I decide to do z has undermined my ability to be impartial.

Therefore

4. X is trying to bribe me, which is wrong.

In logical terms this is at best incomplete, at worst plain invalid. But it may well represent more closely the order of priorities in people's attitudes. *We do not always think logically*. This is another example of a simple truth that needs to be brought more into the open where the management of organisations is concerned.

In some cases, for example where the rationing of health-care is under consideration, someone may have so strong a feeling that the very elderly and infirm should have the option of choosing euthanasia that they will even refuse to accept factual statements which they fear might counter their view. They read a report suggesting that old people's perception may become sufficiently clouded that their verbally expressed wishes cannot be relied on as an accurate reflection of what they truly choose. This is (at face value, at least) a statement that is factually true or false. But someone may well dispute it, not because the research on which the report is based is flawed, but because they disagree with the conclusion. Disputes and disagreements involving ethical values often look like controversies about key facts that are thought to settle the matter (such as in the controversy over abortion, the point at which an embryo might be said to possess human consciousness). But in such disputes, when one move in the argument is toppled, someone simply turns to another, or replaces it with some other idea.

In cases such as the above, it is probably misplaced to seek for a more 'rational', logically based position, for in doing so one might well overlook or oversimplify what someone really believes in (we shall come back to this point later, both when we look at the idea of personal self-knowledge, and also in the final chapter, when we look at some of the destructive effects of management theory). What is probably more fruitful is to consider the key sources of the crucial beliefs. These may well stem from mindsettings, the origins of which have disappeared from someone's consciousness. The label remains, but the garment it originally came with has worn away. This is one way in which the psychological structure of an argument can come to dominate over the logical structure.

We saw an example of this psychological aspect of reasoning when discussing honesty. Individuals were uncomfortable about agreeing that they would deliberately choose to be dishonest, and would try to deflect this conclusion by explaining the situation away 'Yes, but that's only because...' Discussion was then focused around the appropriateness of the word 'dishonest', almost like an intellectual version of pinning the tail on the donkey. What lay behind the behaviour was agreed with little further analysis. The mindsetting that depicts moral concepts as commandments paralyses us when we reflect on our own immoral actions. The plain fact is that we are limited beings who, through folly or selfishness, do a lot of bad every day. The imagery of tablets of stone leads people to believe that investigation below the surface of unethical behaviour is tantamount to condoning it. But unless we examine it, we have no idea why it happens, and hence no idea how to reduce its likelihood.

5.2 Moral capability

The previous section presented a specific feature of ethical attitudes – they do not necessarily, or even characteristically, follow simple rational forms. In the business sphere this may be relatively unsurprising, as many other aspects of business, such as strategic decision-making, or group behaviour, themselves do not always operate in a narrowly rational manner. In this section we will start looking at the underlying explanation for sometimes unpredictable ethical attitudes and behaviour.

The key term here is *capability*. It is tempting to follow the current fashion for referring to anything to do with an individual's actual or potential performance as 'competence' but this will be resisted here. For one thing, 'competence' is used in a jargonistic way in many modern treatments – by contrast, in ordinary use it is damning with faint praise to describe someone as competent. For another, the whole movement of competence-based development, so popular in the UK, is founded on identifying and measuring against a minimum standard. In this discussion this seems an inappropriate focus. The contrast of using 'capability' is intended to indicate that there is no direct comparison with some external standard, and it also seems to be less tightly bound to minimal levels of behaviour.

By far the most influential model in this field is that of Laurence Kohlberg,[1] whose model is outlined in Box 5.1. Although Kohlberg's theory was developed out of research involving adolescent boys it has been

remember that in different societies around the world other groups may be the advantaged ones) may have mixed feelings about equality. They may have doubts about the 'official', accepted, view of their social group (or their organisation) that discrimination on the basis of demographic sector (for example race, gender, age, physical disability, sexual orientation) is unfair. They may resent the suggestion that choices about selection for jobs, allocation of training places, other scarce resources and benefits have not been based on functionally related criteria. But they are very likely to be aware that it is not socially acceptable to express discriminatory views publicly. So they do not expose themselves to potential disapproval by voicing their reservations. Either they try to deal with this in a different way, for example by opposing specific decisions, giving non-discriminatory reasons for their opposition, or they share their views privately with other like-minded WASPs. The consequent suppression of their own feelings is counterproductive – it means that a debate about the nature of discrimination, and the particular circumstances of certain groups, never happens. So we have merely verbal assent to a principle of universalism.

Worse still, this kind of process can lead to *self*-deception. An individual may suppress even their own doubts about such an issue, given enough of a homogeneity of opinion around them. The authority of the external consensus of opinion (or apparent consensus) leads them to downgrade their own views as misguided 'Oh, I obviously haven't got a clear idea of what they're all concerned with. I must be missing something. I'll keep quiet.' They may simply dismiss their own doubts as inconvenient mental slips. An example of this kind of self-deception appeared in a cartoon, published in the late 1980s, which depicted a man and a woman in an intimate embrace; the man is saying 'I like to think I'm a caring, sensitive new man'; the woman is thinking 'Why are men such bad liars?'[6] Here we have what Kohlberg would describe as explicit post-conventional expressions – and self-beliefs – but conventional or even pre-conventional underlying values.

The aim of this section is to get a clear idea about what 'moral capability' might be. The Kohlberg model seems to be too restrictive. One way of gaining a better view of how far an *adult* has a developed moral capability may be by identifying some of the key factors involved. The following two sub-sections will outline two models relating to different aspects of an individual's moral capability.

5.2.1 Platforms

Several times in earlier chapters we have seen that there is a distinction to be drawn between what someone's explicit ethical views are and what these are based on. I shall use the following terminology systematically from here on in this book: how someone's values are overtly manifested, for example they say that they think bribery is wrong or they demonstrably oppose age discrimination, is what I shall call an explicit value. The underlying factors that give rise to this I shall call the platform for the explicit statement (see Figure 5.1).

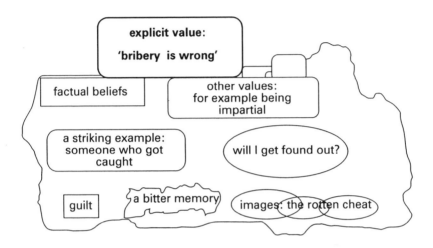

Figure 5.1   The platform on which explicit values stand

There is nothing systematic about the platform for someone's values. It includes a range of different kinds of item, combined in varying ways. This is the application of the model of motivation as problem-solving considered in Chapter 1, when taken down to the level of ethical decision-making. The diagram is not meant to be comprehensive. One might add hopes, fears, role models, and so on. One important aspect that we shall explore in Chapter 8 is which element is dominant – the explicit value or the platform? Sometimes the explicit value leads us to dismiss certain fears for example, whilst at other times a particular image, say of being seen as a hypocrite, determines my explicit value.

Someone is concerned about bribery – they think they are being offered one. They are tempted to accept, but they have great reservations as well. What is going on here? There are factual elements ('am I really being offered this? who is watching? what evidence is there? what consequences will there be for innocent victims?'). Also there are other values that consciously or unconsciously play a part ('is this cheating? is it selfish? am I being hypo-critical?'). There is also an assessment of risk ('what chance that I will get found out? what chance that I could talk my way out of it if I were caught?'). Imagery, metaphors and particular examples can also play a part ('what about so-and-so, who took a bribe last year and got the sack? is this person desperate, or are they a scheming cynic?'). Memories may operate in this latter category ('I remember when I found out we were being undercut by a company paying bribes to customers, it really made me sick').

And so on. The process is complex, dynamic, and only incompletely conscious. One thing it does underline vividly is how difficult it would be to predict what someone would do, even if one had access to many of these elements (some of which, almost by definition, we couldn't discover anyway). For the weightings and tone of these elements are themselves highly variable. Intensity is an important dimension of the decision-making process.[7] Reasoning and other forms of cognitive processing are also variable. As we have already discussed, the degree to which ideas are still vibrantly operating within a relevant context, as opposed to having become detached from their origin, and thus ossified, is also a complicating factor.

5.2.2 Processing, templates and resolution

The model outlined in the previous sub-section indicated the complexity underlying the division between a person's explicit values and what these stand upon. One aspect of the complexity that we alluded to was cognitive processing. In this section we shall look at some (and it is very much a selection) of the features of this process as it applies to ethical decision-making. In Figure 5.2 we see some of the elements of the ethical decision-making process, conceived as a problem-solving process.

The horizontal aspect of the diagram divides into factors that arise specifically by virtue of the immediate situation, and those that might be regarded as longer-term, more permanent features of an individual's make-up. There are cultural as well as individual aspects to this – some nationalities (for example the Japanese) are more prone to take a longer-term view and others (for example the USA) a shorter.[8] Obviously there is an important relationship between the two, but people's behaviour is not comprehensible solely in terms of their long-term, general character traits. Some things 'just happen', in the sense that given our limited knowledge and understanding of the human mind the response from an individual was not completely predictable in advance. Some situations are more or less likely to bring out the open texture of people's responses. Revealing a misdemeanour to a superior is such an example; where the incident is complex and serious, there are many managers whose responses might go in any *one* of a number of directions – bureaucratic, authoritarian, empathetic, legalistic, guilt-inducing and so on. Where so many potential responses are real possibilities, there must be a low predictability on any *one* of them happening. Related to this, part of the reason for distinguishing generic and specific aspects is to enable us to recognise that people sometimes just act out of 'character'. Unusual responses may not be the norm, but where human behaviour is concerned they are not a rarity. So, placid people do fly off the handle sometimes. The unenterprising do on occasion have flashes of opportunism, and so on.

	situation-specific	*generic*
inclinations	emotional reactions to the immediate situation	long-term desires and plans
problem resolution mechanisms	option generation prioritisation	resolution templates

Figure 5.2   Ethical decision – elements

The vertical axis of the diagram reflects the emotional/intellectual division in an individual's thinking. As in Chapter 1, the term 'inclination' covers a whole variety of features, such as feelings, emotions, desires, wishes, needs, and so on (note, in some ways this is an oversimplification, as some of these have their own distinct features). The 'intellectual' factor is difficult to characterise properly – sheer mental ability is clearly not right, for highly intelligent people are as good or as bad as others at dealing with ethical situations. The key issue is what kind of intellectual resource does someone have, long-term and immediate, which might contribute to the resolution of the basic problem confronting any agent – in other words, 'What shall I do in this situation?' In the immediate context, the issue of imagination is important. It contributes to the ability to devise routes through the potential pitfalls of frustrating some of one's inclinations. As we shall see in Chapter 7, it also helps develop new images and frameworks, which themselves can have a potential for stimulating value change. But imagination, though clearly significant, is insufficient on its own – indeed, in some cases a person's imagination can even constitute a disability (for example, it is a significant barrier to heroism to reflect too deeply on the risks that one might be running).[9] Other factors also come into play, such as the strength of the individual's background knowledge of the situation, the assessment they make of the risks involved, and the prioritisation they make of the potentially conflicting inclinations. These tend to interact, as depicted in Figure 5.3.

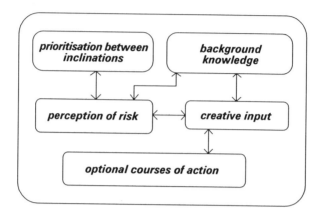

Figure 5.3   Intellective factors in decision-making

What we have here is another derivation from the motivation model of Chapter 1, now cast in terms of the demands, needs, skills, mental resources and abilities that an individual draws upon when they come to do something. As a source of problem-resolution mechanisms this complex may operate directly in a specific situation, in that a particular series of options may be prompted by the particular features of a situation. Equally it may lead someone to formulate generic methodologies for dealing with ethical issues – *templates* or frameworks for determining what someone should or should not do in a situation. Note well that these are more elaborate than simply general principles of action, on the lines envisaged by writers such as Green and Kohlberg.[10] To use the terminology of Goleman (see Part I), a template is a kind of *schema* for deciding between general principles. A general principle, such as 'bribery is wrong' may appear to be immune against compromise but there are always potential complexities, often arising out of conflicts of values. For example, where the prevention of the loss of jobs to a poverty stricken neighbourhood was concerned, some might feel justified in breaking the bribery rule, others might not. How such conflicts are resolved is part of someone's generic methodology for dealing with ethical situations, hence the idea of a template – which includes both general moral values and the ways in which potential conflicts might be resolved – reflects more accurately the role of general ideas in people's decision-making.

Notice that whilst there are four elements identified in Figure 5.2, it is misleading to see them as separate. Each quartile may affect and be affected by any one of the others. My general methods of resolving ethical problems may well be influenced by my emotional reactions in one particular incident (we shall discuss one case involving this below). My long-term plans and wishes may be affected by just one key choice I suddenly think of in one particular situation, opening up for me new possibilities generally.

Notice too that the matrix in Figure 5.2 subsumes the Kohlberg approach. The pre-conventional stage has a centre of gravity in the situation-specific inclination quartile, whilst the post-conventional is more strongly associated with generic approaches to problem resolution. But part of the limitation of the Kohlberg model is that 'conventional' is too restrictive a term to cover properly the variety of cases in which an individual is balancing all four elements of the matrix. Unlike Kohlberg, I would suggest that this central stage is often the most prevalent in the moral and ethical behaviour of individuals in organisations, although the idea of a 'stage' is somewhat misleading. Note, however, that this model is doing a different kind of job from Kohlberg's, for the key issue in that structure is what point on the scale an individual is to be located. In this case, it is more a question of what kinds of reaction, desire, priority or plan someone has and, crucially, how do these fit together?

Someone might say that I am misconstruing this approach. They might say that the adult ethical world, in organisations as in personal relationships, reflects a more universalist frame of reference – convention is not the driving force in people's thinking, key principles are. However, this ignores work that undermines the simple parallel between relationships in organisations from those in non-organisational settings. As Chris Argyris, amongst others, indicated many years ago,[11] organisations often require individuals to act in child-like ways rather than as adults: they should be subordinate, not act outside their own sphere of authority, and are often deprived of key aspects of information that does not directly concern them. Above all, they are not in control. All of these are features of pre-mature individuals in non-organisational settings. This aspect of organised work is as true of empowered, autonomously grouped structures as it is for highly controlled autocracies, for the mechanisms presuming the 'adulthood' of management and the 'childhood' of employees are enshrined in economies and legislation. 'The manager's right to manage' is precisely the embodiment of that division.

We can see, incidentally, why 'competence' in the current understanding of that term is somewhat inappropriate. For what we have here are some very idiosyncratic, highly person-specific aspects – the particular ways in which one individual may generate options in a situation is highly variable between persons, to an extent where comparison does not seem to add anything illuminating.

5.3   A concrete application

In concrete terms, what light can the models identified above shed on individuals and their moral capabilities? In essence it helps with identification of different factors, what the sources of these might be, and how these might interact. Given that the ultimate purpose of this book is to help managers manage the process of ethical change more effectively, these three aims can jointly and individually contribute towards an understanding of how people's behaviour may be influenced.

Let us see how this might be the case by discussing an example. In a moving account, Clive Gilson[12] discusses how he started as a lorry driver in a US bread company, sharing a cab with an experienced, stoic driver called Eric Clark. Clive worked his way up the organisation, and years later was obliged to lay off a number of staff. He discovered that one of these was Eric. Despite his discomfort he had no option but to go ahead with the redundancy. When he told Eric of the decision, the latter was neither angry nor overtly upset. Eric simply explained (for the first time, despite their close association in earlier years) about his war experience (he had been in some of the bloodiest fighting in Anzio during the Allied liberation of Italy in 1944/45) and how he could not understand how 'he was being discarded by the very generation which he had fought for'.[13] Clive Gilson finishes his account by stating 'I suspect that he truly could not comprehend the world, its values and its short memory.'[14]

We shall focus primarily on Gilson, though inevitably, as the account is of an interaction, we will also be looking at Clark. The first and perhaps most important thing to recognise is that this situation presented a challenge to Gilson. It was not one that he could easily locate within his existing value framework and 'explain away'. His emotional reactions are very clearly on the side of Clark. His long-term plans, and his choice of priorities, indicate that the redundancy has to go ahead. But it is clear that for Gilson there is an uneasiness about the situation. His *choice* of priorities is clear, but his *sense* of priorities is not, and there lurks a suspicion that somehow all this is wrong, even though he cannot see a way out of it.

What is problematic is not that Clive finds himself in a situation that he regrets. That is just part of the stuff of life. But his sense that it could be avoided is the difficult area. There is a problem with the *template* Gilson is using. One would suspect that part of that template involves beliefs that somehow people who have made great sacrifices should and do get their earthly reward. Another element would be the idea of cameraderie – people who share a testing set of work tasks should retain over time a sense of the bond this creates. A more sophisticated element is the perception of Clark, a feeling that the dignity of a person's values ought to be respected. This is sophisticated in that it requires an understanding of other people's values that is not simply reducible to a derivative of one's own.

Each of these elements of the template has been undermined, disconfirmed, upset in some way. Clive Gilson's difficulty seems to be that he feels that some kind of action, however palliative, is appropriate, yet he cannot determine what it might be. Hence he is left with an unhappy, ageing man who is being consigned to the dustbin of redundancy (or as we might now put it in more sanitised ways, 'outplacement'). There are several options for Clive here:

- Shrug it all off as a regrettable but unalterable turn of events, too individual in its nature to imply anything about other situations.
- Rearrange the priorities between different elements of one of his templates.
- Add to or subtract elements from one of his templates.
- Reframe some element(s) of one of his templates to enable him either to find appropriate actions to resolve the situation or accept it as it stands.

Paradoxically, the first of these, although the most cynical and defeatist, can represent the deepest form of response. For it says less about the situation than about the template itself – that such overall strategies for resolving problems are not universal, and should not necessarily be viewed as leading directly to actions that would clearly resolve the issue. By contrast, the second and third, though the most immediate forms of 'learning from experience' would represent tinkering, *ad hoc* engineering with general principles and action-rules that is only as good as the last situation encountered. Just as this situation was – to Clive at least – unforeseen, and therefore unplanned for, so future experience will throw up novel cases that fall outside his templates, existing or revised. Both of these responses are single loop learnings – amendments to ' ethical technology' without a more penetrating value. Which is not to say that they are valueless. In any case, though, we cannot 'rearrange' our templates for action at will. We do not choose either our values or our ways of reacting to events.

The last strategy might appear to be an example of double loop learning – learning not just about how to deal with a particular kind of situation, but also what that situation might throw up about the overall way in which resolutions are identified and put into operation. In practice it could be this – it could also be an example of single loop learning along the lines of the previous paragraph. Most importantly, it is the only option that is likely to prompt a recognition that values and guides for action are just that –

guides, not determinants. The negative effects of mindsettings that treat rules as fixed imperatives will be discussed in the next chapter.

What of Eric Clark? His situation would seem to be both more tragic and more simple. There is less of a conflict in his values – it is clearer in his case that he regards what has happened as wrong. He also seems to attribute blame, not directly at Clive, but tangentially in that Clive is a representative of the generation which has done this to him. Yet there is evidence of some conflict in his framework. Earlier in the scenario we are told of Clark's taciturnity. Yet here he reveals important personal information about himself. And for what end? Clearly it will have no influence on getting his redundancy reversed. And there is no suggestion that it is said purely for expressive purposes – to castigate Clive for the behaviour of his generation (though some element of this may be present). It is conceivable that part of the intention is to inform, to let Clive know what kind of person he (Eric) is and was. In doing this, Eric implicitly amends a template; he introduces the issue of communicating more openly as a relevant aspect of his work relationships. This in turn is a consequence of a rearranged priority between different situational approaches, which in its turn has resulted from new or changed emotions and longer-term plans.

We have discussed this case in detail to demonstrate how a person's moral decision-making is a dynamic process, pulling together elements that can act and interact iteratively on each other. This says several important things about the idea of 'moral capability' as a quality (or set of qualities) of a person. First, despite common parlance of some individuals being more or less ethical than others, this only reflects generic elements. Situation-specific aspects introduce an essential element of unpredictability (at least in terms of basing prediction on principles held by an individual). The moralist may act immorally from time to time, and the unethical can and do act ethically. Second, by virtue of this imbalance between the situation and generic aspects, moral capability is an oscillating phenomenon, partially contingent on events, partially stable. Third, and most important, this stable/unstable aspect implies that: (a) for all practical purposes, an individual's behaviour cannot be seen as determined; but (b) there still may be an element of steadiness, relative constancy over a definite period of time. This is what I mean by talking of the model as dynamic – an individual's value system is not anarchic, but flexible generally, and occasionally surprising.

In this and the previous section we have criticised the Kohlberg model of moral development, and suggested an alternative model of moral capability based on the cross-matricisation of the division between intellective and emotional elements, and the division between situational and generic elements. In the next section we shall go on to identify the key cognitive and imaginative capabilities that contribute to moral capability.

5.4   Cognitive elements in ethical attitudes

In the previous section we encountered a broad model of moral capability. It might seem that we could proceed to identify directly the cognitive skills involved in ethical capability, but this is still one step away. The models depicted in earlier sections made a broad distinction between different (but interdependent) elements of ethical capability, but without specifying the precise link between these and the separate skills and attitudes that individuals might possess. Figure 5.4 sheds further light on this aspect.

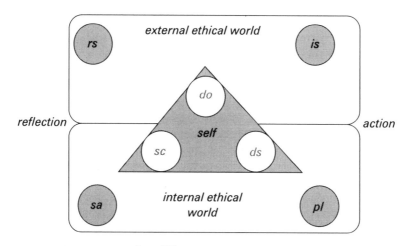

rs – reasoning skills
is – interpersonal skills
do – disposition towards others
sc – self-concept
ds – disposition towards self
sa – skills of self-analysis
pl – personal long-term orientation

Figure 5.4   Personal skills and abilities: context and interaction in ethical behaviour

Each of the elements in Figure 5.4 could be elaborated at length. One thing to point out is that again we have a highly interactive set of items – each can influence and be influenced by any of the others. Some, however, are relatively self-explanatory, such as reasoning and interpersonal skills. Personal long-term orientation is primarily an individual's plans and aspirations – as such it represents a blend of ambitions in the more overt sense of the term as well as more psychologically based aspects such as the desire for fame, power or the like. The 'self'-triangle reflects three different aspects of an individual's contact between their feelings and understanding about themselves and that of others. Disposition to others may be relatively clear – how I understand and react to other people.

What is the distinction between self-concept and disposition to self? Primarily one is intellective (self-concept), the other is emotional. Someone's self-concept reflects how they see themselves; for example someone may see themselves as highly technology orientated, or they believe they have an expertise in managing conflicts, say. On the other hand, the same person may feel that they never take the initiative to use their conflict management skills, or they may feel that they can get too engrossed in technological matters, to the exclusion of their relationships. Obviously the link between these two elements is especially close, nevertheless the difference is there, and reflects an important aspect of how people may be able to develop ethically. For the idea of a self-concept implies that my values may change via cognitive means, whilst that of a self-disposition implies that change is possible on emotional bases. This is an important aspect that will be considered in greater detail in Chapter 7.

How does this diagram relate to the previous models? Essentially what is depicted in Figure 5.2 at the 'inclinations' level is mainly to be identified with the self-triangle, whereas the problem-resolution mechanisms are mainly to be found on the reflection side. The division between situation and generic is not fully reflected in Figure 5.4, except that the action side of the diagram is naturally more closely linked with situation-specificity.

What then are the cognitive elements in someone's values, and in the way they might put these into practice? One model of cognitive frameworks identifies overall patterns of behaviour, such as self-interest, neutralising one's bad behaviour, religious conviction, and so on.[15] While this picks up some useful possible influences on behaviour, these frameworks are of a very mixed type. Religious conviction is a deep-rooted cluster of images, aspirations, beliefs and other factors that go to influence or determine someone's desires. On the other hand there is no similar cluster behind the act of neutralisation. As templates these may have some value, but in that role they are flexible – some people may use them for some of the time, and then use others, but no more than that could be read into them.

Following Figure 5.4, we can categorise the key cognitive elements in ethics as external reasoning, internal self-analysis, and self-concept – so long as we remember that there are bound to be close connections not just between these three, but also with the other elements of the model. We shall deal with them in turn.

External reasoning skills might seem straightforward, although even here there are complications that can easily be overlooked. As mentioned earlier, the role of background knowledge is important – there is some evidence that people reason more effectively when they have some (but generally not too much) grasp of the context of the issue in question. A contextual understanding gives an individual an idea of which are the rigid elements, which are likely to be controversial and which may conceal crucial details under innocuous looking banalities. A separate issue is the ability of an individual to assess deductive reasoning as distinct from the ability to evaluate likelihoods (that is, inductive reasoning). Background is likely to have a more critical contribution to the latter of these, although it might be misleading to say that it is always necessary to have a strong knowledge of circumstances before making judgements concerning probabilities. Sometimes too much knowledge will cloud judgement.

We have skirted around the idea of imagination, but its role in reasoning has been underestimated in the past. In the simplest sense, of visualisation, imagination plays a key role in much deductive reasoning. For example, evidence suggests that good chess players have a particular ability to visualise the arrangement of pieces of the chess board, both actual and future. One researcher showed a chess position briefly to a chess grandmaster, a strong chess player, a weak chess player and a chess novice.[16] The grandmaster then reconstructed the position from memory with one minor error. Accuracy was progressively less good down the scale to the novice, who could hardly recall anything. One might argue that there is some element of contextualisation going on here, as well as good visualisation, and that would almost certainly be right. Nevertheless, it does underscore the importance of imagination in so called 'pure' calculative reasoning. As we shall see later, imagination can also play an important role in the formation and re-formation of our motives.

Internal self-analysis is a more difficult area to pin down. One aspect of this is when an individual might attempt to be a devil's advocate to themselves – externalising, or trying to ask themselves the kinds of question that others might ask.[17] Other aspects are the attempt of an individual to compare themselves with their own self-concept, and the effort to reconcile their own self-beliefs with what others appear to believe about them. One might question whether this is something about which much could be done to develop the skill. Insofar as it is by definition personal, the answer is yes, but only if someone chooses to reveal how far they reflect privately on their own behaviour and values. In practice, the issue is likely to be mirrored in dialogue – what someone may say about themselves and their values.

Imagination again plays an important role in self-concept, which could almost be paraphrased as self-image. Ideas such as the projection of one's own personality as a role that one plays, or such as one's separate role models, demonstrate the function of imagination in this area. But self-concept is more than image. Conception implies an element of 'seeing as', that is, an element of depiction and representation. Someone with a strong sense of self-concept is, of course, not an egomaniac but a person with the capacity to identify and formulate relationships between their long-term orientation and their short-term needs, with the ability to make fruitful comparisons with others, and with the skills of isolating and evaluating the contribution of different elements towards the whole. Self-concept is, as indicated earlier, extremely closely tied to self-disposition – what I feel emotionally about myself is totally bound up with what I think are my abilities, strengths, weaknesses and so on. Often the link is consolidated by the influence of personal long-term disposition. I may have a long-term orientation towards becoming recognised for my expertise – in Schon's terminology, this is a 'career anchor' for me. This career anchor is then both a motive for me and a criterion for self-evaluation. So when I realise that I have failed to develop a particularly high level of knowledge or ability in my chosen field, this could well lead to self-recrimination; in other words, a poor self-disposition has resulted from the comparison between self-concept and personal orientation. In the author's opinion the link between these elements is an unexplored area that could well have important implications for how far adults are able to learn entirely new skills and abilities.

So, in terms of what underlying qualities of an individual cognition are relevant to their ethical development and capability, there seem to be the following:

- **external reasoning**: deduction, probability assessment, background knowledge of specific contexts, imagination
- **internal self-analysis**: externalisation, internal comparison, coherence between self-beliefs and others' beliefs about self
- **self-concept**: separating long- and short-term inclinations, comparisons, separation of different components of one's self-image and subsequent evaluation of these.

What is crucial for the possibility of ethical change in organisations is the question of how far these are amenable to development. This is not directly answerable – for one thing different people are more or less likely to develop in certain ways. For another, the question is not really answerable in the abstract – it is only in the context of certain methods of development that it can be ascertained whether an individual can develop in a certain direction. What should be noted is that there are methods available which purport to develop individuals in each of the above areas – although some are more well established than others.

Perhaps most important, however, is the *particularity* that all of the above underlines. It is not that one method of development may be better than another. It is not just that one way that a method is put into practice is better than some other way. It is not even that one person may be more or less receptive to one approach to implementing a certain method of development. It is that over and above all of these is the *occurrent* nature of people's behaviour. Not being robots (well certainly not very simple ones, anyway), we can and do act in so many different ways, and with so many different options available to all of us, that for practical purposes it is better to see human behaviour as uncertain. Rules of thumb are useful, but no more than that. So changing a person's values is intrinsically difficult, involving many different possibilities, and subject to the vicissitudes of everyday life. Developing an individual in ethical terms can only be based on iteratively trying out various ideas, providing a variety of different experiences, comparison with many different ways of reflection and many different kinds of interpretation. And even then we may not clearly understand what the result is. The suggestion that corporations may go forward by 'sharing values' starts to look, not just optimistic, but frivolous.

5.5   Interpersonal skills – transporting or transforming values?

We have talked in this chapter about the limits of reasoning in people's values. We have also alluded more briefly to imagination. What, though, of interpersonal skills such as effective verbal communication, assertiveness, and so on? Certainly these are highly relevant to an individual's values and how these interact with the values of others. At first one might think that they are primarily a vehicle for an individual to establish links between their own values and other people's, by communicating their own values or allowing others to express theirs. Seen in this light, interpersonal skills are a set of techniques, they are part of the machinery of ethical change, rather than being any part of an individual's personal moral capability. Their prime function would seem to be to transport expressions of value between individuals. But this would be an oversimplification.

For one thing, much of what is considered to be interpersonal is closely bound up with an individual's internal self – both the self-concept and the self-disposition. For example, the writer Anne Dickson discusses how a person can acquire a deeper understanding of her (or his) own being when they can deal more effectively with others.[18] This can operate at several levels, but at even the lowest level it indicates that interpersonal interaction is a good flag of what is happening inside someone.

There is also a sense in which interpersonal skills pertain to one's moral capacity. We only fully understand ourselves by understanding others. Someone's skills at communicating with others, then, is not merely a vehicle for exchanging ethical views, but also a method of developing one's own moral capability. It is a commonplace amongst teachers that the best way to learn something properly is to teach it.[19] Teachers and trainers often say that it is via the process of collating and coordinating material for delivery in a teaching session that they come to a full understanding of what is meant by a certain model, or how it all fits together, and so on. It is via the process of explaining ideas to others that these can become clear to oneself. In a related way, it is by opening one's values to others that one gets a clear idea of what in a deeper sense one really believes – the lower levels of the platform often stay out of sight. But creative interaction with others brings these forth – this can be as much of a surprise to the speaker as to the listeners.

At the deepest level, it is only by interpersonal communication that one can form a self-concept at all. An individual would have no basis for checking their own impressions, feelings, images, and so on, if they did not have some perception of an external reality, including the reality of being human, against which to check. Otherwise, it would be impossible for a person even to recognise whether one feeling was the same one they had had previously. Time, space, knowledge, and the possibility of similarities and differences between people, are all bound up in this. So someone's interaction with others is a key part of their own self-concept.

This chapter has presented several models relevant to personal ethical skills and capabilities. We have focused on the cognitive element in people's values, not because the emotional element is irrelevant, but because it is so often supposed that values and ethics are simply emotive areas. Emotive they might be, but as we have seen, there are considerable intellectual elements to the possession of values. As we shall note later, this has significant implications for the idea of changing the ethics of individuals or of organisations. In the next chapter, we shall look at something that is often seen as a barrier to ethical change before moving on, in the following chapter, to consider an example of how ethical change might work in practice.

Questions

A   What kinds of personal development are conducted in your organisation? How far do they address the elements identified in Figure 5.4? How effective are they? Is there any recognition of the ethical implication of this?

B   Think of an ethical situation at work, one where you did something you now regret. Try to recall what led you to act as you did. What explicit factors were in operation? Now try to relate these to the models presented in this chapter. Try to distinguish: (a) the explicit value; (b) the factual beliefs you held; (c) the risks you felt you might be running; (d) the options that you felt were available to you. Also, what kind of generic framework or template do you think you were using?

Notes

1. Kohlberg (1976).
2. Among these are Robin Snell (1993) and Trevino and Nelson (1995), although to be fair on both of these texts, they do present certain criticisms of the approach, even though they seem to accept the overall model.
3. Obviously they might also behave that way: (a) out of fear; or (b) they are themselves intrinsically boorish. In each of these cases, the comments given in the text would not apply. The point is that the behaviour *might easily* be of a conventional kind.
4. Jean Piaget (1896–1980) researched and wrote extensively in the area of child development, particularly on how logic and cognitive ability develops from a purely sensuo-motor stage (at birth) to a formal stage (at 12–15 years). (See Paiget 1954.)
5. Snell *op. cit.*
6. There are at least two interpretations of this: (a) that the man is deliberately lying for effect, and this is transparent to the woman; (b) that the man is expressing a wish about what he is like, which the woman perceives as unconvincing because it is manifestly untrue. It is the latter interpretation that is relevant to the discussion in the text. Curiously, I have been unable to trace the source of this cartoon.
7. See Jones (1991) for an interesting account of intensity in ethical decision-making.
8. The differences between the time perceptions between individuals from different cultures is explored by in some detail in *The Seven Cultures of Capitalism* (Hampden-Turner and Trompenaars, 1993).
9. For an interesting account of the role of imagination in ethical decision-making, see Ciulla (1991).
10. See Green (1994, Chapter 3).
11. Argyris (1957). More recently, Langer has made similar points (1993).
12. In a case study entitled 'The Termination of Eric Clark' (Frost, Mitchell, Nord 1995 pp. 104–7).
13. *Ibid*. p. 107.
14. *Ibid*. p. 107.
15. McDonald and Pak (1996).
16. My memory of this is from a demonstration on BBC television in the early 1980s. What was emphasised was that the grandmaster is better at chess-like chess positions rather than random ones. This highlights that it is context, rather than some universal skill, that was at work.
17. A phenomenon discussed in the author's own doctoral thesis (Griseri 1989 Chapter 5).
18. Dickson (1982). Despite the title, her book is only apparently aimed at women – it is at least as useful for men.
19. Though I am unable to find any textual reference to this.

6 *Value Rigidity*

In Chapter 5 we considered some of the personal qualities relevant to an individual's moral capability, with a particular focus on the cognitive aspects of these. In this chapter we shall look at one of the key boundaries of ethical change – the rigidities that are built into people's value systems. Far from proving to be a limitation or constraint, these will later be seen as a key resource for promoting ethical change.

6.1 Interpreting changed behaviour – explorations into the labyrinth

Much of the argument of Part I was concerned with the complexities that underlie even quite simple situations. This aspect is explored further here, with a view to understanding what a change in someone's values might actually look like. A large amount of the discussion will focus around ideas brought into management theory from the work of Kurt Lewin.[1] The discussion below will point up how there are very many key issues and competing interpretations that are underdetermined by the evidence normally available to a working manager. The area is a labyrinth through which navigation may well be possible, but on a timescale incompatible with the demands of modern organisational activity. The consequence of this is that although at root everyone's value sets are open to direct influence, in practice there are severe rigidities in people's values, resistances to change. As we shall see, this is no bad thing.

Consider the case in Box 6.1.

BOX 6.1 **A Successful Change Agent**

'I was called in to do some work with a group of reception staff. My client was their line manager. The organisation had put through a culture change programme, improving quality and customer-care, and this group of staff

---

BOX 6.1 (cont'd)

were resisting. I was asked to find out what the problem was, and then try to resolve it. Initially the receptionists were very anti the whole idea of the change. Some talked of it being yet another management fad. One said that management had no idea of the pressures they (the receptionists) operated under. All expressed grave reservations on whether the changes would work, and most said they wouldn't bother trying to help things along, as it would be a waste of time.

After some time it became clear that there was a fairly basic issue underlying much of the resentment. It seemed that their difficulty was with the way the change programme had been implemented. Many other workers had been regraded. This group hadn't – the changes in what they did were not substantial enough to justify more money. The receptionists, who were always at the bottom of the ladder anyway, felt they were being put upon yet again. So they were digging their heels in over the new work procedures.

I had to meet them all several times, first as a group and then individually, before I discovered this. They were very intimidated by their line manager, so it took some time to draw them out. She was quite surprised that they found her intimidating. I facilitated a meeting between two representatives of the group and the line manager. The receptionists were able to put over their points, and the manager acknowledged them. She explained the company rules about grading levels. Someone could be regraded only if there was a change in the main activity of their job, which wasn't the case with the receptionists. The two reps pointed out that they would have to do a lot more than just answer the phone and meet people who came in the front door. They would, for example, have to deal with minor customer complaints, which had not officially been required before, and which they were not trained to do (though a lot of them had done it). The manager thought that if their jobs were as different as they claimed, maybe they should take an NVQ qualification, which would help them develop the new skills required. The reps agreed to put to the other receptionists the idea of a qualification in customer-care as a way of gaining extra recognition and some more money (company rules allow payment of a bonus on successful achievement of a qualification).

A year later, about half of the receptionists group had completed an NVQ. Some of the others had left, and a couple had been moved into different areas. The receptionists had acquired a new sense of dignity and were co-operating 90 per cent with the new working procedures. In a recent in-house survey (1996), 96 per cent of them agreed or strongly agreed with the statement "I think the new quality culture has been a success".'

How successful has the change agent been? It is clear that the primary task has been achieved, in that the current group of receptionists are no longer against the changed culture. Some other staff have been moved, others have left. All good stuff, right in line with the ideas of Kurt Lewin, the touchstone for change management (see Box 6.2) – identify resisting forces and eliminate them or turn them round. The client – or at least her successor – might well feel pleased at the outcome. All also in line with the idea that motivation is often held up by poor responses to 'hygiene' factors.[2]

BOX 6.2   Kurt Lewin and Change Management

Lewin is a key figure in the development of modern organisational psychology. One of his ideas was the representation of psychological items in physical terms. Hence he devised two highly influential models relating to the management of change.

1. Force field analysis

The *status quo* is represented as a boundary. Behind it are forces driving a change, pushing the *status quo* forward. Before it are the forces resisting movement, trying to keep it in place. So, a restructuring exercise in an organisation may be represented as being driven by forces such as senior management, financial stakeholders, efficiency experts, and so on. Resisting this may be staff (fearing redundancies), functional managers who believe it will reduce efficiency, and so on.

Lewin suggested various strategies in the light of this model, including: (a) eliminating resisting forces; (b) increasing driving forces; (c) turning resistances around.

2. Freezing

The *status quo* is now represented as a group of objects locked into a sheet of ice. In order to change anything around, we need to un-freeze the objects. Only then can we carry out any changes, by moving things around. Finally, to ensure that the change is permanent, we re-freeze the ice, holding the objects in place. So, before a manager decides to change the organisation of teams in her division, she spends time discussing the shortcomings of the current situation with the staff (un-freezing). Only when there is a general agreement that change is necessary does she carry out the restructuring. Then she builds in checks and monitoring systems to consolidate the change (re-freezing).

We shall not revisit the question of how far can one fully understand the values of others, and where to draw the line between shared values and compliant behaviour. Nevertheless, that argument should be taken as read in this situation. There are yet other issues, however, that relate to the idea of rigid values. Consider the following questions in the light of the scenario:

- what has been lost here?
- what has been gained?
- where have the differences in attitude gone?
- what has happened to the specific objections to the change programme?
- how has a 'hygiene' factor substituted for a lack of confidence in management?

What has been lost?
It could be argued that some of the elements which have been lost here are things such as: a mechanism for expressing, or processing, or focusing dissatisfaction with the organisation; the opportunity of representing the specific viewpoints held by those who have now left; the group as a vehicle for critique within the organisation. Admittedly many managers would be quite pleased to lose some of these things, but as has been implicit in the argument of Part I, absence of dissent is not the same as the presence of assent. And some difference is important as a driver for the change process.

What has this to do with rigidity? 'Rigid' can often carry a negative reson- ance, but in this context it should be clear that the loss of, for example, the opportunity for individuals to express dissent is not the elimination of a negative, whatever management might feel at the time. Dissent is an expres- sion of a value (although, as we have seen, it is far too easy to jump to conclusions about what value it expresses). There is a temptation for managers to feel that by eliminating voiced dissent they are eliminating the values that they believe are being expressed via the medium of dissent. All too often they are mistaken, in terms of both what they believe the dissenters really feel and what has happened to the values being suppressed. But suppose they were right – what would have really happened? That indi- viduals who disagreed with something just stopped doing so? Clearly not, and this is what brings out why the metaphor of rigidity is being used here – someone's values do not 'simply' change at the drop of a hat. There is a process through which an individual has to go when they change ethically. The resistance or rigidity reflects the fact that values *matter*. This is an aspect of integrity that is all too often missed in current discussions – part of being a whole, integrated person is that my values are deeply linked in with many other aspects of my personality. A change in ethics does not, cannot, happen on its own, but must inevitably affect many other elements. Hence the sheer inertia of these means that we hold tenaciously to our values. If someone were not so tenacious, one might question how far their ethical views were genuinely held at all. This is why I say that rigidity in this context is not to be regarded as a problematic feature of the situation.

What has been gained?

The gains: evidence supporting the idea that dissent may lead to 'something being done'; the subtextual message that if people oppose management they are dealt with in some way – including being eased out; for some individuals, additional qualifications and, thereby, money; for management, the appearance of consent. In terms of value change these do not provide an encouraging basis. The main value emphasised here seems to be an instrumental one. The idea of constancy of values is not especially emphasised or encouraged.

Where have the differences in attitude gone?

It is unclear what has happened to the differences in attitude which members of the group held. Note that 'the group' would be only *apparently* united in their original opposition. Some may have been like that because they have an inbuilt antipathy to the line manager, others have self-consciously opposed management as a negotiating tactic, others may be confused, and so on. There is, then, not *one* phenomenon of changed (or apparently changed) attitude. There may be as many as there are individuals.

So where have the original attitudes gone – vanished? There may be at least four destinations for these original attitudes, which we might call the 'bin', the 'closet', the 'open' and the 'twilight zone'. Individuals may have discarded them, rejected (bin); individuals may conceal their continuing disagreement for fear of it damaging their current job prospects (closet); third, people may have concealed their real views earlier (holding more pro-management attitudes than they chose to admit with their workmates), which they have now found confirmed (open); finally, individuals may have become (or remained) in a state of uncertainty over the issues involved (the twilight zone). Only one of these is much of a healthy situation, the third, and that only because of less open behaviour of an individual at an earlier time. The important thing here is that it is because of the rigidity in someone's values that they will avoid an open strategy – this is as true of the 'twilight zone' case as of the 'closet' one. People often prefer to keep 'shtum' rather than risk a difficult confrontation over value differences.

What has happened to the specific objections to the change programme?

What has happened to the specific objections that the receptionists originally raised, such as the idea that it was just a fad, also remains unclear. Despite the personal agendas of the individuals mentioned above, here is the facet of the situation that did unite them. Conceivably, for some of the receptionists the objections have not gone away. Whilst some individuals have been persuaded by the change agent or by management that the new work systems are acceptable, others have not. So, for those who might remain unconvinced, the objections have gone underground, have in some way been suppressed.

'So what?' I can hear some managers thinking at this point, 'We can't get into everyone's head all the time. The best we can hope for is to get a reasonable percentage of people on board.' Agreed, although we should bear in mind that 'on board' here covers both those who agree with a change and those who choose not to voice their disagreement – remember that people may choose not to participate in open dialogue regarding their values for many reasons: to keep the peace, to avoid prejudicing their career, or out of direct fear of powerful individuals. The main purpose of this analysis – as really with the whole of this book – is not to castigate managers, but to recognise the limits of what they might hope to achieve.

The labyrinth is a perennial – achieving value change does not make everyone's attitudes transparent at a stroke. *Today's solutions are tomorrow's problems*, Peter Senge says.[3] A change solution that suppresses conflicts of values does not resolve these, but is in effect a choice to ignore them. In pushing through a change programme in which individuals are expected to 'buy in' to ideas and values, one is inevitably creating the opportunity for differences to submerge, only to re-emerge at a later date. Note: this is not necessarily a bad management decision – in some circumstances it may be excellent managerial practice to create a situation in which one set of problems is disguised and deferred for the sake of concentrating resources on solving other problems. So long as we recognise that this is what is happening – deferral, not resolution, and as such leaving some need or demand unsatisfied.

How has a hygiene factor substituted for a lack of confidence in management?
This last of the above questions is probably the hardest. It would seem that for at least some of the receptionists the opportunity to get more qualifications, and/or get a bonus, has compensated for the change in work responsibilities. What kind of equivalence in the psychological contract has been set up that an increase in the benefits side of the contact balances an increase on the commitments side? Indeed, what does a psychological contract really mean? Notice that this is not the question: are psychological contracts possible? It is clear that the idea is a useful way of understanding people's orientation to their work and how they may respond to changes in the effort/reward balance. The question is more *how* do psychological contracts work? Obviously, where there is a direct financial comparison the answer is clear – I may accept more money in return for a reduction in job security as a kind of insurance against future loss of earnings. But more qualitative components of a psychological contract are not so comparable. How does, say, an improved relationship with my line manager compensate me for the

loss of a company gym? How can one kind of benefit be measured against a different kind of commitment? There might be several possibilities, including:

- The benefit may directly address a private need of an individual that has been directly created by the additional item on the commitment side.
- The benefit may create sufficient goodwill that an individual forgets – albeit temporarily – the emotional tone of the disbenefit created by the extra commitment.
- Guilt may be induced – management have been so helpful over x issue I can't really keep complaining about y issue.
- A stand-off position is created between management and myself: we implicitly agree to refrain from our respective demands, but the threat remains that if I complain the benefit may be withdrawn, and vice versa.

The implication of this is that the intervention of the change agent may be successful for one of several different reasons – it is not clear at the surface whether we have a simple 'single loop' solution, or whether this was deeper 'double loop' learning. The current wisdom on change management is that resistances are to be eliminated. But as we see here, it is not as simple as even understanding what kind of elimination is involved. This is why the degree and nature of value rigidity is a key determinant of the success of change management. Values are not easily shifted. When values are placed under pressure, when they are questioned, people rarely change their views willingly – indeed, as we shall discuss a little later, it would be disturbing if they were too ready to do so. The more characteristic kinds of response involve some form of *preservation* of someone's views. Sometimes the whole strategy of an individual's response to managerial pressure to change values is to find a way of maintaining their existing values whilst inhibiting or reducing to a minimum the explicit conflicts with managerial requirements. Even when there is transformation, it is almost never a complete clean sheet change – continuities are preserved, but recast and reframed. Resistance should be prized, in a way encouraged – not as destructive opposition, but as a way of drawing out the best aspects of a situation. The Catholic Church used to subject the reputation of a potential saint to the most rigorous scrutiny before agreeing that the person be canonised. A cleric would act as a searching opponent (literally the source of the phrase 'devil's advocate') trying to find reasons not to agree to the sanctification. If the reputation of the person passed that test, they were deemed worthy of the honour. In an more obvious application of the idea, Pascale and Athos[4] have pointed out how conflict and resistance is used in organisations such as Honda, precisely because it produces more informed, more robust, solutions to problems – solutions of greater value because they have already been subjected to searching examination. This is why I say that resistance is to be encouraged – not to stop change, but to give it greater quality.

The scenario also points up, incidentally, the need to learn from one's achievements as much as from one's mistakes – for both may result from incidental, situation-specific factors; but that is a separate issue.

In the light of these questions, it would seem that there are several alternative interpretations of what happened in the change episode outlined in Box 6.1:

- The exercise was a qualified success (the interpretation apparently given by the change agent).
- The expressions of disquiet over the change were solely a negotiating tactic – the organisation has been 'bounced'.
- The receptionists have been bought off.
- The problems have been put to one side, but not eliminated.
- The ringleaders of the opposition have been marginalised or liquidated.
- The receptionists have been deluded into accepting an inappropriate solution to their problems.
- Those receptionists who remain from the original group are even more intimidated now than before.

Clearly there may be other interpretations. The key issue is not simply that it is easy to read a situation in one way only and be blind to the fact that other interpretations are possible, though the example does point this up. What is most important is that different readings of the scenario demonstrate a different kind of *stability* of the values of the individuals concerned. In some cases, such as the second, the real values held by the receptionists to apply to the situation are based on personal material gain. These remain stable simply because they have not been brought out into the open. In others, the values have been undermined directly, for example where the receptionists feel even more intimidated than before.[5]

The image of exploring through a labyrinth, then, underscores the message of earlier chapters that the superficial evidence of values conceals a complex and highly individual set of elements. This means that when it comes to changing values, there is a variety of different kinds of *rigidity* between individuals holding apparently similar views. Rigidity is a mark of the degree to which an issue is important for someone. The resistance it implies is usually seen as problematic for a manager, but really it is a key resource, for it demonstrates the extent of someone's *commitment* to certain values.

Different rigidities – different levels of commitment and therefore different responses to pressures for ethical change. People will change (or refuse to change) their values at varying rates, and through various processes. Depending on these different rigidities there is also a variety of different forms of value transformation.

In Chapter 5 we outlined the idea of a platform of supporting ideas on which someone's explicit values rest. This idea will become more important in the next section, in which we consider value change in more detail. This idea of a platform is a depiction of the various factors that someone's values stand upon. It does not refer in any simple way to the logical structure of reasons for holding a value judgement, because as we have seen, the logical structure of a person's views is rarely the psychological structure, and it is the latter that is important in understanding ethical change in organisations.

The platform underpinning someone's values is an amalgam of different factors that may have led to, and continue to sustain, someone's belief. The link here is a felt one – in the sense that if someone *feels* that a particular factor supports their values, it *does* (not that it lends any external validity, but this is a logical issue, out of place here). As we have seen, other values, factual beliefs, specific examples and many other factors may have a role in this structure. For example, an experienced manager may well hark back to events that happened in her early career, interpret these in the light of her current experience, ponder on the significance of certain pertinent facts, and compare her situation with that of a colleague, all as part of deciding what she should do. It is also worth noting how organisation-wide events can influence the individual. The cultural history of many organisations is littered with symbolic events, often key public conflicts, which take on a meaning far beyond their explicit context. These elements conjointly lend emotional and intellectual gravity to a particular value judgement. The value may not be *defined* in terms of these supporting elements, but it is *understood* in terms of them. What is also interesting, is that whilst some or many of these can individually change, the *totality* is what someone feels lends support to their views.

We can begin to see why the Lewin-inspired imagery of forces being eliminated or turned around can be misleading. Some may indeed be resolved, but what can also happen is that key forces may become oblique, or they may disappear, to resurface later. Changes in the underpinning platform may fail to manifest themselves in changed judgements, or may ossify someone's existing views. Someone's values may seem to change direction only to spawn fresh concerns and difficulties. In the following section we shall examine this further, as well as look at another complication relating to changing values.

6.2   The paradox of value change

In this section we shall mention an issue the resolution of which will be discussed in more detail in the following chapter. The paradox of value change may be expressed as in Box 6.3.

BOX 6.3   The Paradox of Value Change

Suppose that currently I hold to the value of opposing animal exploitation.

This means that, where I am convinced that animals are being exploited unnecessarily, such as when they are experimented on without sufficient benefit in terms of improvements to human life, I will see this as wrong.

Suppose further that at some later time I change my values in this area, so that I no longer feel that animal exploitation is wrong.

If I do this instantaneously there is no problem – at one moment I thought something was wrong, now I think it isn't.

If, however, I go through some *process* of value change, then during that process I must at some point still hold that animal exploitation is wrong, but also be thinking (somehow) that I am mistaken in this. I must in some way believe both that something is wrong and that it isn't.

Like all paradoxes, this one is a problem because of how it is formulated, rather than of what the conclusion actually is. We have probably seen enough to recognise that the resolution of the difficulty lies in understanding the complexity of the platform on which values rest, and that the technology for ethical change works directly on such a platform – more of which in Chapter 7. It is a useful idea to focus on because it emphasises that change is not a moment but a process. Within that process there are contradictory elements co-existing, and this creates conflict. At the same time as criticising a process or system we are continuing to use it. Alongside proposals for a new reporting structure we are expecting people to continue to report 'for the time being' to a manager who is to be made redundant. This creates uncertainty and confusion. Why not change now? When we look at values it becomes even more confusing for staff. 'You say we're going to change to a culture where we all value the customer. But we're not going to change the operation until next year. So when do the values start?' Of course, the values don't start at any time – but that is the very source of the problem for someone.

The idea of a *process* through which one goes when one's values are changing implies an intermediate stage between acceptance and rejection. It represents the middle stage in what Lewin presented as his 'freezing' metaphor, the idea that values and practices have an inbuilt degree of rigidity, and that before attempting any manipulation or change of these it was necessary to unlock people (un-freeze them, in Lewin's terminology) from existing values and practices, and once the manipulation had been made to re-freeze people into the new situation. As an image this is appealing, but it is all too often interpreted by managers as suggesting that there is a single mode of un-freezing, valid for all, and a single mode of re-freezing, again valid for all. The position advanced in this book is that this cannot be the case, so far as values are concerned, for there are far too many variables to take into account. The underlying weakness of this is that Lewin's approach oversimplifies the middle process – the central change activities, at least as far as being a description of individuals and the changes in their own values is concerned (there may be more validity as a model for group-based change).

One aspect of the change process that the Lewin models do not explicitly address is the extent of the change. Some changes are just much more deep-rooted than others. In the area of value change, some writers have identified three different levels of change: α (alpha), β (beta) and γ (gamma) change. Alpha change is similar to what Argyris calls single loop learning – a simple amendment of attitude or belief, without any structural implications for the concept involved. Beta change is where we re-evaluate the parameters of a concept. Gamma change, on the other hand, is where the concept itself changes. Thompson and Hunt apply this to changes in attitudes beliefs and values, coming up with an elaborate model of different ways in which change may be influenced.[6] As the reader may already guess, my objection to this is less on the principle as on the systematic nature of the models involved. The model assumes, for example, a distinction between qualitative and quantitative change. But sometimes a concept is changed *de facto* because of the degree to which its parameters have been changed. So a system in which people are supposed to clock in every morning has radically changed if the proportion of staff doing so drops from 90 per cent to 25 per cent. Nevertheless, this is a useful guide to looking at how deeply change processes are penetrating, whether these are deliberate or, as in the example above, inadvertent forms of 'drift'.

As an alternative to Lewin's model, let us consider different ways in which the intermediate stage might operate. To make the ideas comprehensible, we shall oversimplify considerably, presenting the key phenomenon as a two component state – the holding of a value, and the acceptance of an underpinning platform of factual beliefs and interpretative concepts. On this basis, then, there seem to be three different ways in which a rigidly held value might come to be replaced by another one: decomposition, catastrophe and transition, as depicted in Figures 6.1, 6.2 and 6.3, respectively.

In Figure 6.1 the values change due to the decomposition of the underpinning platform. Factual beliefs may change, the prioritisation between one issue and another may change, the underlying models and concepts that make values and beliefs comprehensible may dissolve and reform. Change in value happens because of the changes in the platform.

The case represented in Figure 6.2 is a more dynamic, sometimes violent situation. A direct competitor value is presented, and the individual may go

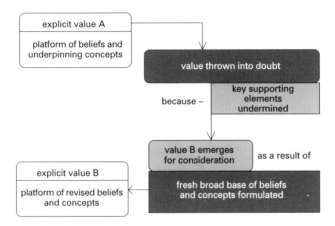

Figure 6.1   Decomposition of values

through an uncomfortable process of trying to retain their original values despite ideas and evidence which incline them in another direction. They may try to find fresh evidence to support their old views, or may try to invent new supporting mechanisms. They may swing wildly from rejecting one or both of the alternative views, until one of these is finally accepted and the other rejected. A fresh platform is erected to support the new position. This kind of process may be public, involving others, or entirely private, becoming really apparent only when it has been completed.

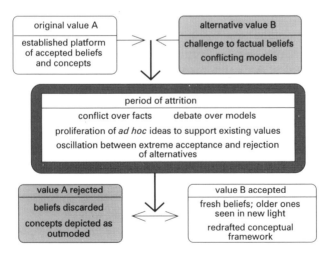

Figure 6.2   Catastrophic change

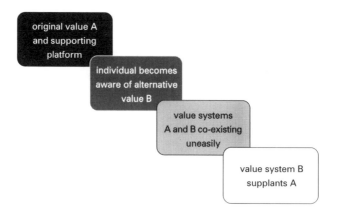

Figure 6.3   Gradual transition

The last case represented in Figure 6.3 is a kind of dissolution, where two sets of values are not perceived to be in *direct* conflict, although some incongruity between them may be sensed. The evolutionary move from one to another may involve changes in the underpinning platform, but the whole process is less fraught with conflict than in the preceding case.

The main implication of these models is that the idea of changing an individual's values covers several different kinds of process. The three outlined above are not exhaustive of all the possibilities, but they indicate the important differences between individuals so far as any external attempt to induce value change is concerned.

The key differences, and interestingly also the key resources for carrying through any change, are the features of someone's value system that lend it a degree of rigidity. Although managers wish their staff would be flexible, in the area of values this can appear suspect. As was mentioned earlier, if someone was too ready to give up their views and adopt those of management we might feel that they were insincere, either about their previous values or about their newly acquired ones. The nature of the rigidity of someone's values is interrelated with the nature of the platform on which the values rest,[7] and dependent on the context within which a challenge may be posed to the individual's values. To an extent also, there may be persisting personality factors that make one person more likely to hold on tenaciously to an idea when another might give it up quite quickly.

What does this say about management behaviour? One implication is that it is insufficient to devise a change strategy along simple Lewin-style lines. Where value change is a component of the process, a deeper understanding of the possible links and contrasts between what is proposed and what has been the norm previously is important, as are the different kinds of underlying sub-structure of beliefs and interpretative paradigms that might go to make up the total value system of individuals. One drawback of the Lewin type of approach to change is to see it as a means of making a break with previous shortcomings. Change construed solely as a way of escaping from the past is – to parody a phrase – doomed to repeat it.

Another point is that any of the three change narratives outlined in Figures 6.1 to 6.3 may apply. Lewin was ambiguous about what he meant by un-freezing – at times a gradualist approach seems to be indicated, at other times a more decomposed process. But either way, it is not wholly appropriate for the catastrophic kind of change – smashing the ice might be a better metaphor here. Similarly, the force-field image helps with catastrophic and decompositional change, but not with gradualism.

Inevitably it raises the question, what can be done to assist the process of value change in an organisation? There is clearly no single formula. One way of evaluating approaches might be to categorise different strategies. In this context the model of intervention outlined by John Heron is useful (see Box 6.4).

BOX 6.4	John Heron's Six Types of Intervention

John Heron[8] outlines two overall approaches that a facilitator or manager could adopt in creating change. The first of these is externally driven, the second is internally based.

Authoritative

Prescriptive	directing individuals as to what should be done
Informative	telling individuals what is possible, what is salient, and so on
Confrontational	proscribing behaviour

Facilitative

Cathartic	creating dynamic experiences that help people make changes
Catalytic	being the trigger for internally based change
Supportive	helping people through the difficulties of change

The value of categorising approaches along the lines outlined in Box 6.4 is that it helps to see how various activities might address certain kinds of issue. For example, where individuals have high levels of rigidity, built up perhaps out of the kind of detachment of mindsettings from their original source, (which we discussed in an earlier chapter), a confrontational intervention may be considered – other issues that might be relevant to the choice would be the kind of change (compositional, catastrophic, transition-based) which it was felt necessary, as well as the kinds of moral skills that the key actors displayed. Suppose a sales team is composed of a number of technically excellent, strong-minded individuals, who are achieving well in their current roles. Suppose too that the overall function of this department needs to be changed, so that they will do less commission-based work and more project-orientated activity – high profile but less for the individual in financial terms. The change is clearly value-orientated – the staff will need to recognise that financial reward is less important, that individual activity will need to be subordinated to the needs of a team, and so on – the changes here are not merely operational (they very rarely are). Clearly a radical change will be needed. Transition will not work. Decomposition may not either. Strong-minded individuals tend to hold their values rigidly, so some external pressure may be necessary. One that simply instructs will be unlikely to be successful. A confrontational approach initially may be appropriate, but how this is put into place will depend on the personal skills of all concerned. How far would the team members go in reframing their own self-concept as high-achieving sales people, for example?

As with all changes of this kind, however, the sheer particularity of the individuals and their collectivity means that discussion such as the above can do no more than hint at possibilities. And the manager on the spot needs to recognise that all change activities have to be provisional, contingent on the wide variety of different factors in operation in the situation.

6.3   Value decay

Most management writing in the area of values and ethics deals with regeneration, corporate upturn through values, success through people, and so on. The inherent optimism of the writing leads one to think that ethical change is all about how to make the future better. Perhaps there is a lot to this – after all, it's what hope is all about. Nevertheless, it would be folly to ignore the less optimistic potential futures awaiting us. Again, we shall start with Lewin's re-freezing analogy. Implicit in the need to freeze behaviour and attitudes into a certain state is the concern that they will slip back to previous forms, or worse still, become unsystematised. In this respect, Lewin is on the side of realism.

In identifying a change in someone's values as a decay, we are treating it as a change for the worse, and therefore indicating that we disagree with it. By contrast, if someone changes their values to a form with which we agree it would be regarded as 'coming round' to good sense. There seem to be two different ways in which someone's value system might be regarded as decaying or degenerating:

- they acquire (or revert to) a value with which we disagree
- the platform on which their values rest becomes in some way undermined or diminished.

An example of the first kind of 'decay' might be: a subordinate who has previously been supportive of management may come to be more directly critical; the manager is likely to regard this as a deterioration in the subordinate's attitude; the subordinate may regard it as having had the scales fall from his eyes. As an example of the second case, a colleague may continue to hold a certain view, say that a high level of income tax is wrong, but they may acknowledge that they no longer see some reasons they formerly held for this as valid. For example, perhaps they originally believed that high taxation makes people on welfare less likely to look for lower paid jobs. Now they see this as too simplistic, yet they continue to hold the basic view on taxation.

The first of these types of value decay is virtually no more than one person disagreeing with another's change of values. By contrast the second phenomenon, obscure in itself, is a key factor in the process of value change, which we considered in the previous section. For it is by means of someone's capacity to retain certain values, even whilst the underpinning platform of associated beliefs and attitudes is changing, that enables us to go through a *process* of change rather than always suffer from direct, instantaneous, 'Damascus'-type conversions. And paradoxically, it is the *flexibility* of the underpinning platform that creates the conditions for *rigidity* in explicit value judgements. As we saw, the link between a supporting platform and the values someone holds is not mechanical; someone can therefore continue to believe something even when their reasons for it give way. The decay of an element of someone's supporting platform underlines what kind of support is provided by other elements – for the value in question may be no less strongly held despite the loss of some part of its support. While this might seem like being dogmatic, there are times when this is regarded almost as a virtue – to have the courage of one's convictions even when their support seems shaky. Almost as if one should be loyal to one's opinions, as if they are a part of oneself. Rigidity, then, is not always a vice – on the contrary, it can be an important virtue, enabling someone to achieve the juggling act depicted earlier as the paradox of value change.

In this chapter we have encountered certain paradoxical ideas: someone can think something is wrong and not wrong at the same time; it can be a good thing to be rigid in one's views; people sometimes persist in certain values even when their reasons for doing so have been undermined; ethical flexibility provides the necessary basis for ethical rigidity; value decay can be a mark of someone maintaining their values. Each of these, clearly, is a paradoxical way of expressing an important aspect of people's values and how these may be open to or resistant to change. But conjointly they underscore

---

BOX 7.1 (cont'd)

the charity is not in a position to offer any substantial collateral as security for the loan. Despite all this, you feel uncertain about the issue. Your training, experience, and values incline you to follow the corporate rules and procedures, which point to the answer in terms of financial prudence, yet somehow you feel a doubt. Somehow you feel that your values are wrong for this situation.

This kind of dilemma is faced by loans managers commonly, and posed just as often by aid project officers. Equally it is the kind of case that often forms the stuff of discussions of business values. The critical twist in this story is the idea that someone might question their own values. We shall use this systematically as an example in the following discussion.

The issue we shall focus on is how there are specific ideas that play a part in the resolution of dilemmas like the one above and that can have an important role in the way people might take steps to change their attitudes. One specific approach, which will be opposed, is the realist type of view which holds that some attitudes just *are* right and others just wrong. This is not due to some theoretical argument that moral realism is unacceptable. Rather it is the pragmatic consideration that the quest to find 'the' correct judgement, which such an approach encourages, can limit and ultimately destroy the possibility of the kind of reflection that is essential for a person to work consciously towards changing their attitudes. The discussion in this chapter focuses on two aspects of the process of attitudinal change: (a) the significance that someone attaches to their own attitudes; and (b) the significance of the collision between an individual's own attitudes and those of other people.

7.1   The paradox of attitude change revisited

The issue posed in Box 7.1 is how a person can contemplate changing their own moral attitudes. Now let us recall the paradox of value change. Look at Figure 7.1. The text there makes it seem impossible for a person to consider that their attitudes might need some rethinking, for that implies that some part of their attitudes is wrong, and how can I hold an attitude and yet think it wrong at the same time?

It may seem puzzling to consider someone taking steps to change their attitudes. But as we saw when we discussed the paradox previously, someone may well go through a *process* that involves a series of changes, often incremental in nature, to various aspects of their values and/or the underpinning platform of beliefs. At some point a threshold is reached at which the pressure of these changes at an underpinning level leads to a qualitative change in the explicit value the person holds. Such a pressure is not a simple consequence of the weight of changed supporting views, for on occasion a single event might cause someone to see things in a fresh light.[1] But in general, the accumulated weight of a number of changed attitudes and beliefs becomes *over time* too great for an individual to maintain their former ethical views. During this time, it seems that conflicting ethical views are operating. The problem of the paradox of ethical change reflects this conflict between beliefs. If we think of attitudes and values basically as judgements of right or wrong, the paradox seems to make the idea of deliberate value change essentially problematic.

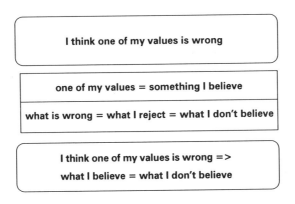

Figure 7.1   The paradox of ethical change

Clearly, this paradox is only apparent. We can and do go through processes of self-criticism that involve considering whether our attitudes are wrong or limited. The paradox arises from the conflict between (a) the perspective of ethical change as a simple transition from one judgement to another, and (b) the fact that ethical changes are not instantaneous. One could say that the problem is dispelled if we drop the first of these assumptions. Much of what follows will emphasise the argument of previous chapters, that changing one's attitudes and moral values *is* a process, extending over time and involving various stages.

As we discussed briefly in Chapter 5, the process of ethical change is essentially related to dialogue. The process of discussion and debate with others is a key factor affecting changes in people's attitudes, although it is not the sole factor, as we shall consider later.

The essential capability that allows a person to maintain their own views but simultaneously consider the possibility of change is that of doubt. The loans manager may continue to hold the view as to whether she or he should offer the loan to the aid agency. But the feeling of doubt marks a pressure for change, a need at least to rethink one's own attitudes and opinions. The point about doubt is that it slows down the process of reconsidering one's views. One does not jettison one set of values and bring aboard another – one resists, one wants to hold on to opinions and beliefs. Doubt allows one to continue life, as a bank manager, as an aid worker or whatever, however much it feeds the process of restructuring one's attitudes and beliefs. The capacity for doubt is a core competence for a good manager. A comment attributed to Peter Drucker, referring scornfully to the early MBA graduates from US universities runs: 'An MBA may sometimes be wrong, but they're never unsure.'[2] In the context, this was unequivocally a criticism. Doubt is as important in some situations as conviction – rigidity, in our previous terminology – is in others.

In the next section we shall see how the interactive aspect of ethical dilemmas can have a significant impact on whether or how a person doubts their views.

7.2   How to drive attitudes underground

I want to turn to two related models to help elucidate the process of attitude change. The first of these helps to clarify certain features of the interactive aspect of attitude change and critique, whilst the second gives an insight into the effects on attitudes of critique.

7.2.1   The OK–OK model

Derived from the work of Thomas Harris and Eric Berne,[3] this model depicts interactions on a two-by-two matrix, which defines four possible categories of 'OK-ness'. Applied to the issue of conflict in attitudes, the model may be formulated as in Figure 7.2.

This matrix represents the possibilities for agreement or disagreement. The quadrants are intended to illustrate the perceived level of concurrence between the views of the protagonists of an ethical debate – they are not statements of whether either or both parties is indeed right or wrong. Needless to say, doubt might occur in the disapproval, concession or impasse quadrants, and conceivably even in the agreement one. The key issue, however, is to try to project what the likely responses of individuals are to each of these possibilities. This is where the second matrix becomes relevant.

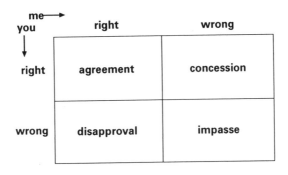

Figure 7.2   The right–wrong matrix – adapted from the Harris OK–OK model

7.2.2 The johari window

Figure 7.3 is known as the 'johari' window (not some ancient eastern mystical sign; it was devised by two social psychologists named Joe Luft and Harry Ingham – hence the joe–harry nomenclature). Luft and Ingham[4] made use of the window to illustrate, among other things, the positive effects of self-disclosure and feedback. The model can, however, also demonstrate destructive effects of criticism and disagreement, and this is where it links with the OK–OK Model.

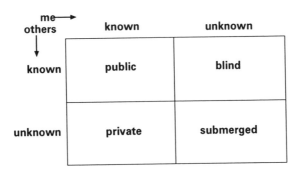

Figure 7.3   The johari window

Consider the individual holding an attitude that is in the public arena – openly admitted by the individual and acknowledged (if not accepted) by others. For example, the loans manager in the scenario we opened with may well give the safety of the bank's funds a greater priority than third-world development needs, and his view on this may be openly tolerated – even if not agreed with – by others with whom he deals. This acknowledgement of the attitude places it in the public area of the johari window.

This has implications for the OK–OK matrix. A publicly owned attitude is one that is allowed to exist openly, even when disagreed with. In one sense, oddly enough, the toleration by others of this attitude places the manager in the 'both right' quadrant, for there is at least a level of agreement that the attitude is tolerable – it is not so outrageous that it is attacked in debate to the extent of either being changed or driven underground. Both the manager and others feel comfortable with the attitudes in question. As a result there is no pressure for moving away from the public quadrant in the johari window.

The situation would be different if the manager expressed a view that the aid worker (or others) felt was highly unacceptable. For example, if the loan was refused on racist grounds, then the dialogue might break down altogether. Either the manager would be forced through argument (and other influences) to give up at least the public expression of his attitude, or he would be excluded from debate about such issues – that is, people simply wouldn't bother arguing with him about it. In the first case possibly there would be attitude change, or possibly the manager's values would be driven underground. In the second it would be almost certainly driven underground through lack of dialogue.

7.2.3 Resistances to change

I want to propose a key feature of attitude change:

> Only if someone is within the public area of the johari window, and in the 'agreement' quadrant of the right–wrong matrix, can there be a healthy change in their attitudes.

If someone feels unhappy either with their own view or with that of another in the dialogue, then there is a likelihood that this will reduce or inhibit their openness in the discussion. To the extent that someone's attitudes stay hidden (that is, in the submerged quadrant of the johari window), or only partially open to all, then key issues may well remain unaddressed.

Consider the effect of criticism upon the manager from someone who holds opposed views. The ideal situation would be one in which someone responds assertively (not aggressively) to this, maintaining their own view in a dispassionate manner, without suppressing any aspects. Needless to say, people often present various *non*-ideal responses, arising from passiveness perhaps, or from some kind of aggressiveness. This shifts the interaction, often downwards to the disapproval quadrant of the matrix, and is likely to have the effect of reducing the public area in the johari window. The reduction may be via an increase either in the blind area of the johari window or in the private area, because the two primary non-assertive responses to criticism are either to withdraw from public debate (increase of private area) or to deceive oneself as to the content of the disagreement (increase of area of blindness).

As an illustration of this, suppose the charity worker accuses the loans manager of being too materialistic. This creates a situation in which both parties are liable to fall into the lower quadrant of the OK matrix, each defending his or her own position and simultaneously attacking the other's. The effect on the loans manager might follow two paths. On one, the manager may think 'They've got their values wrong, you can't invest in unsound propositions.' In doing so, the manager is, in effect, repeating or reinforcing a basic value, but in a manner that is likely to inhibit further dialogue. Hence this will suppress the debate, but not the disagreement, increasing the private area of the johari window at the expense of the public.

On the other hand, the manager might think, 'No, they've misunderstood me. I put people before profit just as much as they do. My way of doing things will help people make greater profits.' Clearly this is a different kind of disagreement. If it is said openly rather than thought privately it could well provide some kind of basis for dialogue. All too often, however, this is likely to remain an unspoken – and therefore untried – thought. In being kept internal, it could reflect a form of self-deception, of a kind of rationalisation, for in thinking so the manager may well be misdescribing his own view. This would be reflected as an increase in the blind area of the johari window at the expense of the public. Similar possibilities are present with the aid worker.

These two models of social interaction, then, provide a framework for describing and understanding how barriers to attitude change can arise. It now remains to consider how they can be removed or overcome.

7.3 Creating the possibility for attitude change

7.3.1 The change process

Figure 7.4 gives an image, derived from Lewin's models of change, of the stages through which an individual is likely to go when their attitudes change. It deliberately oversimplifies the various processes discussed in Chapter 6, but the key idea from that discussion still holds – that a person's value system is best understood in this discussion as comprising a super-structure of explicit value judgements, and an understructure or platform of supporting beliefs, opinions and related attitudes.

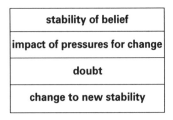

Figure 7.4   From stability to stability – value change

The issues of resistance depicted in the matrices of the previous section arise as part of the two central stages of the above diagram – the impact of pressures for change, and the way in which the resulting doubt is handled. These two stages are where changes in the platform or understructure of an individual's value system occur and are accommodated.

In each of these two stages of the process of attitude change, a *philosophical* approach to ethics can be employed to influence responses. This is not achieved without a bit of liberty-taking with the philosophical views in question – for one thing, in their original forms the two approaches we shall look at were intended as contrary theories. These approaches do not by them-selves yield anything strikingly unexpected. But they do help us explain what is going on in the process of attitude change, and at the very least can help discriminate between some good and bad approaches to attitude change.

7.3.2 Sympathy

The ethical theory of David Hume was very sophisticated, but amongst the several important contributions he made was to emphasise the importance of sympathy in moral responses.[5] Without going into the deep issue of how far moral attitudes involve sympathy, we can still recognise that sympathy can have an important role to play in attitude change. In particular, we can use the idea to help us recognise the value of particular ways of approaching attitude change and conflicts in attitudes towards business activities.

Sympathy enters into the process of attitude change at the stage of the impact of some pressure for change. To return to our loans example, the manager may or may not feel that there is a reason for him or her to change their mind. But when they do, what makes them acknowledge this possibility, without necessarily 'buying into' the attitude with which they have just come into conflict? To put it another way, what creates this kind of doubt? One factor may be a growing or pre-existing sympathy with the situation of some of those who hold a stake in the course of action being considered. The manager may simply identify with individuals whom he or she imagines living in an area with great water shortages, for example. It is quite possible that the dialogue with the aid worker brings this issue to the loans officer's consciousness.

What lies behind this familiar situation is the effect this can have on the position of the individual in the two matrices we considered above. The sympathetic response occurs within the 'private' area of an individual's johari window, and there is no reason, in terms of that framework, why it should facilitate attitude change. But in terms of the Harris model, there is a significant shift. For sympathy is likely to engender a move to a like–like context. The individual may identify a point of similarity with their erstwhile opponent, (agreement) or they depict both themself and that other person as confronted by a moral issue that they have not addressed or satisfactorily solved (impasse). In Harris' terms, we would say that they have reached a state either of OK–OK or of not-OK–not-OK.

Sympathy, then, can facilitate the growth of doubt, in a positive manner, insofar as it reduces or removes the potential adversarial element in a debate. The possibility of the loans manager becoming defensive, retreating into his shell (johari private area) or deceiving himself as to the nature of the dispute (johari blind area) is reduced, because the transaction has been perceived as balanced (like–like position on the Harris matrix).

Much of the above analysis may strike the reader as dressing up the obvious, but recall some of the comments made earlier – the obvious often needs to be said. In any case, there are some less obvious aspects that the model presented earlier does highlight. One of these is the role of self-deception as a potential stratagem. The johari window presents self-deception as a parallel to the process of keeping one's views private. Clearly, field research is required to test out quite what the balance is between these two retreats from rational discussion, but the argument of Chapter 2 emphasises that we have yet fully to understand how great may be the potential of self-deception to ease the discomfort of moral dispute.

7.3.3 Consistency

The idea of consistency I want to cite here derives from Immanuel Kant, the great German 18th-century philosopher I have mentioned earlier (who freely acknowledged his debt to Hume), but has been reinterpreted in the 20th century by, amongst others, Thomas Nagel.[6]

Crudely, this idea is that given a person has a moral attitude in one situation, then they are not consistent unless they extend or transfer that to other comparable situations. For Kant, this meant that a person who made a moral judgement was committed to it as a law of behaviour – applying in all similar contexts. For Nagel, it means that a socially adjusted person will always recognise that a moral judgement they make in their own case applies in the same manner to others. Whilst sympathy operates at the level of the impact of pressures for change, consistency links with the way we process attitudes and reasons. Recalling the model of personal moral skills outlined in Chapter 5, sympathy works in relation to *disposition to self* and how that relates with others, whilst consistency relates with *self-concept* and what this implies about others. As was mentioned in Chapter 5, clearly these are bound to be closely related, but there is further need to recognise that there are two separate components here. One difference between them is that disposition to self will more directly influence someone's behaviour, and hence directly affect their interactions with others, whilst self-concept may work at a subtler level, not so overt in its manifestations, and thus will have a less obvious effect on interactions with others.

How does consistency apply to our example of the loan request? Within that scenario, the loans manager would have to articulate the ultimate reason he had for granting or refusing the loan application. He then would have to consider the range of contexts in which substantially the same issue is raised. If, for example, the manager is tempted to grant the loan, on the basis that the project is a worthy cause, then he would have to consider whether he would grant loans on any worthy cause that applied. Such a question also has a value in the use of scenarios such as the loan application in the development of managers' views, via discussions of whether individuals could take the same stance in different contexts. Consistency is a simple idea, but in practice it can generate considerable discussion and argument.

How does this idea relate to the double matrix model of attitudes outlined above? First, in the right–wrong model it can reduce the likelihood of one or other party viewing the dispute as imbalanced (disapproval or concession) because the idea of consistency by its very nature applies to both parties. Note, however, that it would not necessarily eliminate that possibility. Behind the language of consistency is often a considerable degree of partiality and emotion masquerading as impersonal detachment.

So far as the johari window is concerned, it does force an opening up of the understructure, the often complex edifice of reasons and non-rational supports people may have for their attitudes. One kind of self-deception, for example, involves a person overemphasising a particular kind of example, not recognising that this has only a limited applicability in other situations. The loans manager, for example, may well recall a loan made 'to another third-world aid project' some years ago that was defaulted. This case may come to exercise a disproportionately large influence on the manager's attitudes. Another type of self-deception occurs when an individual misdescribes her own beliefs and wants, as mentioned earlier. The demand of consistency does push the manager into a more open stance, and forces her to consider the degree to which the reasons which underpin her attitudes might transfer to other contexts.

7.4   Consistency and sympathy – their role in changing attitudes

There are clear limitations on the extent to which consistency and sympathy can operate as triggers or catalysts for attitude change. In the case of sympathy there is an obvious shortcoming – it is a feeling, and if a person isn't struck by it then there is no chance of it helping to transform attitudes.

One advantage that the appeal to consistency has is that there is less waywardness of this kind. Anyone capable of understanding an argument can appreciate the demand for consistency once it is brought to their attention. But, as mentioned earlier, issues of partiality and subjectivity can often underpin an argument that is apparently conducted in an open fashion. In the language of the johari window, underlying the material of the public area may often be private, blind or unknown factors.

This brings us back to the issue of self-deception – the mistaking of one's own beliefs, opinion and reasons, sometimes wilful, often completely unacknowledged. This is the single largest aspect of people's ethical attitudes that needs to be addressed. The explicit areas, such as questions of honesty, equality, or valuing people, are so publicly advocated and advanced that it is usually seen as social anathema to question them in public. The practice is different – dishonesty, selfishness and materialism are rife in business and political communities. One function of the requirement of consistency is that it can help flush out covert attitudes.

7.5   Developing individual's views

It was mentioned earlier that dilemmas such as the one in the loan application example have a role in management development. In this area it would seem that consistency has an edge over sympathy, because it is a matter amenable to discussion and debate, which is more tolerable for those from western cultures than the process of reflection, which the development of sympathy would require. But there is a close relationship between the two. The perception of a consistency (or lack of it) is liable to affect an individual's feelings, and vice versa. The ultimate challenge for business ethics must be to harness both factors to help extend and develop the attitudes of today's and tomorrow's managers.

But the two approaches are not really in competition. Their complementary roles mean that these are different techniques for reducing the inertia or stability of someone's current value system. In doing so, they create a degree of pressure on an individual's value system that surfaces initially as doubt and eventually as explicit change. If we go back to the model of personal skills and their relation to ethical behaviour and apply it to the loans manager scenario, we may observe the following:

- his personal long-term orientation currently keeps him allied to the prudent strategy
- there is little evidence relating to self-analysis or directly pertaining to reasoning skills or interpersonal skills
- his self-concept and disposition to self are both likely to be bound up with his professional position
- his disposition to others has led to a degree of unease over the conflict he is facing.

Consistency and sympathy work in complementary ways in that both are means of taking a standpoint that includes others. They start from two separate points, (consistency–self-concept; sympathy–self-disposition) but they both draw the manager into a closer examination of his disposition to others. In their different ways they both exemplify the principle that *the internal mirrors the external*. Consistency works partially by treating the manager's self-analytic capabilities as analogous with his external reasoning skills. This was a point we noted towards the end of Chapter 5. The reasons that the loans manager would need to give publicly for making his decision will either conform to or clash with his internal self-analysis. Where a clash exists, the question of consistency creates the doubt that triggers someone to consider amending their values. The role of sympathy is not analogous, but operates along a line from personal orientation, through self-disposition to other-disposition. Where the manager feels a degree of sympathy for the beneficiaries of the aid worker, what he is doing is comparing his own orientation, and how that informs his self-disposition, with his disposition to others. In other words, the question is 'Given that I would feel bad about this, and given that I basically respect my own feelings, why should I refuse the same feeling for others?' Unless a clear countervailing factor exists to block the transfer of feeling from self to others, the manager will experience a need to equalise the mismatch between self and others.

Yet again someone might say: 'This is dressing up the obvious into an over-theoretical account of quite ordinary events. Doesn't the manager just think "I should treat others like myself"? Isn't this a simpler way of discussing what happens?'

The manager almost certainly thinks something like that. But that response is available *whenever* we are in a dilemma. The account above has tried to get behind why it is that that move of comparison, cognitively (consistency) or emotionally (sympathy) works some of the time and doesn't the rest. It is hardly ignorance – we do not suddenly become unaware that a comparison could be made. It is that certain connections are not made. The mirroring between self-analysis and external reasoning may break down, for example, or the link between personal orientation and self-disposition may be severed (say if the manager feels particularly over or under confident about herself, she may regard this as sufficient difference between herself and others for the sympathetic response not to get started).

This chapter has extended the argument of the preceding two chapters. It has taken two ideas, and two well established, related models, and indicated how they combine with the models outlined in Chapters 5 and 6, to demonstrate how value change may occur. The final chapter of this part will discuss a number of issues that relate to value change and the link between that and an individual's sense of personal worth, for we shall see that this is a key feature of how far change may be resisted.

Discussion

Pick any practice of your organisation that directly affects external stakeholders or customers. Identify exactly how it does affect these external groups. Brainstorm a number of other external groups, and consider how far the practice could be extended to them (or not).

Notes

1. The case of Eric Clark discussed previously is one such example.
2. I have not been able to source this.
3. Thomas Harris (1973); Eric Berne (1968).
4. The original version of the window may be found in Luft (1971).
5. David Hume's major work was *A Treatise on Human Nature* (1888, ed. Selby-Bigge 1957). See Part III for discussion of ethics. Another modern discussion of issues relating to the Human approach to ethics can be found in the many ethical writings of Bernard Williams (for example, 1985).
6. The clearest expression of a 'Kantian' type approach to ethics can be found in Nagel (1979). Kant's own views are most accessibly found in Kant (ed. Paton 1948).

8 *Highest Common Denominators*

The last chapter presented an example of how quite broadly based ideas can have the potential for effecting – or at least assisting – the process of value change in an individual. In this chapter we shall look at an apparently tangential cluster of issues, although we shall see that they consolidate the key points of the preceding argument. They will also, though, give an indication of which approaches to managing people's ethical views are most likely to be effective.

8.1 Fixed and set values

We discussed earlier a concept that I called rigidity of values, which turned out to be an important and often desirable feature – that values don't just dissolve at the first pressure, that people are committed to them. But in fact there are two concepts that come under this heading, two types of rigidity, which we shall now distinguish. The first of these is value *fixity*. This term refers to the direction of influence between explicit values and the platform of additional ideas and feelings on which they rest.

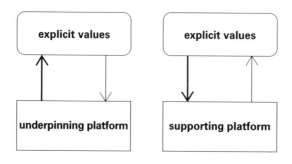

Figure 8.1   Directions of determination

The reader will note that whereas in previous chapters I have talked indiscriminately about underpinning and supporting platforms for values, they are explicitly distinguished here. The reason for this is to illustrate a simple difference in the way someone's values may be linked to their other beliefs. In the left-hand case, someone's values arise from, are influenced by, their other attitudes and beliefs. We might call this *value composition* – that is, the individual's values are made up from and dependent on the underpinning platform. We have already seen one aspect of this in Chapter 6, where one kind of value change was described as decomposition – that is, a composed value changed because elements in the underpinning platform changed. In the right-hand case in Figure 8.1, the prime determination goes the other way – my values lead me to have certain beliefs and attitudes. For want of a better term, we could call this *value imposition*. That is, the individual's values have an overriding influence on other beliefs and attitudes. The more appropriate model of change here would be the catastrophic kind – an individual would not be amenable to changing his view just because some aspect of his stated reasons (that is, some part of the supporting platform) had been undermined.

Let us look at some examples. Suppose someone believed that for management to bug employees' offices was wrong, but changed their mind when they were given evidence that a proportion of employees carried out anti-organisational activities (for example, revealing commercially confidential information to customers) when in the privacy of their own offices. This would be an example of value composition – the influence is from the underpinning platform to the explicit value. Someone who, on the other hand, when confronted with the same evidence, said 'I don't care, bugging's still wrong' would, in this instance at least, be displaying value imposition – the values are not determined by that platform. In extreme cases of the latter people may often deny certain facts, or devise elaborate *ad hoc* explanations, such as marginalising the significance of factual evidence (in the above case, someone might, for example, do this by claiming that the proportions of deceitful employees was not substantial enough to justify the bugging). Obviously, presenting this distinction in 'on-off' terms as in the diagram above is an oversimplification. The difference in reality is one of degree – values will to an extent determine or be determined by the underpinning platform. Equally, it is time bound – people are not often consistent over time, so we must assume that someone may operate with a value-composed system at one time and a value-imposed one at another time. This is true of all talk earlier of 'value systems' – they are systematic for purposes of analysis, but it is rare that the 'system-ness' implies anything about how long a period someone will hold to a certain value.

Nevertheless, the link between someone's values and their other views is radically different in the two cases, and thus the appropriate strategies for change are also radically different. An individual with composed values is open to change where their underlying views can be changed. An individual with imposed values is not, and change must happen from the value statement downwards.

The reader may notice that two of the three models of value change discussed in Chapter 6 have been mentioned above. What of the third – gradual transition? This will become relevant to the second type of rigidity to be discussed. This second kind of rigidity is what I shall call *value setting*. It has obvious links with the broader idea of mindsetting that we discussed earlier. Here it refers to the speed and ease with which someone's values can shift. Where someone's values can be moved easily, when they are able to make alterations, accept different formulations, without too much concern, then we might say that a person can *evolve* their values. On the other hand, if someone holds tenaciously to their views, prepared no doubt to change them if the proof is forthcoming, but not ready to do so at what they would see as the drop of a hat, then we might say they could change their values only by *revolution*. Hence two types of value setting: evolutionary and revolutionary. These reflect the points that were made earlier about mindsettings. They can be flexible useful guides and rules of thumb, but once they lose contact with the context from which they originally drew their use they can become ossified, difficult to shift without a great effort.

Figure 8.2 depicts the relationship between the two distinctions in terms of four types of individual, illustrated here by four famous leaders from the past (note, this is not a theory of leadership – it is just a convenient way of presenting the idea).

| | **Type of value fix** | |
	composed	*imposed*
revolutionary	Abraham Lincoln	Napoleon Bonaparte
evolutionary	Emperor Constantine	Genghis Khan

Type of value setting

Figure 8.2   Four types of value rigidity

The Constantine type reviews his values in the light of changing circumstances and is not overly connected with any of them. He might be suspected of being a little insincere, because he has no great difficulty with value change but he is fairly predictable in the kinds of value change he is likely to experience.

The Lincoln type is more determined. He does not find it easy to change his values, but when faced with changed circumstances he will do so. He may be seen as patient but not dogmatic.

By contrast, the Genghis type is highly dynamic, flying from one wholehearted cause to another. He may change his mind easily, but this is rarely as a result of an appreciation of external factors. He may be seen as superficial or mercurial.

Finally, the Napoleon type is stubborn in the extreme. He is very difficult to shift from his values, and pays little heed to external factors until it is often too late.

We should now consider the managerial implications of this model. Many organisational value-change programmes attempt to change people by appealing to their rational side and hoping that this will create a change in their emotional reactions – that is, changing hearts by changing minds. As we see from the above, this works less than half the time. Equally, an approach based on the alternative – from hearts to minds – is going to be only partially appropriate at best. As with other aspects of facilitated organisational change, such as organisational learning, the key is to recognise that a variety of types requires a variety of different approaches. 'Scatter-gun' strategies are therefore more likely to work than too systematic and controlled a programme, which will win some over and probably drive the resistance of others underground.

Consider what would be the most appropriate way to deal with the issues outlined in Box 8.1.

BOX 8.1   **A Research Team**

The members of a multi-disciplinary team, employed by a local council, were working on a new policy for delivering care services to a local population. They had encountered unexpected difficulties in getting a clear idea of what they were supposed to be doing. Several of the team felt that the whole exercise was unnecessary, and that the key questions had been resolved by previous policy decisions. Others believed that there were fresh aspects that previous work had not resolved. Still others believed that previous work had no relevance at all, and that the team should start entirely afresh.

BOX 8.1 (cont'd)

A facilitator was brought in to help the team members in resolving their differences. During the course of the sessions it became clear that the differences were not technical – they were not soluble by reference to existing rules, legislation or knowledge. Nor were they exclusively ethical, although this was certainly a feature. A cluster of different elements was involved, including ethics, knowledge and rules, but also including different perceptions of long-term strategy, and different views on the causes of some of the needs of the client population.

The facilitator helped the group hammer out seven key statements that represented a substantial part of most people's opinions. Out of the ten members of the team, eight concurred with these statements. Two, however, had serious reservations. To complicate matters, one of the two was the team leader, the other was the most senior member of the team.

Eventually the team reached a crisis point, at which the conflicts became explicit and polarised. The situation began to resemble a dramatised jury room, with the facilitator joining the majority group within the team, presenting argument after argument to the two dissenters, without being able to find any point on which agreement could be latched. Eventually one of the majority, in exasperation, said 'For god's sake, what *do* you really want?' The team leader mentioned the name of a very senior member of the organisation, and almost simultaneously the other dissenter nodded in agreement. It was clear that his job would become redundant once a new policy was brought in, almost regardless of the details. The team discussed this at some length, and then a proposal was made about creating a new role for the individual in question. Almost at once the team leader agreed to this. Just as immediately, however, the more senior dissenter rejected the idea out of hand. In doing so he cast further doubts on some of the agreed statements. After a while one or two other members of the team – but not, obviously, the team leader – seemed now to agree with some of these doubts.

One of the advantages of being an external facilitator is that one does not have to persist with a hopeless cause. The facilitator found a way of winding up the programme not long after, and the last she heard was that the most senior member of the team had dropped out, the person whose job had been in question had been moved sideways, and the team were still meeting to 'set groundrules'.

The box outlines a difficult and unsuccessful piece of consultancy. In relation to the model given above, the most striking feature is the difference in type of resistance between the team leader and the other, more senior dissenter. It is likely that the team leader's values were to a degree composed in this context – that is, her views rested on the underpinning platform, part of which included a concern about the person whose job would become redundant. As soon as this was addressed her position shifted easily. She was something of a 'Lincoln'. By contrast, the other senior member present may well have had a relatively greater degree of value imposition – that is, he was unwilling to agree to the key statements no matter what, and the issue of the redundancy was one of any number of objections he was prepared to raise – a 'Napoleon'-type response. One would guess that he had some further, hidden purpose, but that lay beyond the capacity of the facilitator to detect.

What, though, of the other researchers? Clearly there are critical differences here. The ones who persisted in their original belief were somewhat Lincoln-esque in their behaviour, or possibly even Napoleonic, whilst those who wavered demonstrated a degree of Constantine-type behaviour – less fixed in the sense of being more likely to change their views given changes in the underlying platform of their beliefs and attitudes, and less set in that they were not so committed to particular judgements. There was no one exhibiting particularly Genghis-like characteristics, expect perhaps the facilitator partially, when she turned from a neutral change agent to siding with the researchers. One moral of this scenario is that pliancy and resistance are not simple good guys or bad guys – whilst in general a more pliant individual may be easier to work with, the potential benefits of these two types of individual are more or less situation-specific.

Another lesson to draw from it is the essential fluidity of people's views – as many an experienced chair will say, once a verbal agreement is reached in a committee, it is folly to discuss it too much more. One risk is that further discussion may uncover differences that had been patched over; another, though, is that further discussion may *create* new differences and conflicts in judgement.

From case material general *conclusions* cannot be drawn, but general *questions* can. The above case raises three questions that are generally relevant to the value dimension of organisational change:

- How far is the resistivity or pliancy of the values of any particular actor in the situation a resource as opposed to a constraint on the change?
- How far are similarities in judgements based on similar underlying platforms?
- How far are similar value systems (that is, similar explicit values and underlying platforms) likely to behave similarly with respect to pliancy and resistivity?

The first of these is really a specific version of the Lewin force-field analysis, but illustrates one of the weaknesses of this approach. All too often, when organisations are going through major changes, managers go through a large amount of undisclosed planning, come up with a solution for which they want to gain acceptance, and hence see the key task of change management as 'bringing the staff on board'. In this context flexibility of staff attitudes – in the sense of pliancy – becomes extremely convenient for the manager, who is likely to welcome it. It is also likely to be rewarded as good behaviour.

Equally, opposition, especially when not itself clearly articulated in business terms, is regarded as being negative, awkward, and thus undesirable. But, as Peter Drucker has said[1] it is the obstinate, awkward individual who is likely to have the most important message for the organisation. It is not the case that every change is helped by people willingly flexing into them. If the staff are presented only with a reconstruction of some of the key thought processes which informed the solution that managers are trying to sell, then they are deprived perhaps of the very material that may find a purchase in their own thinking. It is not enough to present a good idea with the best logical reasons behind it. It is also important to create an internal dialogue in which every individual involved in the change has the opportunity to place suggestions and ideas alongside their own underlying belief system. This is what lies behind the idea that people must have a sense of *ownership* of an idea – that they can relate it to their own values and what underpins these. Obviously the easiest way to do this (though sometimes the hardest way to get a clear decision) is to involve them all in the process from the beginning. These are, of course, not new points. But they are confirmed and given an underpinning rationale from the analysis above.

The second and third questions focus on the uncertainty of value identification discussed previously, but take the points further. Not only are managers unlikely to have a clear idea of the values of staff, they are even less likely to have a clear understanding of how those values will operate in different situations; nor are individuals themselves always clear about how far they may be pliant or resistant in their values. In this respect the models in this chapter and the preceding one are descriptive/analytical. Whilst they are valuable in emphasising to managers what could be going on, they are not generally an aid to prediction of what an individual is likely to do or how they might react in a certain situation, basically again for the reason of complexity – there are simply too many factors to take into account. This has some resonance with one of the key claims of Peter Senge 'We rarely see the results of our actions.'[2] If we cannot see the results of what we do, then we cannot easily experiment; we cannot collect data and use it as a basis for understanding the future. Hence we need to model what the situation is likely to involve, and take this as a working guide. This is the main function of the diagrams given above and in Chapter 7 – as guides, rather than maps of the facts. As with all such guides they have limitations on their use, but equally they are better than unguided speculation or spuriously quantified 'data' that often turns out to be founded on elaborate guesswork.

In terms of what managers ought to do, the main issues raised by these two questions are related to information. Managers wishing to manage values in their organisation need to conceive of the relevant data set, from which they draw, on a very wide scale. Tentative change, proceeding itera- tively and involving the staff as a whole, is likely to pull in the key issues and concerns of individuals (although in any other than the very smallest busi- nesses there must inevitably be a high degree of approximation of the totality of people's views). As was indicated earlier, grand strategy is likely to be relevant to some but not all staff. More likely to succeed is a policy of success by means of a series of small wins. Of course, this takes more time.

8.2   The bus fare home

An anecdote recounted to me by an industrial relations lecturer distils the key point of this section. Apparently, the former leader of the TUC, the British labour organisation, Vic Feather (later Baron Hardie), was once asked, after a successful round of negotiations with a management team, why he had not pushed his advantage in the negotiation further. According to the story, his answer was 'Always leave the other bloke the bus fare home.' In a way this is a florid way of recognising that dignity is central to people's experience of events, and its preservation came high in Mr Feather's priori- ties. Ethical changes highlight a critical aspect of this idea of dignity, in a way that recalls the idea of value change as paradoxical.

As we have seen through several different strands of analysis and model- ling, people's values are not isolated thoughts. They are inextricably linked with a variety of other beliefs, attitudes, feelings, thoughts, hopes, and so on. So to change a particular value is most likely to require a series of conse- quential changes in the associated platform – as discussed earlier in this chapter and in the previous one, these may be cause or they may be effect, depending on the level of pliancy or resistance of the values of that indi- vidual. As a reasonable rule of thumb, the greater the ethical change, the more deep rooted the associated changes for the individual. Emotions may be involved, and ultimately elements of someone's personality may be in the melting pot. We have already seen some of the personal tone of the chal- lenge of value conflict when discussing the dilemma of Bernard Atti in Chapter 4, living in two ethical worlds. A different, though no less personal, difficulty is presented in Box 8.2.

BOX 8.2   The Master Craftsman

Simon Dewsbury is a highly skilled artificial intelligence specialist. He works for a small but swiftly growing company that makes robotic devices for disabled people. Simon's particular expertise lies in producing, to order, intelligent aids to mobility for people with motor difficulties. He takes great pride in his work, which he not only views as a social service but also as a form of craft – much as a carpenter or dress designer might. Often Simon will try not only to meet the customer's specification but add something of his own – an extra facility, or sometimes a feature that adds elegance to the design without necessarily contributing anything in functional terms. It is clear that this is a key career anchor and source of fulfilment for Simon.

Simon's boss, Veronica, has recently been given a large assignment, to get her team to produce a whole range of mobility aids for a local health organisation. This will involve working to generic specifications, rather than the customised work the team has done up until now, and to a tight budget. Veronica meets the team, and outlines the task and the constraints it will impose on their work. She particularly singles out Simon's high-class work by saying 'For this contract we'll have to be much more functional in our approach – no more adding little finesses to make the devices look elegant or flashy. We're not here trying to win awards, we're doing the bread-and-butter stuff, so it has to be basic – fit for the purpose, good workmanship, yes, but no more than that.'

Clearly there is going to be a conflict of attitudes here. Is this really a conflict of *ethics*, or is it simply taste?, someone might ask. In my opinion, given that it is a question of value, taken seriously by at least one of the protagonists, and the resolution of which is likely to have significant consequences both for Simon and his ultimate clients, I see no problem in regarding this as an ethical issue. More important is how Simon reacts to the change in practices. Let us start with the somewhat unrealistic assumption that he accepts the changes as stated, and makes no attempt to resist them. How will he feel? Clearly, if his previous behaviour was genuine, then in some sense or another the change to a more functional approach must be some kind of loss for him, related in some way to the fulfilment of being creative or the achievement of doing something special for individual members of the community. So this seems to demonstrate a potential down side of the 'Genghis' response. It becomes a classic win–lose situation, where either Simon finds his fulfilment away from his work (and as a result his psychological contract is diminished to an extent) or he experiences the frustration of not being so fulfilled. Of course, Veronica may be an enlightened manager who attempts to draw out Simon's needs, and provide for them – fine, the loss is counterbalanced, but this is only as satisfactory as the solution Veronica devises. A bigger danger is, as we have seen in earlier chapters, that the manager may perceive acquiescence in a change as the same as whole-hearted acceptance, so there is a good chance that Veronica will think nothing of Simon's sense of loss.

Suppose instead that Simon tries to oppose the changes by arguing the case, demonstrating that to an extent his value in this context is Lincoln-esque – highly set but composed. In this case he will presumably offer arguments why the changes should not be accepted, or how the contract can be fulfilled without sacrificing standards, and so on. Consistent with this would be Simon stating explicitly his own orientation to the work and the opportunities for fulfilment that it gives him. Again there are win–win and win–lose (or even lose–lose) possibilities. Perhaps one difference from the case where Simon responds in a Genghis-type way is that in that case lose–lose seemed built in, whilst here, if a process is carefully followed it may be possible to avoid a lose outcome on one or both sides. Arguably it will be potentially healthier than the previous case, simply because there will have been explicit communication regarding Simon's needs.

But in each of these situations, something dear to Simon is either removed or at least placed under grave threat. What is the *personal* significance for him of the change? There are as many answers to this as there are Simons, but this serves only to underline the point that personal significance there will be, often unperceived by managers, and often, too, poorly expressed or even suppressed by individuals. Unless some countervailing factor is placed into the equation, the situation is perceived as a lose outcome for the individual, and hence part of his dignity has been violated. This is where the idea of 'the bus fare home' becomes important. So far as is possible, an individual should be left with a sense that their own values have been taken into account, and not dismissed. Transformation is infinitely preferable to substitution. The Eric Clark case discussed earlier is an instance in which, amongst several other things, someone's sense of the dignity of their own values has been violated, rejected. Maybe the alternatives have as much to be said for them as Eric's, but that is not generally perceived to be a consolation by an individual in such a situation – in a way part of someone's identity can be at stake in such cases. The more far-reaching the change, the deeper the values are likely to lie, the more they are likely to take on an imposing character, resistant to external influences, and thus the more traumatic the loss.

8.3   Depths of agreement

The issue raised in the previous section is intrinsic to all situations in which an individual is expected or induced to change her values. For values are dear to people – so if they are required to adopt conflicting kinds of behaviour, how does one avoid the sense of loss that someone will inevitably feel?

There are many ways in which the possible loss might be counterbalanced or offset. As we saw in Chapter 6, sometimes a completely different element might be an appropriate psychological substitute (so that, for example, an increase in career opportunities was regarded by some people as compensating or outweighing their lack of confidence in management). But this is side-stepping the central issue. What can we do to help people retain their sense of dignity when their values are to be overturned by the organisation? The critical part of any solution to this is the *level of agreement* between an individual's former beliefs and the behaviour[3] or values that they are now encouraged to adopt.

We need to go back again to the structure of an individual's value 'system' to get a clear understanding of what is meant here. Recall that we divided up an individual's ethical framework into: (a) an explicit set of value judgements or beliefs; and (b) the platform beneath these, which comprises factual assumptions, other related value judgements, and other less easily classifiable attitudes and feelings, all of which might underpin or support (remember the difference here) the explicit values of the individual.

The most obvious sense of agreement would be where an organisation requires an individual to adopt a value that he already explicitly holds. Unproblematic as such, but it is worth noting that this does not imply that there is no potential conflict in values. Someone may hold mutually contrary values, which he has never properly put together. So, a manager might believe strongly in gender equality, but fail to notice that this may conflict with his view on age (say, because of the age issue when women try to balance career goals with any plans they might have for bearing children). Conflicts may also appear because one person holds a value deontologically, whilst another holds it consequentially. Yet another kind of conflict may arise when one person implicitly thinks of a certain value as applying mainly in one kind of context, whereas others in the organisation may conceive the same idea in relation to a different context. Say the company believes in 'loyalty to and from the staff'. A line manager may have a strong commitment to loyalty, as something both to expect from employees and to give them, but they may not extend this to subcontractors. A personnel officer, on the other hand, may see loyalty as a requirement that the organisation should expect *from* employees, contractors and other peripheral workers, but not feel that it is essential for the organisation to offer *to* these groups, beyond legal minima.[4] So even where there is agreement on 'loyalty to the staff' as a key business value, differences may lurk unsuspected.

Once we look at cases where the ethical change involves values that an individual has not explicitly acknowledged or held themselves, then the possibility of loss, and a related possibility of the individual feeling that values are being pressed on them, become much more important. The relation between the value-platforms becomes critical in determining the extent of any commonality, and thus the chance for an individual to accept an ethical change as not severely undermining their deeper concerns – that is, the chance to leave the individual with the ethical bus fare home. Consider the possibility that an individual may disagree at the explicit level with what is proposed by a manager (or by an organisation), yet a potential for change and acceptance is present, because of the connections at the platform level. Clearly, this is far more viable when the individual holds the value in question in a pliant fashion – say as a Constantine – than a resistant one. Resistant values are not, however, immovable ones. It is just that their movement is not predictable on the basis of shifts at the underlying level.

Two individuals may share many underlying elements and yet appear to be diametrically opposed in value terms. Hence, although there is a high potential for conflict, there is also the potential for finding common ground. The same cannot be the case where organisational values are concerned, for an organisation is not a person with an underlying platform that might afford such commonality. Where the individual has a highly composed set of values, in the sense we have outlined earlier, then the prospects for creating a sense of agreement and sharing of value are good. On the other hand, where the individual has a high degree of imposed values then the task is much harder – part of the task might be to understand what is the significance of their factual beliefs. In theoretical terms personality issues are also highly relevant. In practical managerial terms there is often not a lot you can do on this front – people are probably best seen as being what they are. Agreement or the lack of it, then, is deceptive – it is the *underlying possibility for commonality* that provides the best resource for ethical change (where it is appropriate – we should not forget the arguments of Chapter 4 – shared values can be a cover for totalitarianism).

If a manager is aware that people's explicit values are but the tip of a structured iceberg, then that suggests ways to explore the iceberg without having to crack it open all at one go. Ethical change is a process, and deliberate change of values in an organisation should be a highly interactive, and highly iterative process. Sir John Harvey-Jones[5] says 'I believe… that in deciding where you would like to be, as opposed to where you are probably going to end up, you need a great deal of discussion and a great deal of development of new thinking… This process involves large amounts of time and constant discussion with those involved lower down the line… this sort of circular debate, frequently widening out to involve others within and without the company, goes on until all are satisfied that the result is as good as they are going to get.' Harvey-Jones is here talking specifically about strategic change, but in many ways it is almost a perfect realisation of many of the points made in this and earlier chapters. Change takes a lot of work. The passage above seems to be talking mainly about changing minds, but people's hearts are involved too, and it is the heart side, and how it might link with the mind, that is the hardest. The model outlined above illustrates two kinds of factor that an individual might need to take account of when working with a group of people on their values, but it would be a mistake to see it as a *mechanism* for ethical change – again, as Harvey-Jones emphasises, the skills of an organisation's leaders and change agents are paramount for successful ethical change.

8.4 Heights of agreement

'Fundamentally we are in agreement' is a common enough phrase. It is tantamount to saying that we do not agree at all. Fundamentally everyone agrees, where values are concerned. Deep down everyone believes in their own worth, even though this may get horribly overlaid by doubts and the opinions of others. Also, because many words relating to values carry with them a tone of approval or disapproval, it is tautological to value justice, honesty, and kindness, and so on, and to reject violence, insensitivity and indulgence. So at 'the most basic level' we are all against violence and in favour of justice. Of course, the problem is that some acts are both violent and just, some are both honest and insensitive, and some are both kind and indulgent. We have seen part of the reason for this much earlier, and it is not the point of this section to go over the arguments about the difficulty inherent in applying concepts of value, and what different people may mean by them. The issue here is that this intrinsic positive or negative tone of certain terms contributes further to the illusion of 'fundamental agreement' when in reality there is no substantial concord at all.

In the case of managing a change of values, agreement on basics or fundamentals is not the key area for debate. It is in the realm of specific concrete application that the most difficult issues arise, and to which the most attention should be given. If someone's value system is thought of as a hierarchy, with the most basic elements at the bottom, then it is agreement at the highest level that is important. Highest common denominator is an appropriate metaphor – for the issue is how far, once the value systems of the individuals involved have been deconstructed, can one trace the degree of similarity or identity of value. Where the level is at its most basic only, then any substantial concord is going to be an uphill struggle. The further up such a hierarchy such similarities can be traced, the more optimistic one might be of finding explicit points of agreement. But it is also crucial to remember that this has to be a multi-dimensional model, taking account of the degree and type of resistivity there is in an individual's values (as discussed in Chapter 7), and taking account also of the variety and often near insubstantiality of the differing elements that may underlie those explicit values.

The other aspect of the numerical metaphor (that is, common denominators) is that the emphasis is placed on a value system as *deconstructed*. There are two important aspects to this. First, unlike the numeric metaphor, it is not at all clear that an individual's value system has a unique deconstruction. Is there a single way of mapping out the complexity of a person's beliefs, feelings, explicit values, hopes, and so on? It's not clear even whether the question makes sense, even though much of the argument of these last few chapters has worked, for simplicity, from a fiction that it may be possible. But this raises an issue mentioned toward the end of the previous section. Where human understanding is concerned, and especially with values, *analysis changes its subject matter*, particularly when it is explicit and couched in verbal transactions. Just as the committee may suffer a deterioration in understanding if it discusses something for too long, so a person's view of their own values is likely to change if they go through the process of analysing them and/or any underlying structures. So you cannot put your foot in the same stream twice in this context (or at least you *may* not be able to). Someone reading these last three sentences might wonder, what on earth is it all for then, all this stuff on rigidity and the like? It is for development of understanding, rather than to outline a mechanism for value change. As I have suggested earlier, the range of diagrams and models included here have been included less as a battery of tools and more as an illustration of some of the key problems. In terms of the key use for managers and students of business ethics, the main value of the argument is to flag up the complexity of people's values and the various dimensions along which that complexity may run. The problem of collecting soundly based information on what other people really feel and value is, of course, not unique to this issue, although that doesn't make it any easier.

The second point arising out of this idea of deconstruction is to underline that it is not in itself a great achievement to find that two people agree on some particular explicit value judgement, or that an individual accepts the line given by their employer. The key issue, and the prime difficulty, is to identify threads and elements of similarity as far up towards the sharp edge of practice as is achievable. To take another image – it is not a question of whether the fifth floors of two buildings are the same, but of whether the whole buildings are the same – or have appropriate similarities – from the foundations upwards. This is a much harder issue, unfortunately. But it is the way that the issue of values and someone's personal sense of dignity discussed earlier can be addressed.

8.5   Tolerance and compromise

In the final section of this chapter I want briefly to look at two issues that are both important for the management of people's values and are significantly affected by the argument of the preceding sections.

The first of these is the idea of tolerance. This is generally regarded as a key virtue of open, democratic and market-orientated societies (which is not of course to say that it is a key virtue of all societies, even though sometimes in discussing commercial organisations we might be led to confuse the two ideas). It is probably one of those terms that I described earlier as having an intrinsically positive tone, so that it is almost a truism to say that one believes in tolerance. As with all these terms, it is in the 'but' clause that the difficulties occur.

It is not those difficulties of application that I want to focus on, however, but the demand that the ideal of tolerance can make on people. Consider the degree of *challenge* that can be placed on an individual in a concrete situation where the suggestion is raised (either through their own imagination, stimulated maybe by concepts such as consistency or sympathy, or prompted by the views of others) that some practice or behaviour which they think is unacceptable should be tolerated. As we have discussed above, this can present an assault not only on their explicit values, but in some circumstances on their sense of self-worth and their own personal dignity. And what can make this even more difficult is that, unlike situations in which someone's own values are in question, the plea for someone to be tolerant requires them not only to preserve their own values but also somehow to still the qualms they have about some contradictory value. In a way it seems extraordinary that we can *ever* be tolerant of views with which we disagree.

We shall not embark on a philosophical analysis of the concept of tolerance here. What is important is the self-referring nature of tolerance. Unlike, say, kindness, which is a value concerning others' well-being, or honesty, which concerns others' beliefs, tolerance is a value about other people's values. I would suggest that one prime argument in its favour is simply the complexity of the whole nexus that goes to make up someone's values (and hence the virtual impossibility of completely gauging other people's views and concerns). Tolerance, being a value itself, will have an explicit manifestation and also an underlying platform that for some people will be its support and for others its underpinning. For a manager, the challenge of encouraging tolerance in her staff towards different values can properly be resolved only via the combination of the structure of individuals' own conception of tolerance with all that this implies, and creating a perception in them of how complex the similar structures must be in others, however alien their views may seem. The key point is simply that this is *hard*. It is easy enough, of course, to create compliant, tolerant *behaviour* – which may be highly desirable in itself – but tolerant *attitudes* are rather more to be prized.

The second issue to discuss is the idea of compromise. This is often a substitute in people's minds either for value change or for full-blooded tolerance. An individual may be persuaded by their manager that it will be good for their development to take a year-long 'community service' career development break, working for a socially worthy cause. The individual involved disagrees with the idea of social welfare and thinks that everyone should look after their own, but nevertheless he sees that this may be perceived badly if he were to reject the idea. Clearly the individual could simply respond to this with compliant behaviour and no attitude change. That is, he might go along with the placement and not consider whether he had anything to learn from the experience. This might be an extreme response, and maybe a little self-defeating, but a possible one, particularly where the individual had a high degree of resistivity in his value system. An alternative response might be where someone said 'Well, let's see what they've got to offer.' Indeed this might be the healthiest response where an extreme difference of view is concerned. This clearly links with the discussion of tolerance identified above. It trades on an assumption that *I might be wrong*. In that respect it reflects the influence of general ideas such as consistency. What is often supposed in such a case is that a *compromise* has been reached, but I wish to oppose this suggestion. Compromise implies that there has been an equalising of undesirable effects – 'equal pain equal gain' is one current phrase for it. This does the above response a disservice, for the idea of equal pain in this case would be that the individual has indeed suffered some kind of violation of their values (they might have of their rights, if overt pressure has been brought to bear, but that is not the question here). As we saw earlier, violation of values implies loss of personal dignity. What has occurred here may well represent a gain in dignity. Where value change is concerned, compromise is not a positive concept. Indeed, persistent conflict may be preferable to the equalisation of violation that compromise implies.

Notes

1. Drucker (1965).
2. Senge (1990), although he places quite a different significance on this idea.
3. Rightly or wrongly, new behaviour will be perceived as itself embodying a certain set of values. As we saw in Part I of this book, it is an unwarranted assumption, but what is important here is that people will make it nevertheless. It is the belief that matters here, not whether or not it is true.
4. These are illustrations – no general inferences should be drawn about the relative ethics of line managers or personnel officers from the example.
5. Harvey-Jones (1988) p. 38.

Conclusion to Part II

This part of the book has taken us through a number of abstract models relating to how someone might come to change their values. The central concept here is the idea that someone's overt judgements of what they think is right or wrong rest on a complex blend of other values, beliefs, feelings and more. The behaviour of an individual with respect to any possible change is understood in terms of how far changes in that blend determine or are determined by the overt values people hold. Value change is clearly possible, but the ultimate conclusion here must be that it is difficult to predict and perhaps almost as difficult to recognise when it has happened.

In the last part of this book we shall look at what is done in organisations to maintain and enhance people's values – still more from a theoretical point of view than as any overview of the range of current practices. In many ways Part III is an extension of Part II, as the underlying issues remain – how are values identified? what in them can be changed? what are the triggers for change?

PART III

Maintaining an Organisation's Values

In the first two parts of this book we have seen that the understanding of people's values is a highly complex issue, and that consequently the process of value change, whether self-generated or initiated by management, is difficult to comprehend and vastly more difficult to steer with much degree of control. In this final part we shall look away from change-driven attempts at value management, and consider the incremental, day-to-day actions that can be used to try to maintain the values of staff in an organisation. 'Maintain' may suggest that it is a case of keeping things the same – this is rarely the case. The business environment changes, and so do perceptions of external stakeholders. Maintenance is therefore more about keeping a steady level of change in line with these external non-controllable changes. In some ways the discussion in this final part reflects general management and HR management processes, unlike the earlier parts, in which Organisational Behaviour (OB) was the key contributing business discipline (although there will certainly be some OB here as well). We will find that the complexity of the structure of people's values makes serious managerial activity difficult at best and self-defeating at worst. In Chapter 9 we will look at the value and usefulness of codes of ethics. Chapters 10 and 11 consider two key HR issues, those of reward and learning, respectively. The final chapter considers the role and value of 'ethics' as a business field.

9 *Organisational Principles and Codes*

There are many treatments of codes of values in the literature, and I shall not attempt to go over the same ground in this chapter.[1] The main theme of this discussion is that the existence of such codes often obscures their relevance and potential function. Clarifying these is liable to clear up some of the misunderstandings, but at the end we can be left with something that is not significantly greater than the sum of its parts.

The most immediate question is: What do we mean by a code of ethics? This in turn can be resolved into two other questions, namely (a) What function can a code play in the behaviour of an organisation? and (b) What codifying activity goes on?

9.1 Functions of a code of organisational ethics

A formal statement of values for ethics, be it officially called a 'code' or not, could be doing several things. Before listing out possible functions, it is useful to think about what prompts an organisation to bring an entity such as a code into existence in the first place. Any of the following can be a trigger for the production of a code:

- an organisational disaster
- discovery that the competition are doing it
- external regulatory body suggests/requires
- senior management have been on a seminar
- new staff question existing corporate behaviour
- internal doubts about practice.

The existence of a code is somehow a response to one or more of the above (amongst others). Roughly, the above list moves from the highly reactive to the highly proactive responses. So, trying to cope with an organisational disaster, or keeping up with the competition, are prompted by external events (that is, re-active), whilst internal doubts, or the organisation taking seriously the views of new staff[2] would be proactive – trying to foresee what the external environment will throw up later.

So we have, in the above, a dimension of what triggers the production of a code. Consider the following:

> The more proactive the trigger for the production of a code of ethics, the more substantial and longer lasting the effects on corporate behaviour.

This is a speculative general statement about codes. As a formal hypothesis it would merit a full research project designed to test out its validity.[3] Some examples may illustrate the point behind the assertion.

Example 1: A good idea, let's adopt it as well

Dave Sessions, CEO of Bontex Plastics, is a member of a local professional association. He goes to one of the meetings and listens to a talk from a fellow entrepreneur, who describes her own company's statement of values and the benefits it has brought the company, giving staff a much greater sense of involvement. Dave is sold on the idea. He goes back to Bontex, calls in the management team, and announces that the company needs a set of values, into which everyone will 'buy'. He announces that he wants to see Bontex 'recognised by the customer and the community as a good buy and a good player'. Two managers are tasked to produce a draft by the next meeting (the following Monday).

This is a caricature in name only – such examples exist. There are several points at issue here, and some of them will be discussed later on – the key point relevant to the current discussion is that on the face of it we have here a clear example of a reactive trigger. The CEO cannot be said to be uninterested in the idea of corporate values and ethics (quite the reverse) but the manner in which the values statement has been prompted suggests strongly that the full implications have not been thought through. Ownership by the staff, for example, is crucial for a code to have any hope of really touching people's attitudes (as distinct from achieving compliant behaviour), and it is obvious that this has not been considered. Hence there is an inbuilt weakness in the generation of the code.

Example 2: Do we know what we're doing?

Fuzzy Sounds Ltd is a successful record label. It has been importing blank CDs for recording from a supplier in Brazil for several years, and it also purchases paper and card for printing the sleeve notes from a Canadian timber company. The company sells a large volume of albums by several chart-topping bands with distinctly 'green' sympathies. One of the senior marketing executives feels that the company has a potential weakness in the contradiction between the message that some of their recording artists project and the company's own behaviour. He suggests that they draw up a code of practice that will help them to decide which suppliers to use, and may provide a possible defence if any unecological sourcing comes to light later.

Clearly this is partly consequentialist-driven and partly sheer prudence – there is no direct evidence that the executive cares one way or the other about the ecosystem; however, he does care about the company. The fact, though, that it is prompted from within, rather than being perceived by the staff as something imposed on the company by individuals or events from without, creates a greater likelihood that the code will be more closely focused on the actual business needs of the company as recognised by the staff, rather than purely in the terms of, say, the CEO.

These are fairly straightforward examples, but they indicate the relationship between genesis of the code and its pull on the organisation. It is interesting that the different level of ethical commitment in the two cases has taken implementation in the opposite directions. In the former, there is a definite moral conviction that has led to a strong drive to create uniformity of values. In pushing the company in that direction, the chief executive has overlooked the varying degrees of resistivity (as discussed in Chapter 8) that may be present in the value systems of the staff. The moral imperative has blinded his own perception. By contrast, the more instrumental approach in the recording company example leads to a more analytically based understanding of how best to implement the value change implicit in the production of a code.

This suggests two further general points relating to the function of a code of values or ethics in an organisation:

The production of a code is in ethical terms a non-neutral act; it cannot but change the pool of values in the organisation.

The degree of ethical commitment held by the key actors in an organisation is an important but double-edged resource where the production of a code of values is concerned.

Neither of these is an earth-shatteringly novel point in itself, and in some respects they are not specific solely to ethical change; but jointly they emphasise that how a code of values comes into being is a significant organisational event, with implications for culture, power, history and politics being implicit in the process.

How does all this contribute to an understanding of the functions of a code of ethics in an organisation? There is one further issue to acknowledge before answering this. Some texts discuss the *benefits* of a code of ethics.[4] But this is not the same as the *function* of a code. 'Benefit' implies that something is a positive consequence, but it does not identify whether it is a central rationale for the existence of its cause. 'Function' on the other hand, does suggest that without this particular kind of consequence the practice would have no real meaning, however useful its spin-offs might be. So a key question is – when considering particular benefits of having a code, are they part of its core rationale, or are they useful spin-offs, side effects? Consider some benefits that have been claimed for codes of ethics:

- they can have a motivating effect on employees
- they may provide a defence in legal cases
- they can clarify policy where difficult decisions have to be made
- they can be a focus for discussion and debate
- they can reassure customers as to the company's best efforts
- they can set a standard of behaviour for all employees.

Which of these are chicken, and which egg? Obviously, the answer may be different for different organisations. The great mistake would be to attempt to have all of these as the egg – that is, as the primary *raison d'être*. For example, it would be *helpful* if a code of values reassured actual or potential customers – this is a marketing issue. For the code to set a standard for employees, HR issues need to be considered. The two may not coincide. For example, a code that states 'No employee may offer or accept personal gifts from customers, clients or suppliers external to the company' is a useful statement for employees, but may have less value for potential customers (indeed, for those from certain cultures it could be a clear disincentive). The point is not that there can be different views about whether accepting personal gifts from clients is right or wrong. It is that this kind of issue is differentially relevant to, and differently perceived by, different stakeholders.

Take a second example: 'People are our greatest asset. We will value and respect each other.' As was noted earlier, the problem with this is that it sounds halfway between an injunction ('value each other – now! get on with it!') and a statement of fact. But more importantly, it is an employee-directed statement. It has little relevance for the supplier or client, unless the organisation is highly integrated vertically across its value chain (when the relationships between individuals working for the company and those working for suppliers/customers are unusually closely linked). Also, how far does this help with clarifying what someone should do in a difficult or obscure situation?

These examples are not meant to undermine the idea of a code of conduct *per se*. They are intended to demonstrate that such statements and documents should be seen as directed at particular groups. A code cannot be designed for all stakeholders.[5] Each and any of the benefits outlined above may well be valid as the main function of a code of practice – the point is they cannot meaningfully all be so.

Ultimately, the triggers for a code to come into being fall into two macro-categories, as below:

- to enhance services and/or operations
- to solve a problem.

Any of the benefits outlined earlier might function as fulfilling one or the other of these. So, in setting an overall standard for employees the organisation might see what it is doing as solving a problem of how to systematise behaviour across the board. Alternatively, it might perceive what it is doing as part of a continuous improvement strategy. Equally, the provision of a defence for legal purposes may be seen as solving the problem of how to forestall further litigation or it may be regarded as enhancing the ability of the organisation to operate without incurring greater legal risk.

Previously we saw the proactive *versus* reactive distinction as applying to *triggers* for the production of a code. We now see proactive *versus* reactive *expectations* of a code of ethics, a more dangerous phenomenon. The danger is perhaps encapsulated in the following comment made to me by a middle-ranking employee of a multinational organisation. 'The great feeling we had after the statement of practice had been circulated and discussed was – been there, done that. Now shall we get on with the business?'

The danger here is that the degree of value resistivity seemed to be unaffected by the creation of a code – so the company had the classic situation of behavioural change without attitudinal change. But underneath that is another, related danger – that the code was seen as an end-point of the process. This is the reactive expectation referred to above, that the code solves a problem. The suggestion is almost, 'Well, that's alright now, we know what we ought to be doing' as if this marks the place where resources that had been tied up in ethics can be released for other uses. This reflects again the danger of too narrow an interpretation of images of change influenced by the Lewin freezing metaphor, drawing the mistaken conclusion that once something has been 'locked in' then it will stay that way. Codes of practice or value do not influence behaviour in that way. If they are regarded as problem-solving they are almost doomed to suffer drift – the slow ebbing away of commitment and gradual incremental transformation of people's behaviour into quite different forms.

The degeneration of codes of values and other corporate statements into forgotten documents that gather dust or prop up a wobbly desk is a well attested phenomenon.[6] What the above analysis adds to this is that the key error is not simply that managers do not give their full commitment to the code, or even that codes are not properly implemented. It is that the existence of a code is seen in the wrong light – it is regarded as important as a *statement*, rather as if once stated it goes in the staff manual (which it often does, of course). A hyperbolic reaction against this might be that once a code is in the staff manual, it's dead, and a new one should be devised. Whilst that might be too strong a view (and too big a luxury for most organisations to sustain the overhead of continuous ethical debate) it is nevertheless important for an organisation to consider what kind of life a code should have once produced. We can probably sum up these points as follows:

A code can be seen as the *distillation of the values of the company*, or as a *move in the process* of managing values; it is the latter which is the more proactive, and hence more effective approach.

9.2   Sources of codes

The previous section indicated that a code or statement of values is far less useful as a definitive *statement* of what is acceptable or unacceptable behaviour than it might be as part of a *process* of discussion and consultation. Basically the reason for this is that it helps individuals to focus on their own perceptions and beliefs, and thus helps to unloosen levels of value resistivity and enables individuals to relate what is proposed with what they personally adhere to ethically – the process of doing this is part of what is meant by 'increasing ownership'. This is not purely an ethical issue – it is in line with what has been claimed as one of the main benefits of a mission statement.[7]

The next main question to ask is what kinds of genesis of a code of values are appropriate? Which, of the many different ways a code might come into being and become part of business policy and practice, are likely to enhance the way values are managed in an organisation, and which are likely to be ineffective? Clearly, some attempts at producing a code of ethics stem from an implicit or explicit perception of the issue as purely task- or problem-focused – that is, the issue for management is just to have one. One consultant told me that he has more than once been approached and asked 'Are you the person who helped XYZ company to produce their code of ethics?' When he admits this, he is then asked 'Can we have a copy?' The suspicion must be that the enquirer hopes to 'copy' the code of XYZ. It is almost as if the content or the attunement to the organisation is irrelevant. We shall pick up an aspect of this in the final chapter. For the moment the main point is simply how inappropriate this is, and how ineffective any such move must be for corporate transformation (of course, that may not be the intention of the person wanting a copy of the code – they may want only to be seen to have a code, no matter what; but no-one should be in any doubt that achieving such an ambition is nothing to do with business ethics).

Consider the following possible ways in which a code may come about (we shall ignore the idea of cribbing one from other companies!):

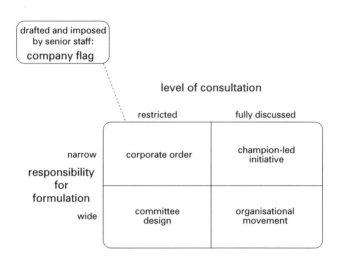

Figure 9.1   Origins of a code of values

The key dimensions of the production of a code of values depicted here are the range of players involved in its formulation, and the extent of the consultation process that follows this.[8] In one sense this is an oversimplification, because consultation will often – and should always – bring a degree of redrafting of the code. Nevertheless, the initial draft is crucial, for it sets the framework for what the document will involve and how it will impact on behaviour. The figure shows one extreme deviant case – in which senior management basically do it all themselves and just tell the staff that the new value statement is such-and-such. I call this the company flag approach because it is likely to have about as much influence. In a few cases, where there is generally a high level of confidence and respect for an autocratic management, the 'flag' may well have some impact. Otherwise it is either a window-dressing exercise (where little attempt is made to enforce the values) or an extreme version of the corporate order (when the new values are enforced – of course this means that compliant *behaviour* is achieved, but not necessarily agreement in *attitude*). A little less extreme, but sharing the same essential features, is the 'corporate order', where the issues and framework of the values statement is defined by a small group – possibly senior management-driven, and the consultation is narrow, either in organo-geographic terms (focused on a small sample of staff, or from very specific segments of the business) or in logical terms (where the task is seen as selling the idea rather than listening to find improvements). Neither of these approaches – the 'flag' or the 'order' – is to be recommended as a means of managing the ethics of an organisation – though they might be very useful for totalitarian purposes.

The other three categories outlined in Figure 9.1 reflect different clusters of management style, organisational culture (type and degree of saturation) and communication structures. Having stated this, however, it is not a contingency model. Essentially, the most appropriate method of putting together a code of ethics is likely to be the bottom right-hand corner of the diagram – that is, where a good range of people are involved in its formulation and there is subsequently a wide discussion of its content. To call this a movement is perhaps going a little over the top, but it captures the fact that the code is not tied to any particular interest or power group, and it also reflects the idea that the values have some degree of commonality (though all the caveats we have thrown up previously about shared values still apply). This is the only approach that is going to give individuals the opportunity to fill out in their own minds what the words of the document mean. It is also the only opportunity for individuals to bring the complexity of their value systems – underlying platforms of views as well as explicit beliefs – to bear on the statements of the code and find some points of contact.

This is not to say that the 'committee design' or the 'champion-led' approaches have nothing to be said for them. Depending on organisational circumstances they may sometimes be the only ways that anything can get done at all. Nevertheless, they contain seeds of difficulty – sometimes more than seeds. What I have called the 'committee' approach (that is, a wide range of people involved in formulating the code, but a restricted degree of consultation across the workforce subsequently) will undoubtedly provide an opportunity for those involved in the formulation to present different ideas; if the implementation is restricted, however, then the benefit of this is lost. Even though a wide range of people may be involved in the drafting of the code, it will not include the whole staff (unless it is a very small business). So those individuals who have not had the chance to have their views represented in the formulation stage will find it hard to establish bridging points from which they can draw a sense of ownership.

Similarly, the championed code, perhaps the nearest to a classical leadership role, may well create a sense of ownership, but without building in a full understanding of what is being owned. A small group of individuals, perhaps just one respected and charismatic figure, put together a code and then disseminate it widely, communicating with individuals at all levels to gain a fuller sense of understanding and ownership, amending where important concerns are expressed, and explaining and selling the benefits of what has been drafted. The code may create excitement and commitment, but superficially. If access to the depths of individuals' value systems has not been built in, it may not be clear to them how the statements of the code could satisfy concerns that reside in their underlying platform. The best efforts of the champion(s) may fail to establish connections with what the code states and what individuals feel is most important to them. Worse, the sheer personal power of charisma can lead people to dismiss their own doubts and reservations – they may simply write off their own feelings as 'sentimentality'. High levels of articulation can be their own worst enemy at times, but even when it is not a case of the dazzle of smoothly polished communication, the manner in which a field is initially set out can often overshadow people's perceptions of what is relevant, to the point where they may suppress their own views and instincts.

To take an example, few organisations have any dialogue on the nature of personal transactions and relationships within the business. Hence the issue of how individuals relate at work is defined in a managerial framework. Relationships are discussed in terms of trust, respect, honesty, and so on. Recent litigation in the EU and the US, amongst others, have pushed issues such as sexual harassment and bullying into consideration, and hence some codes are likely to reflect these, often as a subheading under 'respect'. But the framework is still managerially defined, and reactively at that.[9] Now consider other aspects of personal relationships. Outside a work context, a key virtue that people often use as a measure of someone they know well is kindness. Yet in the work context this is almost universally absent from any discussion. Is this because kindness is not present? Hardly. It must be because this is not perceived as a relevant personal quality. One might bemoan this as a consequence of a male-orientated business environment in which heroism, courage and struggle are much prized, and more stereotypically 'female' qualities such as nurture, kindness and sensitivity are downplayed, but this locates only part of the issue. Kindness is an important dimension of interpersonal relationships, and hence it cannot but be highly relevant to relationships in the organisational context. But it is defined more or less out of existence. The managerial imperatives of task accomplishment have inhibited any opportunity for it to find expression. This is what I mean by the idea that people may suppress their own instincts and feelings because of the agenda they find already set for them. Obviously not all championed codes of values are explicit manifestations of this phenomenon, but it is a perennial danger for this kind of approach. Key aspects of people's concerns may inadvertently be swept away, and the excitement generated for what is put on public display can lead people to overlook this.

9.3   Codifying as an activity

We have seen, then, that there is only one really healthy source for a code of ethics, if it is to be a useful tool for managing values in an organisation, namely one in which a wide range of people are involved in its formulation, followed by wide discussion and dissemination around the organisation before it is finally adopted. It might be added here, as was argued in Section 9.1, that 'finally adopted' should be in name only, and that continued review and redraft is the ideal. Even one individual's ethical system is complex and thus liable to continual change. How much more true this will be of the values of a collective. In this section we shall look at the process itself of identifying and agreeing key elements of a code of values. In so doing, we shall gain further insights into the issues of identifying and changing values generally.

Nature of statement production

		Reflection	*Reformation*
All		selected	summarised
Proportion of workforce involved	*Majority*	voted	composited
	Key players only	placed	reframed

Figure 9.2   Different ways of codifying an organisation's values

What does 'codifying' really mean? Depending on the kinds of genesis of a code and the strategy for generating one, there are several possibilities, as depicted in Figure 9.2. We are getting into very fine realms here, but this level of analysis is necessary for certain key issues to be brought out clearly. In this diagram, the way in which elements of a code of values or ethics might be generated is presented in two dimensions – first, the proportion of the workforce involved in the process, and second, the extent to which the code reflects actual statements of participants in the process as opposed to presenting a reformulation of people's views. There would seem to be six possibilities but in reality only five are at all likely to be practicable – selection of statements of value from those offered by the whole staff is impractical in numerical terms and, even if adopted, would lead to a degree of autocracy in that a key group of decision-makers would most likely make the choice as to what statements were included in a code, even though these may have been offered by the staff as a whole.

The model depicts, then, five characteristic ways in which statements that go towards a code of values or ethics might be arrived at. The putting together of a number of items for such a document is a process in which at one point one of these ways may operate, at another a different one may, so comments below about a whole code being put together via one of these five is an oversimplification for convenience.

A couple of examples may bring out what is meant by the labels for each of the five types involved. First, a public highways authority may ask the staff to contribute ideas towards the formulation of a code of practice. Suggestions are made, and a group of staff drawn from all parts of the organisation sift through them, putting like ones together, theming, noting where there is near or exact duplication, and finally arriving at a draft code comprising entirely of statements contributed by the workforce. In the process some naturally have been discarded, but the leader of the team involved has been able to put together a code based almost entirely on the actual suggestions of the staff – only a very small amount of rewriting has been involved where several very similar suggestion were put in different terms. In this example the main codifying mechanisms are 'voting' (that is, basing the decision to include a statement on statistical evidence of representativeness) and to a lesser extent placing – as decisions have been made about inclusion by a small coterie of individuals. There is also a slight element of compositing – rewriting a statement to take account of a number of other related statements.

In the second example a consultant is brought in to help a shipping line formulate a code. The consultant works with a small group of employees, most of relatively senior standing. Many individuals are interviewed, many suggestions are encouraged, focus groups are run, and other methods are used to garner data about the values people hold in the organisation. The consultant then produces a draft, with the help of the working group. This is based on the general consensus of opinion. The consensus is reached on a majority basis: an item is included where enough staff have expressed an opinion, tempered by a recognition of the key objectives of senior management, but attempting to be as all-inclusive as is consistent with producing a manageable statement. Here, the codifying is primarily of a reformulating kind. The consultant freely rewrites the material presented to her/him. Some of all three types are present – an attempt is made to summarise views of all the staff, in places an overall compositing based on frequency is adopted, and the views of specific key players are taken into particular account as a means of reframing the views presented.

The main conclusion to be drawn from the model is that *accuracy and representativeness are inversely related*. The more a code of ethics precisely mirrors what people actually state to be their beliefs,[10] the less certainly it covers the views of many.

To explain this, let us look more closely at the two examples given above. In the first, there is a degree of accuracy within the code in that the statements used are ones actually produced by the staff. However, these have been selected from a large number of submissions. Only in the event of the improbably happy accident that many people presented the same evaluation in identical or near identical wording can the selection of a set of items for inclusion be regarded as unequivocally representative. Otherwise – and this is the rub – *someone has to make a decision as to how similar the value statements are*. This is the crucial issue here. If someone is to interpret two statements as expressing essentially the same thing, they have to make substantial judgements about what may underlie the statements. In other words, they have to infer a similar set of relevant elements in the underlying platform of beliefs. Suppose one statement suggested by someone reads 'The company should promote equality of opportunity between people regardless of colour, race, age, gender or ability.' Someone else may have written 'The business must respect the needs and reward the efforts and abilities of all no matter what demographic groups they belong to.' Let's ignore minor differences – for example, 'business' in one, 'company' in another.[11] Clearly these two would get themed as equal opportunities or diversity statements. It is easy to feel that the hearts of the two writers are in similar places. But there are key differences between the two statements. For one thing, the first gives a list of groups, whilst the second does not. One question to raise is whether the writer of the second means just the same list as appears in the first, or a smaller, or a larger list. Also, the former statement talks of promoting equality of opportunity, whilst the latter refers to respecting needs and rewarding efforts and abilities. These are vague terms. How far would, for example, training and development be covered by either or both? Hopefully both writers might have implicitly felt that their statement covered training, but it requires an *assumption* to this effect. The explicit statements people make often take for granted part of what forms the underlying platform of beliefs from which their statements spring. Explicit agreement does not necessarily imply similarity in the structure of the overall value systems.

What has been said here, in the context of codifying as reflection, stands even more true for codifying as reformulation. And it is likely that in the real world some degree of reformulation of items suggested as components of a code of values is always present – indeed in some organisations the idea of reflecting what members of staff suggest would be judged to be quite out of place. So the way in which a code of values gets put together is intrinsically flawed.

We come back again to the complexity of values, and the great difficulty of getting through this complexity within the timescales required for effective managerial activity. We have focused here very closely on the process of codifying, and as a result have come to a somewhat purist conclusion – that there are potential weaknesses in the process. In the demanding light of managerial reality, a light that cannot afford to be too pure, one might well be tempted to brush such weaknesses aside. I do not wish to inveigh against this in one sense. Life is too short to get a definitive view on everything – in some cases life may be much much too short to hope to get anywhere in understanding the deeper element of people's values. The key point here, as with so much of this text, is that we should not blind ourselves into assuming that because we don't have time to investigate something, the bit we haven't investigated doesn't matter. It does matter that we are likely to re-interpret other people's value statements in terms of our own value systems. This is not the same as saying we impose our own value judgements on what others say. But it does imply that we try to interpret what others say in the light of our own platform of underlying beliefs, not theirs (virtually by definition we have at best a dim understanding of others' platforms, for they are like the vast bulk of an iceberg beneath the surface of the ocean).

The idea of a code of values is probably the most well known method of trying to systematise, communicate and manage the collective values of members of an organisation. In this chapter we have examined in close detail the idea of a code as a key tool for maintaining the values of an organisation. Almost as a side issue we saw quite early on that 'maintenance' is a misnomer – developing a code is yet another change strategy. We have also seen here that the cause which prompted the development of a code can work against its explicit purpose (if the latter is even recognised). More latterly we have also seen how different sources of a code can be important determinants of how effective it is likely to be, and finally that the manner in which items are codified can conceal great differences between individuals in how values are conceived. One key issue that we have not explored is that a code is by its very nature constructed of explicit evaluative statements – where does it fill in what in individuals counts as an underlying platform? Obviously it cannot, and this would be a further weakness of a code as a management technique. If we have to summarise the argument of the chapter, it is highly sceptical – values are not easily grasped by codes. In the following chapter we shall look at other key management techniques that might be used to help manage organisational values.

Questions

A   How far can your organisation be said to have a set of values that members are required or encouraged to adopt? How does this link with your view of the cultural saturation of the organisation?

B   If your organisation has a code or statement of values, find out how it has been developed. Evaluate the balance between the accuracy with which it reflects people's views and the degree to which it reflects the views of all the staff.

C   If your organisation does not have a code, how does it ensure that members know what values are encouraged or required? How far could a code assist in this process?

Notes

1.   The reader is referred to, amongst others, Campbell and Tawadey (1990), as well as Webley (1992, 1993).

2.   Though, sadly, the learning for an organisation that the immediate perceptions of new staff can provide is usually dismissed – 'Oh, they're new, they'll soon learn how we do it round here.' For all the love of culture, it must be recognised that it remains a potential threat to innovation.

3.   Which it has not to date, so far as the author is aware.

4.   For example, Webley (1992).

5.   Even if it were possible, which it is not, unless one adopts so tight a definition of 'stakeholder' that only shareholders and employees count.

6.   Rather like the fate of many mission statements, with which ethical codes are closely related. For an interesting discussion of how to improve the effectiveness of codes of ethics, see Weller (1988; also available in the Campbell and Tawadey volume).

7.   Namely, that a mission statement is more valuable to an organisation as process rather than result.

8.   Walter Manley provides an interesting practical discussion of how codes may be drawn up, although it ducks the issues raised here (Manley 1992).

9.   Though it is still better that organisations do have some kind of policy in these areas than none at all.

10.   Obviously all that has been said before about the relation between what people say their values are and what their value system as a whole might be, still stands here.

11.   It may be less trivial than it looks, but space precludes a discussion of the contrast.

10 *Process, Result and Reward*

In the last chapter we saw how the idea of a code of practice or statement of values had inbuilt problems – unless it is conceived as part of a larger scale process it is unlikely to help in creating the opportunities for individuals to identify points of contact between their own value systems and what is being advanced within the code.

Thematic in that discussion, as with earlier chapters, was the issue of behaviour *versus* attitude. What do managers really want from their staff in the way of ethics? In this chapter we shall move further into the arena of managerial expectations and consider this issue of actions and intentions, as well as the crucial motivating factor of reward. We will find confirmation of much of the argument of the previous chapter, and we shall see that systematic organisational reward methodologies may undermine what is central to genuinely ethically worthy behaviour.

10.1   It ain't what you do...

Let us recall some points made in Part I of this book. An action cannot be treated simply as a narrowly defined piece of behaviour. Whistleblowing, for example, is often regarded as anti-organisational behaviour because it brings misconduct into the public domain. But the same narrow behaviour – for example, writing to the press outlining how the company has been violating safety standards – may spring from several different intentions, and it is the *act-in-its-intention* that is crucial, both from a moral and from a managerial point of view. Imagine a disciplinary inquiry in which someone is charged with the offence of misconduct on the basis that they revealed damaging information about the company publicly. A person who confirmed this and said 'Yes, and you deserve it, I'm going to spread your name in the mud' is clearly going to be perceived very differently from one who says 'I had to do this, as people didn't seem to take my warnings seriously, and it could have led to even more damaging consequences if there had been an accident.' Not that the latter justification would count as a satisfactory defence in all circumstances, but it is certainly to be differentiated from the former example. For one is a case in which the whistleblowing behaviour is a form of deliberate damage to the company, whereas the other is an attempt to prevent too much damage. The implication of this for managing values is to raise the question: what should managers manage – behaviour or attitude? Consider the two examples given in Box 10.1.

BOX 10.1   Two Kinds of Manager

Example 1: Vera Mason is a successful entrepreneur, who has built up a multi-million dollar business from scratch, specialising in the recycling of paper refuse. She has strong, clearly expressed values, centred around two concerns: one of maintaining a high level of ecofriendliness and the other of operating in an open and scrupulously fair way to employees, suppliers and customers alike. The company has a statement of core principles, which includes both evaluative judgements and mechanisms for resolving problematic dilemmas. Vera is known for her strong managerial style. She had no compunction in dismissing two male employees who admitted making gibes and sexual innuendoes to some of their female colleagues. Her comment was 'I don't care that there was no obscenity. I don't care that there was no physical aspect, and no obvious malicious intent. I even don't care that the women involved didn't object, at least officially, though I think they ought to have. What matters is to keep some kind of integrity. We have a duty to treat everyone equally no matter what. In any case, we're an American company and Federal law won't tolerate that kind of thing. I'm sorry for the two guys but that's the price they pay for sexism.'

Example 2: Sevando S.A. is a successful French meat processing company. The Sevi brothers, who run the company and jointly are the majority share-holders, have a strong sense of the quality of their products – patés, sausages, and meat pies are the core product lines. The company has a strong export trade. Conscious of international differences over meat production and the treatment of animals the Sevi brothers have insisted that all constituents of their products be clearly labelled, fact sheets are available in their main outlets, and they have an information office that answers all and any queries on how animals have been treated, manner of killing, and so on. In this way they have been able to maintain good sales of traditional products (for example, *paté de fois gras*) for the local market whilst developing new lines such as white meat derivatives for export. In the summer of 1996 the company was hit by a scandal: it seemed that there was mislabelling of some products. Whilst there was no suggestion that this was deliberate, there was criticism of the fact that adequate controls had not been put in place to prevent this. The brothers were also criticised for not taking decisive action quickly enough, and some French papers were outraged that no dismissals were made. Jean-Jacques Sevi, the older

> **BOX 10.1 (cont'd)**
>
> of the brothers, said 'Yes, we had some problems, and it took us some time to get to the bottom of them, but we have now put these right. Disciplinary action is not suitable. Okay some people may not have been diligent enough, but there was no deliberate attempt to fool the public.'

Now there are many similarities and differences between these two cases. At this stage I want to make no comments on the kinds of reaction the two sets of management had – in the one, a disciplinary response, in the other a response designed to improve operations. We shall come back to that side later. What I shall discuss here is what is perceived to be the ethically relevant phenomenon. In the first instance, although there were overtones of sheer prudence (the reference to potential litigation) there would seem mainly to be a focus on the behaviour as such. Indeed, the manager goes out of her way to exclude issues of the contextual circumstances and consequences; these are dismissed as irrelevant. The fastening of the label 'sexual harassment' on the behaviour is the determining feature of her response. By contrast, the second example provides a more mixed response. Denunciation is absent, and there is a greater sense of a complex situation with several ethical uncertainties handled away from the glare of publicity. Intention is explicitly referred to as a key factor. The error of mislabelling is diminished in favour of the issue of honesty.

Neither of these could be regarded simply as the 'right' response. Probably every reader may have their own reactions to the situations. But the examples do tell us a significant amount about the ethical views of the managers involved. In the one case a manager seems to see things in very definite terms, and as a result seems to project those terms onto the other actors in the situation. That is, Vera Mason sees the situation in the light of her own clear-cut views on equality and fairness, and regards what happened as 'simply' a breach of those terms. The breach is put in a balance against the various other issues such as perceived harm to the victims, levels of obscenity, and so on, and found to outweigh these. Hence her response. The Sevi brothers, on the other hand, find that the breach of one of the central planks of their business is counterbalanced by the contextual issues such as lack of any perceived intent to mislead. So their reaction is one of mitigation.

Someone may object – 'But these are hardly the same degree of gravity – in one case it is merely an operational error, whilst in the other it is a case of the dignity of women.' Possibly, but this only reflects the values of the reader – for people of a strong religious persuasion, meat can be a big issue:

try persuading an orthodox Jew, or a Muslim, that mislabelling pork as beef is a trivial matter; try suggesting to a Hindu that it doesn't really matter if on one occasion they ate the remains of a (for them sacred) cow. Though these reflect very different kinds of value to secular western mores, and spring from different cultural origins, they both can be serious for one group of individuals and trivial for another.

To return to the main point, the main inference to be drawn here is that the way in which an organisation processes values, and in particular the extent to which *specific behaviours* are focused on, as opposed to underlying attitudes, will be strongly influenced by the value systems of the key power brokers in the organisation – usually, though not exclusively, the managers. This creates a difficulty for the way in which values may be managed in an organisation. As has been argued above and in earlier chapters, someone's explicit value judgements, and the explicit choices they make about what to do, are the tip of an iceberg. Underlying these, sometimes as cause, sometimes as effect, are a large number of additional feelings and beliefs that intermesh with each other and with the explicit value judgements a person makes. A specific item of behaviour, such as whistleblowing, is not just different in its significance between different individuals. At different times it may represent a different response from the *same* individual. A person who publicly criticises senior management in an open seminar may be motivated by a desire to get back at them for some perceived injustice. Some months later, at a similar event, their confidence may be restored, and they may be publicly critical simply out of a desire to get the right solution to a problem.[1] Concentrating on the act itself, rather than what underlies it, is not the appropriate vehicle for ethics – the intention behind it is essential for an understanding of what someone is doing.

But what the discussion of the two examples has indicated is that in some circumstances, generally depending on the ethical stance of the key players involved, a particular kind of behaviour may well be focused on by them and regarded as the prime vehicles for moral praise or blame. As in the Vera Mason case, an act such as sexual harassment may be treated as ethically right or wrong without any consideration of the intention that may have lain behind it. I do not want to suggest that such acts might have the potential to be right, depending on the intention with which they were done. But clearly, such behaviour may in some circumstances be gravely, seriously wrong, and in other circumstances rather less so. An older man brought up in the early 20th century in the UK may see certain kinds of language he uses in his dealings with women as harmless, legitimately affectionate even. This may be unfortunate if the language in question is perceived by women as patronising. But this must be sharply distinguished from someone who has been brought up since the 1950s in the West, for whom the nuances of language and behaviour are more apparent, and so it must be presumed that there is a clearer understanding that the use of such terminology is likely to offend. One could say that in the first case there are mitigating circumstances. Fair enough, so long as it is borne in mind that all cases have their own particular context, and hence the issue of how far one set of circumstances mitigates and another set does not is a managerial decision, not an automatic outcome.

So we have a tension between the analysis given here, which emphasises the importance of context and intention if someone's behaviour is to be understood in ethical terms, and the tendency amongst some managers, often those with keenly held ethical views, to look at the act in isolation from what underlies it. It is not enough simply to write this off by saying 'Oh well, such managers are just wrong.' They may be, but their wrongness is a defining feature of how some organisations operate. The focus on behaviour to the exclusion of underlying attitude and intention does not just manifest itself in somewhat harsh decisions by individuals. It will strongly influence both the nature of any codes of practice adopted in the organisation, and how seriously these are taken, as well as which parts are regarded as crucial and which are seen as relatively peripheral.

What is the source of this tension? Primarily it will lie in a confusion latent in the idea of value management. On the one hand this implies something about ethical development, creating a learning organisation in which individuals are able to take responsibility for their own actions and reflect clearly both on how their acts may be perceived and what their underlying intentions and feelings may be. On the other hand, though, is the need for operational control. An ecologically friendly organisation can ill afford to have operational slips that result in them selling, even accidentally, unecological produce. Hence tight control is often necessary to maintain the strict criteria required either by management or possibly by external organisations such as governmental or industry bodies. The fact that there is a double focus – ethical and operational – on the activities within the organisation is what may lead to the confusion, and can result in a situation in which behaviour in the narrow sense is tightly controlled, to the exclusion of the broader issue of intent and context. This is not to judge all organisations in which there is a strong imperative to conform to specific modes of behaviour as inherently confused. It is a perfectly reasonable part of running any business that there be tightly defined rules that regulate closely the activities of employees. The potential confusion may occur when those rules happen also to have an ethical overtone, when operational control can be easily mistaken for ethical management. As much of the above has indicated, the management of an organisation's values is a developmental issue, not an operational one (we shall look in more detail at the role of learning and development in the management of a organisation's ethics in the next chapter).

10.2   Old bottles, new wine

In the previous section we saw that some managers may take a narrow focus on *behaviour* as the basis for the management of values. This was criticised on the grounds that people's actions have to be understood in terms of what they intended. This in turn is deeply caught up not just in the explicit value judgements that people make but also in the platform of attitudes and beliefs that lie underneath the explicit.

There is another, more practical, reason why it is inappropriate to concentrate attention on particular kinds of behaviour. This is that it is not flexible enough to meet the complexity of modern, global business management where different ethical norms are brought into contact with each other, and where often, as a result, both may be changed.

Let us look again at the Vera Mason case. The concentration on behaviour in that example manifested in itself in Vera dismissing two members of staff when there was at least a *prima facie* case for saying that the behaviour was not that serious.[2] Whether or not the principle is explicitly enshrined in the company code, it is clear that sexual harassment is a non-negotiable issue for Vera, and by extension (presuming that we have here a highly saturated organisational culture) for the organisation. By 'non-negotiable' is meant that it is not open to being overruled by other considerations. Very likely Vera holds this as a deontological value – that is, one where the very act of sexual harassment is wrong, no matter what kind of context it is placed in or what consequences follow from it.

Now suppose that two of Vera's employees go on a sales trip to a country with a different set of values concerning relations between the sexes. For example, in some Mediterranean countries there remains a very 'traditional' approach to women, where a significant level of respect is accorded to older women and to mothers, but where younger, unmarried women are regarded (often by other women as well as by men) as being in a sort of sexual market. No doubt to someone brought up in the USA or in the UK this may appear somewhat discriminatory; but the point is not to identify a set of values with which the reader may disagree, rather it is to indicate that within such a culture the different values of the employees of Vera Mason are placed under a challenge that the explicit prohibition may not equip them to handle. Accepted, there are many discussions of the limits to the idea of 'when in Rome, do as the Romans do',[3] but what may be overlooked is that the attitudes the employees may encounter are not simply a lower standard, but a different one. Hence what a man from such a culture might regard as mild banter may seem outrageously over-familiar to the Americans.

But equally what the US sales reps will do in the name of treating men and women equally might seem discourteous to a person brought up in this other culture. So a simple rejection of the behaviour that the sales reps encounter will be inappropriate. Some form of adjustment has to be made, whereby the individuals involved draw a line that in some way represents the non-negotiable, and up to which behaviour in some way or another is tolerated or compromised. Sometimes the line is entirely mental – no attempt is made to change the behaviour of the local residents, but the individual chooses to ignore or avoid those aspects of which they disapprove. This kind of thing happens to almost every traveller in one way or another. The key point here is not whether there is a direct contradiction between the organisational ethos from which the sales reps come and the more complex situation that they find abroad. Rather it is that the focus on specific behaviour overlooks this kind of tension, so that the employee abroad often finds herself in a compromise that could prove embarrassing back at home. So, too directive an approach to value management may not help individuals when they are confronted with the challenges of different ethical norms of a foreign culture.

The other side to this is when values change. Social attitudes do not stand still, partly because of features such as the sales reps mentioned above encounter. A set of ethical requirements that focuses on the specifics of behaviour may become obsolete as the world moves on from the context within which they were couched. This is much more than simply society accepting that something is right at one time and then later regarding it as wrong. As mentioned earlier, a code of values has to assume a certain kind of underlying platform in the minds of the staff. The less visible changes in someone's value system are precisely those that occur at this subterranean level. But these are the areas that give specific value judgements their substance. It is not, for example, simply sexual harassment that is unacceptable, but the further implications about respect and the expectation of women to be able to control their own destiny that make it so.

The organisation that focuses on values in purely behavioural terms is likely to find that these will age. Sometimes this will be in the simple sense that the organisation requires something which is not generally approved of any longer; sometimes it will be a case of being out of step without any particular evaluation being in conflict with societal norms. So, where a company that has a strong ethical line on, for example, providing the fullest information about its products to customers, this is likely to link in with underlying assumptions relating to safety, consumer confidence, openness, and so on. Without any general change in social values regarding providing information, this network could grow tired if those related concerns such as openness and food safety became less acute. Similarly, a stipulation regarding, say, the commitment to maintain lifelong employment has a greater level of significance – and thus a different kind of underlying support – in an environment where work is scarce, or welfare meagre, than in more fully employed or more generously supported economies. A variety of other values can also cluster around this idea. So, for example, it is not surprising that in Japan, where full employment is still seen as socially desirable, there is also an emphasis on mutual loyalty (at least for the 'salarymen' – the corporate employees who still make up over 30 per cent of the total workforce). 'We stand by you, so long as you stand by us.' This implies that job mobility is frowned upon. The corporation invests in its people, but it expects the long service that comes from loyalty to the company as a return on its investment. Legislation does not require this, but it is an ethical expectation. It can be inappropriate, however, to treat this cluster as a non-negotiable framework. At the time of writing, for example, some Japanese conglomerates have had to loosen the commitment to lifelong employment, primarily due to economic changes. In those employees who were used to seeing lifelong commitment as a fixed value, the change has caused resentment. As times change, so will our values, because what underlies them will be changing. The organisation that operates as if its current values are eternals will almost inevitably suffer because of this at some point in the future.

An example from a non-business context may illustrate this point further. Arthur Miller's play *The Crucible* examines the panic that ripped apart a community during the witch-hunts in Salem, Massachusetts in the late 17th century.[4] A village becomes gripped by the belief that the devil has taken hold of it, and has centred on a group of young women. These, partly out of group hysteria, partly out of more calculating motives (the ringleader is depicted in the film as trying to take revenge on an older man who had slept with her previously), make ever more wild accusations, incriminating almost all who resist them. Part of the drama is the paralysis that prevents the community from satisfactorily resolving a conflict between two mindsets, one rooted in mediaeval beliefs about witches and conjuring the devil, the other a modern, legal approach to fact, evidence and testimony. In the end it is the primitive that wins out: law fails to save the innocent despite the beliefs of those administering it. The play exemplifies that values change not simply because moral beliefs change, but because whole systems of which they are a part change. *The Crucible* presents the growing pains of a society trying, sometimes unsuccessfully, to free itself from superstition.

The argument of this and the previous section has been that the emphasis on the *result* of ethical reflection – the value judgements themselves – has limitations as a mechanism for managing ethics effectively in an organisation. It does not take account of the key role of underpinning beliefs and attitude that may contribute almost invisibly to a specific value judgement. Consequently, it fails to provide a methodology for individuals to cope with the conflicts of value that arise when alternative value systems are faced, and it fails to assist an organisation to come to terms with the continuing subtle changes in attitudes and beliefs that characterise all societies, not the least being the modern hyper-acceleration of communication via global trading.

An objection: 'This argument makes it look as if any organisation that makes specific ethical demands on people is being naive. What about the Body Shop? That has a strong set of values, reflecting a wide range of concerns. But the idea that management might fail to understand the underlying values of the staff is misplaced here, because the company *selects* people on the basis of their support for these values.'

There are two issues here. First, there is nothing in the above argument that implies that strongly held values are inappropriate in a business context. It is the degree to which an organisation might be tied to specific value judgements that is the potential weak spot. Second, it is quite correct that a company such as Body Shop, which selects on the basis of adherence to core values, is much more likely to be able to manage the values of the workforce. This, if anything, reinforces the above points – it is precisely because more than mere lip-service to certain value judgements is sought that gives an organisation such as Body Shop the capacity to continue to modify its core values in the light of changed circumstances. Clearly, though, there is a danger that an organisation which requires overt adherence to a set of core values may end up selecting people on the basis of what they express rather than what they really believe. Where this might happen (and this is not to suggest that it does at Body Shop) then the organisation will run the risk of falling into the kind of totalitarianism discussed in Part I.

In some respects the argument presented above is consistent with the kind of view presented by Kohlberg and his supporters[5] but it comes from a different kind of starting point. Kohlberg presumes that the more general the ethical structure the more developed it is, and then he draws from this the conclusion that it is appropriate to aim for a value system in which individuals are less bound to individual value judgements and more concerned with overall principles. The argument here, however, is that values of whatever sort rest on a large supporting network of ideas, and the concentration on specific value judgements ignores the fact that change is as likely to happen at the lower level as at the higher.

A closer kind of view is that of Bolman and Deal,[6] who state 'In an increasingly pluralistic and secular world the solution is not for organisations to impose a narrow ethical framework on their employees. Such an approach would not work and would not be desirable if it did.' Although their analysis is based on different, more Kohlberg-influenced, lines, the key issue of how values link with the context in which they operate is an important feature of the above quotation. The analysis given in these two sections has built upon that, and taken it in a broader interpretation that includes not just the external context but also the internal context of what lies beneath the explicit value judgement.

These last two sections also mirror the argument of the previous chapter, that ethical codes are valuable only as process, not as result. Here we have seen that the end-point, the code or ethical directive, is not particularly effective even in its own terms. We shall now look at another issue that is central to the management of people's ethics in organisations – reward.

10.3 The fruits of virtue – intrinsic *versus* extrinsic reward

Harvey-Jones again: 'In the reward area, I believe public recognition is almost as important as financial reward. Public praise is very seldom given... We are quick enough to admonish... but all too seldom do we actually give praise, ...even more rarely when an outstanding effort has been made but has not succeeded... We have in my company a system of good work bonuses which are totally unsystematized... the receipt of such a bonus has an effect far outside the regular annual rise... the importance of the good work bonus, or the public recognition, is in its very unexpectedness.'[7]

The quotation above picks out some important themes. First, the contrast is made with financial reward – in organisational terms, reward is seen as so bound up with payment that the two terms are almost regarded as synonymous. Second, the idea of praise as a reward, and its rarity in day-to-day organisational life. Third, there is allusion (more overt in the full text from which the above is extracted) to the idea of reward not for achievement but for effort. Lastly, the idea of expectation is posited as a key factor in people's perception of what counts as a reward.

This section is not intended to provide a full-scale critique of organisational reward strategies. Rather it is targeted at the idea that reward is a key means of influencing people's behaviour and hence a crucial tool in the process of managing people's values. First, what is a reward? For the transfer of something, be it financial, emotional or material, to be regarded as a act of reward, the following conditions would seem to be individually necessary and jointly sufficient:

- The item transferred must be perceived as a benefit, at least by the person who transfers it.
- The transfer is a form of recognition that some action by the person to be rewarded has been worthwhile either in effort or outcome terms.
- The selection of that individual for that action to be rewarded is non-arbitrary.
- The reward is for something over and above normal expected behaviour.

These proposals sharply distinguish between reward and payment. The financial consideration involved in a contract of employment is better described as a compensation package, *reimbursing* an individual for the use of their labour power, rather than *rewarding* them. A useful way of clarifying this is to consider the opposite – punishment is generally taken as the contrary to reward. Yet the withholding of someone's normal pay is not necessarily a punishment. Though it could be as a result of disciplinary action in some circumstances, more often than not it is simply breach of contract. As the Harvey-Jones example illustrates, there is something of the *celebratory* about the idea of reward. The final comment emphasises that this is not a simple transactional element, but involves something that goes over and above this – as a means of recognising behaviour that itself has gone over and above what is normally required.

Another point in the Harvey-Jones quote is salient to much business practice. Praise is rare and expensively won, criticism is cheap and frequent. The emphasis on the negative is inevitably destructive in all but the most unusual cases – most people feel that what they are doing is justifiable, so denunciation is almost always perceived as unfair. So a blame culture is unlikely to result in significant improvements in behaviour, but will certainly have a lot of resentful people wandering around – probably spending a fair amount of the organisation's resources making sure they don't get blamed the next time. There is a link with the emphasis on specifics. As Francis Aguilar points out, blame cultures harp on about what should not be done, but they take what should be done as a given, hence it is not generally perceived as standing out from the norm, and so is rarely singled out for praise or reward.8

One key distinction that is drawn in this kind of discussion is that of intrinsic *versus* extrinsic motivation. This distinction has some resonance with Herzberg's two-factor model, but links motivation more specifically with what is internal to the work itself as opposed to what is outside it. Laurie Mullins characterises the difference as being that extrinsic motivation relates to 'tangible' rewards such as pay, promotion, or conditions, whilst intrinsic is related to 'psychological' rewards such as challenge, achievement, appreciation, being treated considerately, and so on. He also reflects that whilst the latter groups is often under the control of line managers, the former is usually not.9

The main problem that this distinction highlights is probably best illustrated by Figure 10.1. In each box, there is a type of reward mapped against the cause of the reward. Each of the four has been classified in terms of the frequency with which such a type might occur, what it may be given for, how clear the criteria might be and how easy it is to decide when they apply.

The problem this displays is that tangible reward (or punishment) is most frequent mainly because it is easy to apply, less open to direct challenge. This in itself is a result of looking at specific acts, but means that the tactic is most easily applied when rules are broken. In short, it helps create a blame culture, because this is so easy to administer. By contrast, none of the other categories are easy to apply – there is a potential to challenge them. For acts-in-context the structural problem is that no-one can be too sure what goes on in someone else's head, and the hard-pressed manager is not going to waste too much time trying to find out (not because they may not want to, but because it just takes too long). So the difficulty of establishing context diminishes the likelihood that it gets done. A further problem with giving a tangible reward for an act-in-context is that the merit of the reward is likely to be unclear – one person's hard work is another's heroics. For a psychological reward of either kind there is the additional issue of what actually counts as a reward – it will vary from person to person depending on a number of factors.

	what is perceived as ethically relevant		
reward type	specific acts	acts-in-context	
tangible	frequently assessed	rarely assessed	when assessed
	breach rather than conformity	heroics	what is rewarded
	clear criteria	unclear criteria	criteria
	unambiguous application	ambiguous application	ambiguity
psychological	rarely assessed	rarely assessed	when assessed
	extremes of either	potentially any behaviour	what is rewarded
	clear criteria	clear criteria	criteria
	ambiguous application	ambiguous application	ambiguity

Figure 10.1   Ethical rewards

The problem, then, is how to reward ethically praiseworthy behaviour? The mechanics of fairness, embodied in some of the proposals outlined earlier in this section, work against the flexibility necessary for rewarding people for what they have tried to do, rather than for what they have achieved. Once selections are made for reward then appeals are likely, unless the criteria are very clearly spelt out. But these cannot be spelt out in a way that will take full account of the platform beneath the explicit value judgements and choices someone makes. On the other hand, if the rewards are psychological, although appeal is an inappropriate reaction there is the potential for resentment, and the possibility of a high level of misperception of what is or is not a reward. All of the following have been recently suggested to me as potential rewards for conformant behaviour: sponsorship for a course, an international assignment, promotion, a particular desk, even!

What is a manager to do then? Should s/he give up the idea of trying to reward ethically worthy behaviour? Obviously the answer to this must be no. Nevertheless it is a process fraught with difficulty. There is no glib answer, but the central issues must be: (a) how can one establish what counts as a worthwhile act when the contextual issues have been taken into account (including what has gone on inside someone to generate the intention in question)? and (b) how can one establish what will be perceived by individuals and the work team as fair, not just as a reward for one individual but as something withheld from others?

One last point concerning reward mechanisms, particularly where they are related to tangible rewards. There has been some suggestion that the effect of performance-related payment is relatively short-lived. The payment is perceived as a positive benefit, both in financial and in psychological terms, but over a period of time (relatively short – some indications are that it is a matter of weeks only) becomes seen as the norm. The expectation is created that the following year will bring the same level of reward (an expectation that line managers find difficult to resist, because of the potential demotivation it can engender). I want to suggest that this finds a parallel in tangible rewards for ethical behaviour. Where specific reward is given, the pressure is to see it in pure act terms. One situation represents a considerable achievement in moral terms for an individual, and hence a reward is given. The next time a similar situation occurs, however, it is not likely to be so great an achievement – the individual has thought through how to deal with it. So they will have, in a sense, devised a kind of mental technology to process the issue. The same outcome, therefore, represents a different act-in-context, but it is a brave manager who refuses the prize. So there is a gentle, downward decay into a kind of transactionalism, whereby all acts of a certain kind are deemed to be 'worth' a certain 'price'.

In this chapter we have looked at two issues. The first is the question of whether managers should look to behaviour in itself as the object of ethical management, or the behaviour as understood in a certain context. The second issue is the question of what counts as an appropriate reward mechanism for ethically worthwhile behaviour. The two issues are related in that the temptation for managers is to focus on acts themselves – these are clearly definable and thus more directly open to being influenced, as well as providing a simple basis for rules and rewards. The problem is that ethically valuable behaviour is rarely definable in simple terms – intention is always a key contextual element. Also it is easy for an act-orientated management style to degenerate into marking the points at which rules have been violated, creating a blame culture, with all its destructive effects on motivation.

Whilst these may seem like rather pessimistic conclusions, they are not entirely so. All managerial activity involves the ability to fulfil corporate objectives whilst steering through a variety of different pitfalls, be these financial-, technical- or people-orientated. In identifying the problems associated with rewarding individuals and with the prime vehicle of ethical evaluation, we have not provided solutions, but we have flagged up some key issues that managers will need to take into account when formulating their solutions. In others words, we have helped to provide criteria for action, rather than suggest actions in themselves.

In the next chapter, we shall look at what might seem a separate aspect, that of organisational learning, but it will twist back to some of the points outlined here, and hopefully help to provide some more positive options for those concerned with managing values in an organisation.

Questions

A How is ethically praiseworthy behaviour rewarded in your organisation? How is it recognised and singled out for praise?

B What happens in your organisation when members are perceived to have violated the ethics of the organisation (without actually breaking any disciplinary rules)?

C How far is *behaviour* rewarded (that is, compliance) as distinct from *intention* (that is, morals) in your organisation? How far is disagreement and ethical conflict allowed – is it ever praised?

Notes

1. The great danger thrown up by attribution theory is that management may form a view about what motivates this individual on such flimsy evidence as two isolated events.

2. Notice that under different national legislative frameworks such a move may or may not be open to her. In a country where there is tight legislation on sexual harassment any leniency on Vera's part might be itself subject to legal contest. In some countries (such as the UK), if a practice is defined within the corporation as a sackable offence then that in itself allows the manager to take this action, whether or not legislation requires it.

3. See Chryssides and Kaler (1996) Chapter 9.

4. My own familiarity with the play is derived from its film version (Miller, 1997).

5. Kohlberg (1976).

6. Bolman and Deal (1991) Chapter 10.

7. Harvey-Jones (1988) p. 91.

8. Aguilar (1994) pp. 112–14. He complains that '...rewarding ethical behaviour is one of the least exploited opportunities for ethical leadership'.

9. Mullins (1996) p. 481.

11 *How Stakeholders Learn an Organisation's Values*

In a ground breaking article[1] Alan Mumford pointed out the vast range of opportunities that everyday organisational life presents for learning. This formed the basis for a model of learning from experience that he and Peter Honey proposed and expounded, and which has been extremely influential on how development processes in organisations are conceived and understood.[2] The central point that Mumford emphasised, which will provide the keystone of the argument in this chapter, is that people do not learn in neatly compartmentalised periods. It is not an activity that people can turn on at one time and turn off at another. It is more like a pathology. This is highly significant for any attempt to manage the ethics of an organisation, for it means that whatever is done in pursuit of creating a greater sense of value cannot but be put through this mechanism of continuous learning. This has general implications about managerial behaviour, but it will also be seen to have some surprisingly specific consequences.

In Chapter 4 we looked critically at value management in terms of the objective of securing a level of consensus. This was primarily fixed on the idea that managers might attempt to control the development of people's attitudes, but in doing so they would almost inevitably treat these in simple, explicit terms, overlooking the complexity to be found within an individual's value system. We have encountered echoes and extensions of this point in later chapters as well. In this chapter I want to focus on some of the opportunities that are presented to a manager by this propensity people have for continuous, almost uncontrolled learning.

11.1 Managing learning

Learning is traditionally seen as a directly manageable process. Organisations have training and development managers, learning centres, courses, mentors, action learning sets, and other bits of soft technology all intended to ensure that individuals have the appropriate capabilities for effective job performance. The central plank of this panoply of management processes is this issue of ensuring that people are able to do the job, their current one or a future range of jobs. Only relatively recently (say, the last 15 years) has the management of acquired attitudes and values come to be seen as a legitimate objective of secular and non-militaristic organisations, mainly in the wake of the 'discovery' of culture as a relevant concept for organisational analysis.

It would be going too far to suggest that all this is a waste of time. But it is legitimate to indicate what kinds of assumptions are being made about learning here, whether these are really valid, and what this implies about the way people acquire or change their values in relation to their experience at work – or elsewhere. Note that the discussion is focused on learning as it pertains to values. Hence issues such as how people best acquire skills of dexterity, for example, or become fluent in other languages, is not particularly relevant (although the discussion may throw up some implications for these).

Recall first some of the elements relevant to people's values, as discussed in Chapter 4. These included:

- underlying values, feelings, concerns
- strategies for applying values in concrete situations
- factual beliefs
- perception of general conventions of argument and debate.

How are these learnt? The answer may seem clear in the case of, say, factual beliefs – we would seem to learn these by coming to conclusions on the basis of how we synthesise evidence from a variety of sources, including experience, raw data, other people's interpretations, documentary and other textual sources, and so on.

In a different way strategies for applying values may be learnt – someone may hold a particular value and in different contexts conclude that it implies this or that about the situation. As things turn out, they may realise that certain factors that they thought were relevant happen not to be so, and that other things seem more pertinent than was previously believed. So they develop approaches out of trial and error.

Certainly we learn about conventions on argument, analysis and debate through experience and reflection. Someone in her first job quickly discovers that meetings are conducted in a certain fashion, and that certain kinds of move are appropriate, and others not allowed. As she gains greater experience of the variety of organisational practices, she discovers that the conduct of meetings varies from organisation to organisation, and is strongly conditioned by the nature of the industry as well as by the nature of the national culture. All these elements are also components of what is learnt in this sense.

It is not clear whether we can talk about 'learning' underlying values. These seem to be things we just have – we may vary them, we may drop them or pick up on new ones, but the acquisition is not obviously a learning process. Nevertheless, whether something is developed, acquired or jettisoned will certainly depend on what the individual learns in the other areas.

11.2   An example

So far we have described loosely how the idea of learning links with the acquisition of values. Let us consider a concrete example in these terms.

| BOX 11.1 | **Interview with a Regretful Manager** |

Interviewer: Tell me about the most difficult situation you have faced as a manager.

Manager: I was under pressure to achieve results, and we had this bloke who was, well he wasn't very good. He wasn't a weak performer in the normal sense of the word, but the rest of the department were very enthusiastic, worked way over their official hours, really put themselves into the job. This man, I'll call him X, he was a bit of a time server. He got his basic work done alright, but he never gave that bit extra, he never did any development work. He wasn't at all popular with the others and he complained a lot – frankly a lot of the time he was a pain in the backside. I discussed it with my line manager, who said if he wasn't pulling his weight along with the rest of the team he'd have to go. I did say I couldn't put my finger on any exact misconduct or incompetence that would stand up in an IT [Industrial Tribunal][3] but my boss said he'd find one. I stressed that I needed total back-up if this was to work, and he said he'd give me it.

Interviewer: And?

Manager: We found a loophole to give him his marching orders. I discovered he'd originally been employed about eight years previously on a contract that allowed him a limited amount of flexi-time. We'd changed all that when the new payment scheme came in 18 months ago, but hadn't really enforced it. It wasn't relevant for most people because they worked long hours anyway, and it wasn't really that much of a do with Mr X. Occasionally he took a Friday afternoon off, but I didn't

---

BOX 11.1 (cont'd)

often notice because it was my day in lieu of working weekends. Well we stopped it – he was just going out one afternoon and I asked what he was doing and when he explained it was his flexi-time I just said he couldn't go. Well he did, so we disciplined him, gave him a final written warning. The next Friday he did the same – it was obviously deliberate, so we sacked him.

Interviewer: So what happened then?

Manager: He went to a Tribunal and our case was thrown out because we hadn't followed the proper procedure. I was then scapegoated for being the person who had started it all. My manager copped out of taking any responsibility. X got a good pay-off, I was disciplined, and I suspect it barred me from promotion within the company. I did try to discuss it with my manager, about the total support and all that, and he said he had given me it, but I'd gone too far. When I heard that I gave up.

Interviewer: What do you think you learnt from this?

Manager: Well, I learnt a lot about people I worked with. I thought I knew my boss, but I realised I didn't at all. He was much more of a slippery customer than I ever believed. I also found out a few things about my team. I thought they didn't give a monkey's about Mr X, but they really closed ranks when we sacked him. And I suppose the biggest thing I learnt was never to trust someone in the workplace, however much you think you know them.

The kind of experience that the manager in Box 11.1 had is probably familiar to any readers who have been involved in disciplinaries relating to individuals who are weak but not hopeless – organisations are often tempted to push such people out rather quickly, and it often ends in tears for all concerned. The rights or wrongs of this are not under consideration here. It is the learning that is central. Before thinking about what the manager learnt, let us focus on *his* manager, the boss who seemed to give support and then seemed to withdraw it. We shall suppose below that the account given by the junior manager is an accurate description of what happened.[4]

What might have been going through the mind of the line manager? Clearly, many things relating to saving one's own position, avoiding too much blame, and so on. But in learning terms, what would the manager have thought was going to be the result of his actions? It is implausible to suppose that the manager would have thought 'Now he'll never trust me again, and he'll probably be totally resentful, and probably somewhat difficult to manage over the next few months.' Hardly likely that this would be intended. Might the boss acknowledge that this might be the consequence but decide that this was a price he was prepared to pay? Possibly, but if someone had gone that far one might think that they would take a few steps to limit the damage, perhaps by taking the team manager aside after the adverse result and talking them through what had happened, and maybe by attempting to avoid disciplinary action. In the situation as recounted there is no way of telling whether something like this was considered and rejected. I want to suggest that sometimes another response occurs – that the senior manager, out of embarrassment or out of guilt, overlooks this aspect altogether. A risk assessment is made that this side of the events doesn't really matter. 'He'll get over it', or some such thought, insulates the senior manager from what has happened to the attitudes and values of the more junior one. In some such cases, then, a senior manager is likely to overlook, disregard, the potential negative learning that may have taken place.

Now consider what the junior manager has said about what he learnt. First, there is factual material that he has picked up – he probably exaggerates when he talks of not trusting his manager at all; what he means is that he could no longer trust his manager in serious situations where their interests may conflict. What does the UK colloquialism 'a slippery customer' really mean here? Standard use of this phrase suggests that it is difficult to pin someone down (hence their opinions 'slip' out of someone's grasp like a wriggling fish). In this situation the boss was pinned down, but it transpired that what he said was not honoured. This might be evidence that he had not meant it in the first place, but it is at least as likely that he had meant it at the time and went back on it when he saw what the consequences were – dishonourable certainly, but here we are just trying to understand what might have gone on, rather than judge it. Probably the most plausible interpretations of what the manager says are: (a) that he cannot predict with any great confidence how his boss will behave in difficult circumstances; or (b) that he *can* predict with some confidence that his boss will not honour *promises* and will violate trust. For the purposes of this discussion these two have the same importance, though they are obviously very different assertions. In both cases, though, it is clear that the junior manager will in future hark back to the memory of this event when considering what to expect from the more senior manager.

The junior manager mentions the views of his team. He has learnt something about them, but this is also likely to provide an additional finesse on his general views about people's loyalties at work. So there is a specific factual element as well as a generalisation affected here. What he does not mention is what they may have learnt about him. In this respect he mirrors what we have said above about his own manager.

The junior manager also talks of learning 'not to trust people' in a more general sense. This would be an odd statement to make, were it not for the fact that many people do say such a thing! How does one learn not to trust people? Is it the same as learning not to trust the safety of thin ice? Is it clearer to say that he has *chosen* not to trust people? In some ways this may be so, but bear in mind that the idea of not trusting people is an explicit value judgement. The learning is concealed in the underlying platform. What might be regarded more plausibly as the learning here is that his previous factual beliefs about the likelihood of people violating trust have been confounded. He has learnt that trust involves in some contexts taking a bigger risk than he previously supposed. At this point, his other views, beliefs and feelings have not adjusted to this new belief. Hence the manner in which he conceived of trust has for him lost one of its key supports. Not surprisingly he feels that this means that trust has no support at all. In practice it is likely that some reconciliation of beliefs will occur later – probably he will find a way of re-interpreting trust differentially, between individuals he feels more confident of, and those similar to his boss.

A lot of learning has gone on here and, as alluded to above, we have not really looked much at what the senior manager may have learnt, and not at all at what the other staff may have concluded. The key problem here is the mismatch between what is thought to have happened and what really has happened – in learning terms. The junior manager has drawn conclusions that may have some justification to them regarding his own actions in the future. He has not at all reflected on future actions of others. The senior manager in his turn may or may not have considered the implication of what he has done, but this has not been manifested explicitly.

We could summarise the above analysis, so far as the junior manager goes, as follows:

factual beliefs – changed regarding predictability of the line manager
underlying values – probably unchanged
strategies for applying value – changed due to realignments in the underlying platform
discussion and argument – changed in contextual terms.

The disturbing thing about this scenario is the lack of recognition of how *out of control* learning is. If asked, both the junior and the senior managers would claim, quite sincerely, that they were concerned about the way their staff develop; they might well talk about the courses they send the staff on, and the various other procedures that we dubbed earlier as 'soft technology'.

They would doubtless be offended by the idea that their day-to-day actions were anti-developmental. Yet in terms of creating a positive ethical culture this is a conclusion that is difficult to resist. The junior manager seems unaware of any learning on the part of his team, or of his own manager. The latter is unlikely to have reflected to any great extent on what the junior manager thinks of it all. Both have behaved in a way that is damaging to any cause of promoting a greater sense of value within the organisation.

This is not a story about bad management – thought the scenario is hardly one of high levels of practice. It is rather one of how an apparently non-learning type situation in practice makes a considerable impact on people's learning, and not a particularly beneficial impact, at that. We shall develop this further in the next section.

11.3   The pathological learner

What is meant by the idea that learning is out of control in organisation? Clearly not that managers cannot do anything about what people learn. They can and they do, in the form of explicit training and development activities as described earlier. What is meant is rather that this does not scratch the surface of what people learn in the work situation (or anywhere else for that matter). Learning is, for want of a better phrase, a natural part of the human condition. People are continually developing theories about a whole variety of different aspect of their circumstances, adducing evidence (sometimes repelling contrary evidence) reforming their views, testing them out, and so on. Most of the time this goes unnoticed, and is not managed or promoted, arising out of everyday experiences and activities. I shall call this 'incidental' learning. Much of what is learnt is regarded as too trivial for someone to bother formally recognising it as such. Someone gets a new desk lamp; they have to find out what is the best angle and position for the lamp to be in. This is trivial, and hence ignored almost all of the time, but it is learning nevertheless. It is the recent acknowledgement of the huge amount of learning which passes by unrecognised that has led to the idea of accrediting prior experiential learning (APEL) in the UK and the USA. The idea is that many people have gained significant levels of understanding and capability through their life experiences that have not been regarded as appropriate for formal recognition in the past.

Not all unrecognised learning is quite so mundane as the lamp example might suggest. There may be learning of new skills, new work methods, new opportunities. For this discussion the key categories covering a great deal of the incidental learning that may take place in an organisation are:

● factual beliefs about organisational processes

- factual beliefs about people's behaviour
- links between different elements in someone's platform
- contextualisations of values and value systems
- appropriateness of different strategies of application of value judgements.

Incidentally, these are not independent. I may learn something about how appropriate my application of a certain value is and at the same time be developing a fresh understanding of how context bound my values may be.

We have seen how an example of bad management practice can lead to a wide range of learning, most of which is not conducive to good relationships in the organisation (and therefore is unlikely to promote high levels of performance). Let us consider delegation as a management practice.

A manager comes to one of her staff and asks him to take the responsibility for producing the next quarter's performance figures, which are required by the board. This person has been selected because he is well motivated, generally competent in the relevant skills, and it would be a useful development activity for him. The manager explains the process she normally goes through to produce the figures, and checks that the employee understands. She also discusses with the employee tolerances of error, areas of potential difficulty in getting accurate data, and so on. She then agrees a reasonable deadline for completion of a first draft, sensibly keeping a good period of time in reserve in case it has not been done properly. The manager periodically checks that everything is going smoothly, and when the draft is produced by the employee she finds only a few areas for improvement – these mainly centre around the fact that the employee has tried to make some improvements to the process; the line manager disagrees and asks him to do it in the way that he has been shown. Delegation has been successful, and the employee is generally happy to take this on as a regular part of his work.

This is a regular kind of management event – very much described in functional terms, and in those terms successful. It is not obviously a value management field. So where is the learning here relevant to the management of values? Obviously there is a lot concerning task completion, but that is not likely to influence values. The key elements that are likely to affect value management are:

- mutual perceptions between the employee and the line manager
- perceptions about the importance of the task being delegated
- beliefs about capability and performance.

Possible determinations of these elements are as follows:

- **mutual perceptions between the employee and the line manager**
  - trust of the line manager that the employee will cooperate with the job
  - trust of the employee that the job being delegated can be done

- **perceptions about the importance of the task being delegated**
  - the line manager feels that the job is important enough to explain to someone else to get it done properly
  - the employee may feel that it is a job which the line manager does not want to do
  - the task may be perceived as intrinsically undesirable

- **beliefs about capability and performance**
  - the line manager believes that the employee is capable of doing the job
  - the employee is flattered that they are seen as capable of doing the job
  - after producing the final draft, the employee is less flattered because what he believed to be enhancements to the process have been rejected.

Of these three categories, the last is of peripheral importance, mainly restricted to the issue of the role of praise and encouragement. More important are the first two categories. Mutual perceptions between the employee and the line manager are a lifeblood of organisational performance. Relationships between a manager and the people she or he manages tend to ebb and flow with the vicissitudes of organisational life. Nevertheless, a manager can help to steer these in a certain direction, for example, by taking pains to recognise achievement and minimising the attention paid to weakness or substandard performance. Equally a manager may inadvertently allow events to steer the relationship in a negative direction simply by overlooking these. This is part of the lesson of the regretful manager described in Box 11.1: both managers fail to take explicit notice of the possible implications of their acts for others, and in doing so fail to take any opportunity to manage the learning that inevitably does take place.

One area in which the manager in the delegation example runs a risk of incidental learning running counter to what she would probably want is in the area of the attempted enhancements that the employee made, and that were rejected. The chance is that the employee might perceive the action in one of the following ways:

- the manager does not like me taking control
- the manager always wants things done her way and no other

- the manager doesn't understand what I was trying to do
- the manager doesn't like taking risks
- the manager correctly avoided a difficult situation arising.

Note that one of these is a positive perception (and even then someone might feel aggrieved at the manner in which the correction was made) and the others are negative. As we said before, good management is hard! The point is that whilst the manager may well have a good reason for preventing the employee making too many changes right away, in doing so she runs a risk that there will be a negative impact on the employee's attitudes. One kind of event of this kind is probably tolerable, but several in a short space of time may well change the employee's overall perception of his boss.

The question of how the delegated task is perceived is much more variable. A keen and self-regarding employee might well feel that it is vitally important (that's why it has been delegated to them!), whereas one with a more retiring disposition might perceive it negatively. The issue is not so much whether either is right but more the fact that it may be difficult for a manager to establish clearly which is the case, and it is probably too fine an issue for many managers to take the time to find out.

But consider what may be the knock-on effects where someone does perceive this as an undesirable task, or even one that, while not intrinsically undesirable, is one that the manager wants to off-load. It creates the suspicion that the manager is not 'really' interested in the development of the employee but has used this as a smokescreen to dump a dull job. It may lead the employee to assume that the manager is restructuring her own work for reasons of personal advancement, for example.

The nub of this section is that people will form perceptions and opinions about what is happening almost compulsively. Managers often act in a way that is myopic to this aspect, not necessarily because they deliberately choose to deceive themselves as to the feelings and motives of their staff (though sometimes that might be true) but because *they simply don't think of it*. Learning is not generally regarded as pathological, so it is not considered a likely consequence in many organisational situations, and thus the management of it is relegated to formal activity intended to produce certain outcomes. Incidental learning is ignored by this, and is therefore a major problem for managers – one that they do not even know is there. The most dangerous assumptions are the ones we don't know we're making.

One important footnote to this analysis, as with the other points made in this chapter: what goes for employees goes also for other interactive stakeholders.[5] The customer whose impression is not considered when receiving a less than perfect service is a classic and well known kind of example – they walk away, of course, sometimes leaving the organisation little idea of what was done wrong. It is less well recognised that suppliers are often in a particularly privileged position to evaluate the performance of an organisation, and suppliers are sometimes also customers. So this is not simply a point about employee relationships, but a wider one about how values of all parties may be managed well or badly.

11.4   Transparency

Consider the model of how people arrive at explanations of organisational events given in Figure 11.1.

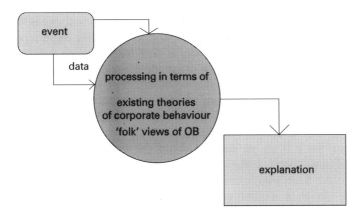

Figure 11.1   Organisational explanations

Three large items are connected by some very thin threads. The supply of information is crucial to the process of how people explain what is happening in an organisation. This is interpreted or processed in the light of people's existing beliefs and theories of how well management is disposed towards the staff, and in terms of people's own personal ideas of how organisations in general work. From this they come to a conclusion, an explanation of what is going on. Now, one key implication of the incidental learning model we have discussed above is that this process occurs *no matter how complete the flow of information is*. In other words, people will form views about what is happening whether they have a large amount of information or a little. This is not irrationality in itself – though it would be if people did not accept that their views are often highly underdetermined by the evidence they have before them. It is rather an inevitability – what I said earlier was just part of the human condition. In the light of this, consider the two versions of this process illustrated in Figure 11.2.

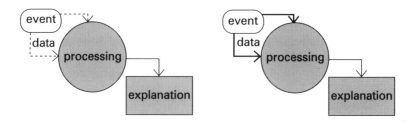

Figure 11.2   Over- and under-determined organisational explanations

The single difference between the two examples given above is that in one there is a meagre flow of information, and in the other there is a full flow. Crucial to the management of values is that *the processing will go on all the same*. Whether managers provide a lot or a little information makes no difference to the process of forming explanations, it changes only the quality of those explanations. As nature abhors a vacuum, so the human mind abhors the unexplained, and will fill the vacuum with some kind of account, however sketchy or under-evidenced.

However, there is an asymmetry about the process, which makes things yet more complicated. Individuals have beliefs about how much information to expect from managers for given types of event. Where decisions or events are trivial, it is often presumed that there will be no filter on information, and where something is sensitive it is often presumed that there will be a strong control on what information is provided and when. It is a great condemnation of management styles of the past that such assumptions have grown up, but they have and are now a fact of organisational life. These beliefs are themselves neither entirely rational nor irrational (regrettably they are unlikely to be based on nothing at all).

Where information is restricted, not only will people's spontaneous capacities for forming explanations go to work but also the very fact of information not being readily available becomes part of the situation. In simple terms, people will presume that if they're not being told then there must be some significance to this – usually it is presumed that the news is bad. This is likely to operate at all levels. Certainly, at the strategic level people immediately begin assuming that there are redundancies in the air, but it is just as relevant at the operational level of line management, where the presumptions take on a more individual aspect (for example, *I'm* not being told because *I'm* going to be made redundant). In the kind of situation depicted in the left-hand example in Figure 11.2, therefore, not only will individuals seek to explain the situation on a basis of limited information, they will also do so with an additional belief that the lack of information is significant. 'They must be up to something, because we don't know what's going on.' This is the stuff of complete fantasy sometimes, but it is a key to much mismanagement of organisational climate. Perhaps the worst contributor to this is the 'need to know' culture. If people are excluded from information deliberately, they will take it as confirmation that what they are being isolated from is important and, 'obviously', detrimental to them.

What does this imply about managerial behaviour? Simply that transparency is to be promoted in organisations for reasons other than that it is ethically desirable. Far more importantly, it is the best way of having any chance of managing the values of the stakeholders of an organisation. This is not to say that every manager should reveal every item of information to all and sundry. Commercial confidentiality is crucial for organisations – not just in a competitive environment either, though that is the most obvious field. But what the above discussion does emphasise is that where confidentiality is required there is a potential risk of misapprehension, one that particularly works against the effort to manage values. Part of this is because openness and honesty are generally perceived in the abstract as desirable, as virtues. Any behaviour on the part of managers that limits information flow is certainly perceived as a lack of openness, whatever the justification a manager may offer for this. Also, though, the restriction of information is often perceived as tantamount to dishonesty. People feel that if their manager conceals information from them, they are in effect acting in no essential way differently from when they lie. At first sight puzzling, the response is based on the assumption that honesty is less about telling the truth *per se* (though that is included as a necessary condition) and more about preventing deception, a point we discussed in Part I. Seen in this light, failure to tell some or all of the truth results in people being deceived (or at least running the risk of being deceived). Hence the manager may be perceived as being dishonest because she has made no attempt to minimise or prevent her staff adopting incorrect beliefs.

This section has not explored transparency in detail. The concept itself is not as clear as some accounts might suggest – for example, the extent to which a manager takes into account the existing background knowledge of his or her staff may well affect whether what they do is transparently presented or not. Hence there is an issue about whether transparency is a feature of how a manager acts or represents a feature of the relationship between one party and another.

Nevertheless, the key message of the above discussion is founded in the idea that transparency represents the full flow of information from managers to other stakeholders. As we have seen, this is less a virtue in itself and more a necessity for effective management of values.

11.5 Leadership

In the final section of this chapter I shall not attempt a full-scale analysis of leadership and its role in ethical management. I shall look at one or two specific aspects and relate them to the discussion in this and previous chapters.

The first of these is the idea of leadership and example. One of the most frequently criticised statements is 'Do as I say, not as I do.' This represents a clear personalised version of the conflict between someone's espoused theories (that is, what I say) and their theory in use (what I do). It is generally seen as poor leadership style, and I have no disagreement with this. The point I wish to make is that this springs naturally from the analysis given above. Someone's acts are decoded, interpreted, in the light of: (a) the information provided on that particular situation; (b) what people already believe about the manager concerned; (c) the interpreter's own value system, in particular the specific breakdown between their explicit beliefs and what underlies these.

People seek explanations primarily for the *actions* of those around them. The statements that are made are not normally taken as definitive, but are generally treated as one piece of evidence to fit in with what else is available. Where there is a misfit between statement and behaviour it is not usual that the verbal evidence outweighs the physical. When a member of staff witnesses a particular act by a manager (the point could as easily be made the other way round, of course) they put together the evidence of what they see with the other categories of evidence outlined above. So the behaviour takes on an interpretation. If the manager denies the interpretation, the denial is placed against the interpreted behaviour – only if the denial is vehement, or if it squares with the previous theories of that manager's behaviour, is it likely to topple the impression that the action has created. This is why 'do as I say, not as I do' is so singularly ineffective – it tries to point to the weaker source of evidence to overturn the stronger.

The other side to this is that whatever a manager might say, the example of their behaviour is creating the theories that the staff will have of them. Where these theories are unflattering, it is rare that the manager will have any access to them. So managers are often likely to be deluded about how they are perceived by others. Clearly, techniques such as 360 degree appraisal have a potential to break through this, though there can also be barriers to honesty even given this approach.

The last point I wish to make is that the emphasis on leadership tends to overplay the functions of power and authority in the cluster of roles that leaders are often expected to play, and minimises the extent to which value management, and particularly the management of perception and learning discussed above, operates in the behaviour of effective leaders. Krech *et al.* outlined a model of leadership that identified fourteen different roles a leader might play.[6] A selection of these may give a flavour of how far good leadership involves management of values:

- external representative of the group
- purveyor of rewards and punishments
- arbitrator
- exemplar
- symbol for the group
- ideologist
- father figure
- scapegoat.

It need hardly be mentioned how far someone's behaviour under these headings will influence the values of the team the person is leading. But following the argument of this chapter, it probably hardly needs adding now that this is not a simple mechanistic cause and effect link – 'If I do this, people will see me as [for example] a father figure and respect me.' The crux is that the various behaviours of the leader will be fitted together to form a model of what kind of person they are. This will be conditioned by the culture of the organisation, the organisational theories-in-use to which the individual members of the team subscribe, and their own personal levels of perception, which in turn are strongly influenced by the structure of their own values. In short, managing values is a complex business, and the effective leader is one who recognises this and realises that it is a long process, slowly built up over years and easily wrecked by a few ill-chosen words.

Notes

1. Mumford (1981).
2. Honey and Mumford (1986), although they acknowledge their debt to Kolb (who in turn has acknowledged his debt to Lewin).
3. For the reader unfamiliar with British employment law, industrial tribunals are a legal mechanism in the UK for dealing with individuals' employment disputes. They are rather like small courts that deal with employment matters such as unfair dismissal.
4. Not really a realistic assumption, but convenient for the purposes of this discussion.
5. I use this phrase to exclude parties who may have some interest in the operations of an organisation but do not have any interactive relationship with them – the most notable example might be the generations of the future, who may well be significantly affected by what an organisations does now, and hence (with a stretch of the term) might be considered as stakeholders, but by definition they have no dealings with the organisation.
6. Krech, Crutchfield and Ballachey (1961).

12   *Ethics as its Own Worst Enemy*

In this final chapter we shall turn away from the issues relating to how an organisation can (or mainly cannot) manage the values of its members, and consider the question of how 'ethics' as a field impacts on business practice. We shall see that the influence is largely an unfortunate one.

12.1   The 'ethics' industry

Andrew Stark, in an article in the *Harvard Business Review*, complained that business ethics as a subject of study had largely failed to have the impact on management practice that he (at least) hoped for.[1] He bemoaned that the field was too theoretical, had yet to become an ethics of practice, and that whilst it was long on discussions of right and wrong, it had not come to terms with those of right *versus* right (or, as the material of Chapter 2 might suggest, less wrong *versus* more wrong). In a not dissimilar style of critique, though coming from the other direction, Bruce Macfarlane has more recently argued that ethics as a component of the business education field can all too easily be too narrowly vocational in its orientation, with the result that it loses its distinctive critical edge, becoming 'little more than a strand of corporate strategy in disguise'. This echoes in much gentler fashion some remarks made by Peter Drucker, '"Business ethics"... is to ethics what soft porn is to the Platonic Eros. Soft porn too talks of something it calls "love". And in so far as "business ethics" comes even close to ethics, it comes close to casuistry and will, predictably, end up as a fig leaf for the shameless and as special pleading for the powerful and wealthy.'[2]

Clearly the existence of radically opposed criticisms of the same area suggest a subject matter that has yet to settle down. Whilst it is true that there has been speculation about ethical issues of business activity for as long as there have been ethics or businesses, it is fair to say that it has only relatively recently been seen as a distinctive feature of business activity or education. Whilst this is better than being ignored altogether, the development of a field as a feature of business education can be a mixed blessing.

Consider the kind of process that a subject will go through in becoming a part of the business curriculum, a process which creates a whole industry around it. A few key researchers or writers begin alluding to a subject area as holding some value for general business understanding and practice. Trailblazing initial research identifies more concretely the potential of the discipline to improve some aspect of business. Individuals begin to study the subject at undergraduate or MBA level, so textbooks are written for those students. Teachers begin more detailed research into the area, and produce their own research monographs and journal articles.[3] One side of an industry is created – an academic side – but there also grows a demand for this study to become more closely attuned to the practical needs of business (like the Stark comments mentioned above). So a secondary industry grows up, concerned to turn the academic field into something directly applicable. Whether or not this secondary element develops rapidly or slowly depends on external influences. In the case of business ethics, senior managers and legislators were brought to the field as a result of the various scandals of the 1980s and 90s (they don't seem to abate – during the period during which I have been writing this book there have been reports of misconduct in several large UK financial organisations). Leading the ranks of the secondary element are 'gurus', consultants, business school academics who turn commercial, and more popular writers.

It is generally this second tranche of activity that brings the area into public view. In doing so, the features of a market in business 'knowledge' create their own demands on the subject of study. For example, items of such 'knowledge' acquire product characteristics – such as a life-cycle. This can create the impression that management theory is a series of fads and fashions. Not that this is necessarily always detrimental. As Abrahamson has argued, the existence of management fashion does not suggest that the fashions themselves are trivial. But he does suggest that these are at least as often the results or symptoms of the general business environment than they are determinants of greater levels of business effectiveness.[4] Thus national and organisational cultures, technical contradictions, changes in labour relations and macro-economic fluctuations can all in their different ways affect the growth, surgence and demise of management ideas.

A second market-driven feature of the 'management knowledge' industry that is relevant here is the issue of high value *versus* high volume. Cast in terms of management ideas, this means high quality ideas that have been tested either empirically or analytically, and that carry with them all the necessary provisos about the multi-disciplinary and multi-functional nature of organisational management, as opposed to simpler, sloganised, but much more clearly and comprehensibly expressed perspectives that may have a less complete supporting background. High value also implies high cost – not in the sense of price, but in terms of the cost to the consumer as measured by the effort needed to establish the connections between the concept or technique in question and other elements of their management practice or business understanding. Put simply, if it's sound it's probably hard to master.

Yet another aspect of this is the need to publicise and promote management 'knowledge'. The 'guru' becomes especially important here. In an intriguing study of the business process re-engineering (BPR) phenomenon, Bradley Johnson demonstrates how the language and behaviour of key gurus played a central role in the growth of interest in the idea. Johnson argues convincingly that the best ways of understanding their role is by comparison with 19th-century evangelists and with dramatic performers.[5]

This market-based analysis of the generation, celebration, and ultimate demise of management ideas works at different levels and speeds depending on the nature of the idea. So a technique or perspective such as management by objectives (MbO), total quality management (TQM) or BPR may well have a life-cycle of merely a few years. On the other hand, a wider field such as work study may have a considerably longer one.

This is not intended to suggest that such ideas and techniques have no intrinsic value. On the contrary, a market can come into being only because potential consumers perceive some value in the commodity offered. But the analysis, though incomplete, does underline that the very existence of management ideas as commodities has a significant effect on their impact on business.

In concrete terms, how has this affected the growth of interest in business ethics? In the next section we shall explore the effects. The two aspects that are most important are those that were described earlier as consequences of management 'knowledge' being subject to market forces, that is: (a) the high turnover of ideas; and (b) the secondary market of high-volume, low-cost material.

12.2   Market-driven hypocrisy

How does the turnover of management ideas impact on business practice? At least three separate dysfunctional effects can occur:

- degeneration of management capability
- constant out-of-datedness
- low quality ideas not properly implemented.

Management capability

Management ideas are intended to be tools to help the manager to operate more effectively. Many books on business ethics try to offer a toolkit at some point.[6] The danger here is that the use of a toolkit can lead a manager away from developing her own ability to analyse situations. When in doubt, she reaches (not always metaphorically) for the book, and reads off the solution. Obviously this is not always how authors intend their texts to be used, but the high-volume approach, and the inevitable low cost (that is, easy-to-read style) that this requires creates such a possibility. In constantly using a particular approach, taken from a text, as a solution to a management problem, the manager is not necessarily being lazy, but she is certainly deferring the need to think through herself the appropriateness of the answer. In using someone else's expertise, the manager fails to create the conditions in which she will learn from her experience – by trial, error and eventual success. The person mentioned in Chapter 9, who phoned up a consultant and asked if they could use a copy of some other corporation's code of values, is an example of this tendency, one that much modern management writing encourages rather than inhibits.

Out-of-date

A turnover in ideas means that at any one time there will be concepts and techniques that are brand new, others that are mid-cycle, and others that are perceived as out-of-date. This has nothing to do with how useful they may be, and everything to do with the forces that drive changes in management thinking. Because even the flimsiest of introductions of an idea into the practice of an organisation takes some time, every managerial practice can be regarded as having been superseded by some other, hot off the presses. Hence every organisation could be regarded as operating with an out-of-date set of managerial tools.

New ideas, relatively (or sometimes absolutely) untested, can be seen in black-and-white terms. The exposition of a concept or technique is usually made in abstraction from the contextual variables with which it would interact. So the mode of presentation of the idea is: if we do this, that happens. The old ideas, now in operation, can be seen in all their greyness, subject to qualification, constraint, and dependent for their success on the interaction of many other variables. So their mode of presentation is rather different: in these circumstances, with these resources, with this staff, given our existing levels of service, customer base – and so on, and so on, – when we do this, that happens. Hence the new becomes a potential saviour, a clear, black-and-white solution to all the problems we've been having with this limited, grey, old and above all *compromised* technique we've got at the moment. Not only is the multi-functional and integrative nature of the management task abstracted and oversimplified to the point of fiction, but furthermore the processes, techniques and ideas that go to make up the operations of the organisation are all diminished precisely because they are implemented. The temptation is then for managers to see what has not been put into operation as different – this is a mistake. Management ideas are good and bad, but this is rarely the reason why they are introduced, which is much more to do with the nature of the knowledge market that we discussed earlier.

Low quality, poor implementation

So, as a result of the apparent drabness, mediocrity and essentially compromised value of the old, the new seems to hold a seductive power – a concept which abstracts from that drabness and is therefore all too often perceived as an appropriate solution. As Abrahamson points out,[7] the market for management ideas grows significantly when the economy is in a downturn, or when a manager is having technological difficulties or experiencing labour problems. In other words, the approach read in the book or seen in a 'living Technicolor'-style presentation acquires the perceived attribute of being a solution to those labour problems, or diminishing sales. But as I have mentioned above, the new idea is actually almost always presented in isolation from how it will be implemented, and hence the most critical issue is omitted. This derives from management ideas as commodities – they have to be presented as somehow differentiated from other similar 'products'. What is common to all these 'products' is the fact that they have to be integrated with the complex of organisational processes and systems, so *that*, ironically, is what gets left out. The idea is thus highly oversimplified. In appearance it looks like a brand new, magic box of tricks that will solve the most intractable of problems. In reality it will be only as good as the latent management competence of those who will implement it.

These are general points, as applicable to new approaches to marketing as they are to managing values. The main implication of all this for values and ethics is that managers are likely to become enthused about new possibilities for explicit values without recognising that for every individual the larger and more significant part of their value system is the platform discussed in previous chapters, the underwater, majority segment of the iceberg. One example of this was the 'green' fashion of the late 1980s. As a result of a focus on environmental issues in the developed world, retail businesses, particularly in the food and petrochemical sectors, become imbued with 'greenness' overnight. Company logos were changed, corporate colour schemes were amended to ensure that lots of deep green could be included, the ecofriendliness of various products was emphasised, and promotional activities became focused on ecological attributes. But in fact these companies hardly changed. Many were in any case trying to make their operations more ecologically friendly as required by legislation. Many others made no attempt to make significant changes. Some introduced new lines but retained the old lines alongside – so that in the UK it was possible to buy organically grown produce, such as carrots, as a specialist line, whilst the 'ordinary' carrots were still available (usually much cheaper) and often displayed some distance away in the store to reduce the likelihood of direct comparison. Petrol pricing structures quickly adapted to the new demand for unleaded fuel, with the introduction of different unleaded grades, a top grade being comparable in price with the old, leaded, high octanes. Thus petrol companies could satisfy the public concern, but retain their existing product range, maintaining or even enhancing revenues without easing the overall cost burden on consumers or national economies.

Strong though such a judgement might be, it is difficult to avoid the conclusion that here was a cynical attempt to exploit a new feature of customer's attitudes, without making any serious changes to operations. How can such hypocrisy have come about? In part, it results from a failure to understand the key division of people's values into the explicit judgements and the underlying complex or platform of other supporting or underpinning beliefs and feelings. But this in turn does not get a grip in this situation unless there is also the prevalence of ideas that are presented to the business community in simple – too simple – terms. In the above situation, the whole idea of environmentalism can become reduced to the single image of 'green'. This can seem like an excellent form of communication – as the saying goes 'Keep it simple, stupid!' But the weakness of keeping it simple is that for a management concept, which has to be operated in the multivariable complex of organisational practices and extreme levels of uncertainty in the business environment, simplicity is bordering on falsehood. Thus 'being green' seemed to food retailers to be a matter of purchasing organically grown fruit and vegetables, eliminating CFC aerosols, and so on. Some, more enlightened, corporations recognised that business processes may be implicated, thus paper reduction and energy conservation programmes were introduced. But few considered their company car policies, even though a significant proportion of the air pollution in USA and UK cities could be attributed to company fleets.[8] Fewer still considered the implications of their food purchasing policies for soil conservation, despite the established connection between intensive farming and land exhaustion. Even fewer would have taken account of any consequences of credit management and capital management policies in green terms. Yet the notorious tendency for large organisations to keep their small suppliers waiting for payment of invoices inevitably increases the number of small business failures, which represents the loss of an input of resources – that is, waste. Similarly, the practice of many large organisations of utilising excess cash by placing it in short-term, high-yield investments contributes, albeit indirectly, to the increasing demand for good short-term results for equities and securities at the expense of the long-term development that is characteristic of much of the non-Asian financial system. This is not to say that all such practices are wrong – simply to point out some of their consequences, and the conflict between these outcomes and the stated credo of ecological responsibility.

It is not that all large corporations are hypocritical (but nor can we absolve all from such a charge). The example is meant simply to show that a simple idea, neatly encapsulated by an attractive slogan or, in the above case, by a single colour image, can actually operate against the deeper development of a value. Once the organic carrots are on the supermarket shelves, senior managers can say 'Well, we're green. We're alright. We've covered that aspect.' In practice they have hardly scratched the surface. Simplicity, that ideal of good communication, is the enemy of managerial understanding.

Ricardo Semler echoes many of the points made above when he discusses the transferability of Japanese management ideas to other cultures. 'If you must borrow from Japan, don't forget to fill a 747 with enough Japanese to fill your factory.' He then goes on to relate how he came across a group of workers in a Japanese shipyard based in Rio de Janeiro singing the company song. 'If by succeed you mean that half the people at the shipyard were exercising because they thought it was the best route to promotion, then it was a success. If the goal was to integrate the employees, build respect for their leaders, and meditate on the importance of the company in each worker's life, then they are on the wrong side of the ocean.'[9] In other words, the simplicity of the idea of a high commitment unitary organisational culture deceived managers into believing that it was simply transferable.

There is a related issue relevant here, which has been referred to previously. This is the ethical 'halo' effect. To remind the reader, this is the tendency for individuals to put on an 'ethics halo' when discussing values, responsibility, and so on. As has been mentioned before, we're all in favour of virtue, and against sin. So a dialogue that is couched in those terms leads people almost inevitably to reflect on their ethical concerns and feelings rather than on the actualities that may often conflict with these. It is extremely difficult to focus on one's own unethical acts, and even when someone does become aware of them, embarrassment and self-justification tend to produce the classic attribution effect discussed in Chapter 1; people identify the locus of control in such a way as to place themselves in the best light possible.

The combination of halo effect with the excessive simplicity of some approaches to management, and to business ethics in particular, makes managers want to be what they are not – thoroughly virtuous ethical beings.[10] As a result of this, self-deception leads managers – and non-managers as well – sometimes to adopt positions that are wholly unrepresentative of their real behaviour. For example, one study found that the more senior a manager was, the less tolerant she was of fraudulent behaviour.[11] One reading of this, naturally, could be that senior managers are more ethically concerned. An alternative, however, is that they are too divorced from the day-to-day operational details of their business, and hence become too idealistic.

We can castigate this as hypocrisy if we wish, but it is a hypocrisy that virtually everyone who is alive has practised in some form or another. It is also worth recalling that to *call* someone by such a term is almost bound to create fierce defensiveness, precisely because the individual concerned perceives their behaviour in more sympathetic terms. There is a clash of loci of control that blocks agreement about the nature of the behaviour under discussion, even when the individuals concerned might have the same basic value system, platform and explicit judgements as well.

In this section we have seen how the market for business ideas has a critical influence on the nature of those ideas, and the consequent impact on managerial behaviour is, by and large, to oversimplify. The implications of this for the management of values are that managers tend to misrepresent their own behaviour and attitudes, and tend to project themselves and their organisations in terms that are usually literal falsehoods. Put like this, it may seem highly culpable behaviour, but in practice it is a natural, if somewhat unfortunate, consequence of the structure of values and the nature of the knowledge market. In the following section we shall look again at the whole idea of 'theory' and how it relates to managerial practice.

12.3   Theory and practice

In this section we shall look at the idea of theory in management, and what it has to do with the behaviour and practice of professional managers. We shall see that there are positive links and negative ones.

First, we might question whether some types of management theory should exist at all. Several times in earlier chapters we have alluded to the apparent redundancy of much theory in the business area. It seems that often a great deal of argument, analysis and research is necessary to tell us what we already know. I shall not give a full-blown defence of the practice of theorising in management studies (or any other branch of applied social science), but there are some considerations that make the idea of researching into what everyone knows 'as a matter of common sense' less foolish a practice than it might seem at first sight.

First, not all theories are that obvious. It may seem pretty redundant to go through elaborate studies to establish whether or not people would prefer to have positive or negative relationships with their line manager, for example. But the idea that such relationships have a greater potential for diminishing rather than enhancing motivation is a substantial viewpoint that at the time of its initial presentation to the business community carried a high degree of novelty.[12]

Second, even where theories do present an obvious point, it is usually in a novel context. For example, the now ubiquitous references to organisational culture are not in themselves reflecting a discovery of a phenomenon that went unrecognised before the late 1970s. Individuals who moved jobs were aware that one organisation might well feel quite different from another, and respond differently, despite similarities in sector, size, business, and so on. What changed was the understanding of how this might affect and be affected by other organisational variables, and thus how managers might be able to manage it.[13]

Third, where field research leads to the confirmation or rejection of theories, there can be a substantial gain simply from having a clear body of evidence supporting a common-sense position. As mentioned in Chapter 1, common-sense positions are, by their very nature, taken for granted. No-one questions that, for example, the most satisfactory way for organisations to meet the needs of their stakeholders is by trying as hard as possible to survive. It seems almost crazy to think otherwise. But eighty years ago it would have been crazy to suggest that the most effective way for an organisation to operate was to give as much power and opportunity as possible to the workforce (not that this is universally accepted these days, but it is regarded as a tenable position when once it would have been rejected out of hand). The idea of questioning the survival instinct of organisations probably *is* crazy – but there has been no formal test of this.[14] Any material that demonstrated the benefits of doing this would therefore represent a substantial gain, for without this kind of confirmation there must remain a doubt that this is a form of flat-earthism. OK, the doubt may be remote, and hardly nagging, but so was the idea of a round world for a long long time. So 'proving the obvious' is a valuable result.[15]

The conclusion to be drawn, then, is that the degree of similarity between common sense and theory is not in itself a useful comparison. Some theories and concepts are very similar to commonly accepted ideas, others are far away from them. Neither is better or worse for that. There is, however, one important point of asymmetry: where a theory is far from 'received wisdom' there is the task of understanding how and why what is commonly accepted is so far away from what theory suggests. But other than that, the validity of a theory is unaffected by how close it is to current practice and attitudes.

This is different from whether an idea carries any *face validity*, which is a different question altogether. 'Face validity' is how acceptable an idea or concept may be to individuals. Clearly, approaches that are remote from existing practice are likely to have a harder job gaining some acceptance than those which look like an extension or confirmation of what people think anyway.

This leads into the second main point of this section. How people respond to ideas in business is less due to validity as it is to do with how acceptable the ideas are felt to be. This in turn depends more on how the ideas can be fitted in to someone's overall conceptual framework than on the soundness of the supporting evidence. Recall Figure 5.2, where we mapped out certain elements of the ethical capability of individuals. Capability in this area was depicted as resulting from the interaction between problem-solving mechanisms and inclinations. What were dubbed 'resolution templates' are a key part of the practice side of someone's conceptual framework; for they represent the kind of *managerial praxis* that someone employs. By 'praxis' I mean a personal theory-in-action that someone uses to get on with their life. Long before anyone learns anything about the formal theory of dynamics, they may learn how best to throw a stone so that it will skim along the top of a still pond. Similarly, before someone encounters any formal theory of organisations they develop their own understanding of factors such as power and culture (often this builds up initially from experiences at school). When I say 'theory' I do not wish to imply that always someone has a fully worked out account of organisations (or skimming stones) but that they have some kind of image of what underlies the experiences they have and the methods they may employ. We don't just develop technologies (hard – throwing, or soft – interacting in organisations) we try to explain them as well. This is another aspect of what in Chapter 11 was described as the pathological drive of people to learn. People theorise most of the time. An important consequence of this is that in doing so, they are creating potential bridges or barriers to ideas that may come to them from elsewhere.

Take an issue such as how far managers release or withhold information.[16] Each manager will have an explicit value judgement on how far information should be shared with or concealed from staff, and an underlying platform of thoughts, feelings, and so on, which will support or underpin the judgement. Part of that platform is a set of links between what the manager believes he should do and a complex that includes both a personal set of beliefs and concerns about issues such as how people respond to being given important items of information or how far disclosure risks loss of information control, as well as factual beliefs about the impact of that loss on competitiveness, labour relations, and so on. It is not that some managers are just more secretive than others. It is that the greater or lesser degree of secrecy inevitably affects and is affected by other elements of the individual manager's attitudes and beliefs and values.

With an issue such as that outlined above, praxis is a kind of rule of thumb. 'I wouldn't tell the staff any more than I have to; once you tell one the whole town will know. I remember when I told just one person about a poor set of results, and before you knew it the union rep was in my office, demanding to know about the redundancy plans.' Here we have a rule or guide to action, very crudely articulated, but resting on prior experience, which itself has been processed in a certain way. We see, then, how a template for resolving ethical dilemmas is thus elaborated on the basis of a 'theory' on predicting people's secrecy behaviour (in this case resting on maybe one critical incident). So the impact of a management idea, such as high consultation as a means of improving worker commitment, has to be made to fit with these factual beliefs underpinning the manager's current practices on information management. A template is unlikely to be entirely jettisoned. The existence of the beneath-the-surface platform creates an intrinsic conservatism to people where values are concerned. Therefore a novel idea or approach has to find some kind of connection with how the individual thinks currently. The existing platform of beliefs is a barrier to too novel a conception, and provides a convenient conduit for more familiar ideas.

At this point you , the reader, might well be saying 'But what you say here doesn't fit with what you said in the previous section. You argue that managers are too prone to get hold of new ideas and put them into practice without thinking through what is involved. Now here you're saying that someone doesn't easily take to new ideas, and that people are essentially conservative with values.'

This does look paradoxical, but there is no real conflict. The point of the previous section is that people do take on ideas without having thought through how they will impact on what is actually out there in the organisation. Here I am saying that people don't take on something new unless they feel there is a link with what they already think or feel. In other words, people grab ideas without looking at the reality, but the ideas they grab are the ones that seem to fit with what they already believe. So there is no conflict, but it does emphasise the importance of face validity as a determinant of organisational change. We can summarise these points as follows:

- The inherent value of a management idea is not necessarily connected with the manner in which it is adopted by managers or organisations.
- Critical to the acceptance of a management idea is the kind of 'face' validity that it possesses.
- Face validity is determined by the fit between an idea and the underlying platforms of beliefs and values that an individual already holds.

Going back to the market aspect of management knowledge, an implication of the three statements here is that the best marketed ideas are ones in which managers can find a wide variety of resonances. The slogan or image that is consistent with a wide range of concerns and ideas is more likely to be successfully adopted by managers than one that has a more limited set of perceived connections. At first sight this seems reasonable – a survival of the most suggestive. But the key here is that the associations are perceived. The process is not dependent on how rich *are* the links between ideas, practices and realities, but how rich are the links that people *see* between them. Writing style, and expressive proliferation, can easily carry the weakest of ideas – and possibly the weakest ones are the best for this – into many hearts simply by the imagery and nuance of language employed. Too specific a message is likely to be restrictive on the range of chords struck in people's own minds and hearts. So a broad – dare one say, vague – idea has a greater chance of being accepted. A good writer, like a good orator in classical times, is more likely to have a powerful impact on societies and organisations than a good thinker. Of course, good presentation is important, but the risk of creating spurious 'understanding' by means of facile but seductive associations is a significant one.

Theory clearly should and does influence practice. What we have seen here, though, is that the influence it may have is less to do with its intrinsic value as an idea about how organisations might operate more effectively, and more to do with the kind of presentation they receive. This is in some ways not greatly different from other applied studies, but that of course does not diminish the importance of the point. Theory in a practice-driven area such as management is as much to do with how people perceive the ideas involved as it is with their essential worth. How people perceive ideas is in turn as much to do with how they are presented as it is with what is actually meant.

This underlines the points made earlier in this chapter. Managing values, and the whole idea of business ethics, are vulnerable to being hijacked by highly effective presentational material at the expense of good quality ideas. Quality in this context is directly connected with creating understandings of how the many elements and factors affecting values and behaviour in organisations interact.

12.4   The future of ethics as a business discipline

In this final section I want to outline how I think ethics might impact on organisational management in the future, although I fear that it will continue to be subjected to the forces described in the previous two sections. This may result in the same kind of process that sociology, psychology and other behavioural disciplines have experienced when applied to management, of being reduced, in the name of accessibility and comprehensibility, to a shadow of their own reality.

The history of management thought over the last hundred or so years is one of continued re-evaluation of the relationships between human and technical aspects of work. The ultra-rationalism of the 'scientific' management theorists, such as Frederick Taylor, conceived of the management task as essentially mechanical. The only behaviour of workers that was recognised as relevant to corporate life was effort directly aimed at productive work – all else was ignored or castigated.[17] Human relations and socio-technical systems approaches first recognised that people do not conceive of their work solely in mechanistic terms, and then attempted to identify how personal and organisational processes and needs may be made more compatible with each other. The 'discovery' of culture led to the development of more integrated models of how people contribute to organisations, such as total quality management and human resource management.[18] The idea of managing values as a tool of corporate strategy comes from this source of management theory, which could conveniently be located as starting around the early 1980s. By contrast the idea of *ethics* as a separate tool of management related much more closely to specific behaviours is much more a phenomenon of the later 1980s and 90s. Conventionally the genesis of this is perceived as the major scandals of the time – issues such as insider trading, the persistence of tobacco companies in refusing to acknowledge that cigarettes are harmful to health, and ecological disasters stemming from environmental irresponsibility are often cited as key demonstrations of the need to influence the ethics of people's behaviour.

Macfarlane[19] identifies two dimensions of the study of ethics in business: one is whether the study is about business or for business, the other is theory as opposed to practice. He argues that part of the business ethics curriculum must include reflection about business, rather than merely providing tools for business. By contrast, a writer such as Pearson seems to be firmly in the 'for business' category, and at times seems to see business ethics as a unified field with a well defined and agreed set of aims. Talking of three different groups of people interested in business ethics, he says 'these three groups are not wholly separated; many individuals belong to more than one constituency. Moreover, many share the same broad aim, though their detailed agendas may have been somewhat different in emphasis.'[20] Given the argument of this chapter, if there is such a commonality it would be a worrying thing, for the prospects of developing a sound and detailed 'for business' form of business ethics that takes account of the multiplicity of the relevant elements and issues are, in my opinion, poor.

What contribution can 'ethics' make? First, the two non-overlapping waves of concern about values and ethics mentioned above suggest two different kinds of contribution that the field can make. One, the traditional 'ethical' one, is related to the drive to improve the image or business, and the need to ensure that individuals stay within agreed standards. It is essentially a compliance function, stemming ultimately from the wish to answer questions of what should be done (that is, normative). The other, the regard for managing values that originated in the early 1980s, is a broader field that is more to do with interpreting behaviour. Until recently the primary format in this area was also normative – 'create shared values', 'praise the staff every day', 'walk the talk', and so on. In being written with an excessive *for* business focus these approaches have neglected that some underpinning study is needed. There must be some material *about* business for tools, concepts, and normative directions to have some basis other than just simple preferences. The need here is to gain a greater understanding of what values people really hold, how these behave under the pressure of corporate communications and initiatives, and how far value management is really possible at all.

The present text has leant more towards this second field. Whereas the narrower study of ethics draws primarily from philosophy and to a lesser extent from areas such as political theory, the approach here has been a study of values drawn from philosophy, organisational behaviour and human resource management. The key relationship between them is that it is not possible to establish what people ought to do and hope that this will have an impact on how organisations operate until one has a good idea of what people actually believe and how these beliefs may be amenable to change – or may not. Ethics requires an understanding of values. The theme of this book has been largely sceptical of the possibility of getting sufficiently clear an idea about people's values as to be able to manage these with any great degree of success in an organisation. Perhaps this is a feature of the age. We may be at the equivalent stage with the theory of organisations that medicine was in when leeches and blood-letting were standard cures, and surgery was seen as a lower and extremely risky activity. My own prejudice is that the sheer quantity of data we need to collect on people's attitudes is so large and so potentially variable, both in its content and its interlinkages, that for practical purposes we may have to accommodate ourselves to a permanent pre-scientific stage in this field. If we at least accept our limitations, that may be a good start.

Notes

1. Stark (1993).
2. Drucker (1981); Macfarlane (1996).
3. The reader will doubtless be aware that these comments are somewhat self-referential.
4. Abrahamson has a balanced view on management fashions, seeing them as having strengths as well as weaknesses. One area where the present discussion varies from his is in the genesis of fashions, which has been presented in two stages – an initial academic or technical one, followed by the development into a fashionable 'knowledge product' (1996).
5. Bradley Johnson (1996).
6. Thus, Trevino and Nelson give their 'Eight Steps' (1995 p. 71), and Laura Nash (1990) has several boxes of questions at different points, intended to help the manager get through what she calls the endemic roadblocks of business ethics.

7. Abrahamson *op. cit.*
8. I owe this insight to Tony Emerson – see Emerson and Welford (1997).
9. Semler (1993) pp. 272–3. This quote probably epitomises much of the argument about deep understanding of values.
10. A phenomenon Sartre called 'bad faith' (1957) and Kierkegaard 'double mindedness' (1944).
11. Harris (1990).
12. The reader may recognise here an obtuse way of referring to the work of Frederick Herzberg (1974).
13. Although the argument of this text has been largely sceptical of the idea of managing culture, as a large part of this is managing values.
14. To the author's knowledge.
15. It is of course a myth that there is a single body of ideas that everybody agrees is 'common sense'.
16. An interesting normative account of this issue is to found in Pompa (1992).
17. So the rational economic behaviour of groups of workers to try to keep unit rates up, by a combination of activities which deflected management from recognising that an individual could perform at a higher level of output (at least over relatively short periods of time) was decried as 'soldiering.' See Rose (1988).
18. In one of the guises of the latter. For an account of the different meanings of the idea of HRM, see various contributions in Storey (1991).
19. Macfarlane (1996) p. 171.
20. Pearson (1995) p. 24.

Conclusion

In this book I have tried to give some substance to the idea that values are too complex to manage directly. The question we are left with is: what should managers do about it? One option is unacceptable – to give up. We couldn't do this even if we wanted to – everyone is managing other people's values every time they make just about any kind of comment.

The best attitude to take away from a text such as this is simply to log it and then keep it on one's mental desk – don't file it away, because the ideas and their value for you will then fade. But keeping it on your mental desk doesn't mean watching for definitive changes in how you manage individuals – or cope with being managed – so much as evolving a change in perspective, a change in the way you see what is happening. Above all, I would suggest that the central issue is the extreme frailty of our knowledge of any but the most superficial aspects of someone's personality. So-and-so is a quiet type. What makes them that? What experiences led to the quietness, and what beliefs does so-and-so hold about their own quietness and indeed of the value or significance of quietness? Ethics as presented here has been more a branch of applied psychology than of business strategy.

What does all this imply for management development? Above all there should be a far greater emphasis on interaction and personal development. The manager who has internalised how difficult it is to be sure what others really feel or hold dear is already one important step along the way of being more sensitive to others. This is crucial for business success – good salespeople, for example, get sales because they can sense what a potential customer really wants, and they show the person how their product or service will meet that. Good strategic managers know that all the paper planning in the world will go for nothing if they cannot take the energy and commitment of their staff with them in a new venture – hence they have to question what the staff really want, and what would be the key benefit that would make an idea acceptable. Managing means managing values. Managing values means understanding them. Understanding them means knowing the limits of your understanding.

This is not something you can teach. It can be encouraged and developed, but that is a voyage of self-knowledge. It is not captured by the presentation of a battery of tools and techniques (the standard source of solutions to management problems). Values and ethics are basically too dear to be made technical. But they are far too dear to be ignored. The new global economy we are moving into will ensure that. What it will also do is force each of us continually to re-evaluate our positions. This will create great changes in national, organisational, and personal values, and as a result the lives of our grandchildren will be very different from ours – not solely in technical terms, but in personal terms, just as the kind of lives those of us in the EU and USA lead are far more cosmopolitan than those of our recently industrialised grandparents, whose lives were themselves far different from *their* rural grandparents. The world is changing – we must give ourselves the capacity to change with it and ahead of it.

Bibliography

Abrahamson, E. (1996) Management fashion, *Academy of Management Review,* 21(1): 254–85.

Adams, Dawn (1995) Psychometric testing through the eyes of some users, *Selection and Development Review,* 11(1): 5–6.

Aguilar, Francis J. (1994) *Managing Corporate Ethics*, New York: Oxford University Press.

Argyris, Chris (1957) *Personality and Organisation*, New York: Harper & Row.

Argyris, Chris (1993) *On Organisational Learning*, Cambridge, Mass.: Blackwell.

Bain, William (1993) Advancements in empirical business ethics research methodologies, paper delievered to British Academy of Management conference.

Bartolome, Fernando (1991) Nobody trusts the boss completely – now what?, in 'Ethics at work', *Harvard Business Review*, Boston: Harvard Business School Press.

Belbin, Meredith (1981) *Management Teams: Why They Succeed or Fail*, London: Heinemann.

Berne, Eric (1968) *Games People Play*, Harmondsworth: Penguin.

Bhide, Amer and Stevenson, Howard (1991) Why be honest if honesty doesn't pay' reprinted in 'Ethics at work', *Harvard Business Review*, Boston: Harvard Business School Press.

Bolman, Lee and Deal, Terrence (1991) *Reframing Organisations*, San Fransisco: Jossey Bass.

Bronstein, David (1980) *The Chess Struggle in Practice*, London: Batsford.

Campbell, Andrew and Tawadey, Kiran (1990) *Mission and Business Philosophy*, Oxford: Heinemann.

Carr, Albert (1968) Is business bluffing ethical?, *Harvard Business Review,* Jan/Feb.

Chatwin, Bruce (1987) *The Songlines*, London: Viking Press.

Chryssides, George and Kaler, John (1996) *Essentials of Business Ethics*, London: McGraw-Hill.

Ciulla, Joanna (1991) Business ethics as moral imagination, in R.E. Freeman (ed.) *Business Ethics*, Oxford: Oxford University Press.

Cole, G. A. 'Personnel management in theory and practice', London: DP Publications.

Cook, M. (1993) *Personnel Selection and Productivity*, Chichester: Wiley.

Deal, T. and Kennedy, A. (1982) *Corporate Cultures*, Harmondsworth: Penguin.

de George, Richard (1993) *Competing with Integrity in International Business*, Oxford: Oxford University Press.

Dickson, Anne (1982) *A Woman in Your Own Right*, London: Quartet.

Drucker, Peter (1965) *Managing for Results*, London: Heinemann.

Drucker, Peter (1981) *The Public Interest*.

Emerson, Tony and Welford, Richard (1997) Defining the problem: diagnostic tools to explore the evolution of unsustainable practices in organisations, in *Corporate Environmental Management 2: Culture and Organisation*. Earthscan.

Festinger, L. (1957) *A Theory of Cognitive Dissonance*, Illinois: Stanford.

Forsyth, D. R. A.(1980) Taxonomy of ethical ideologies, *Journal of Personality and Social Psychology,* **39**(1): 175–84.

Frost, Peter, Mitchell, Vance and Nord, Walter (1995) *Managerial Reality*, New York: HarperCollins.

Gergen E. (1991) *The Saturated Self*. Basic Books.

Goleman, Daniel (1997) *Vital Lies, Simple Truths*, London: Bloomsbury.

Green, Ronald M. (1994) *The Ethical Manager*, New York: Macmillan College Publishing.

Griseri, Paul (1989) The Master of the Passions?, PhD thesis, Canterbury: University of Kent.

Hampden-Turner, Charles and Trompenaars, Fons (1993) *The Seven Cultures of Capitalism*, New York: Doubleday.

Handy, Charles (1993) *Understanding Organsations,* 4th edn, Harmondsworth: Penguin.

Harris, J. R. (1990) Ethical values of individuals at different levels in an organisation, *Journal of Business Ethics,* September: 741–50.

Harris, Thomas (1973) *I'm OK You're OK*, London: Pan.

Harvey-Jones, Sir John (1988) *Making it Happen*, London: Fontana-Collins.

Hatch, Mary Jo (1997) *Organisational Behaviour: A Postmodern Perspective*, London: McGraw-Hill.

Heron, John (1984) *The Facilitator's Handbook*, London: Kogan Page.

Herzberg, Frederick (1974) *Work and the Nature of Man*, Cleveland: World Publishing.

Hofstede, Geert (1991) *Cultures and Organisations*, London: Sage.

Honey, Peter, and Mumford, Alan (1986) *A Manual of Learning Styles*, Maidenhead: Honey.

Hume, David (1888) *A Treatise of Human Nature*, Selby-Bigge L.A. (ed.) (1957), Oxford: Clarendon.

Johnson, Bradley (1996) Re-engineering the sense of self; the manager and the management guru, *Journal of Management Studies*, **33**(5): 571–90.

Johnson, C. and Blinkhorn, S. (1994) Job performance and personality test validities, *The Psychologist*, 7: 167–70.

Jones, T. M. (1991) Ethical decision making by individuals in organisations, *Academy of Management Review*, April: 366–95.

Kant, Immanuel (1948) Groundwork of the metaphysic of morals, reprinted as Paton, A.J. (ed.) *The Moral Law*, London: Hutchinson.

Kierkegaard, Søren (1944) *Either/Or*, trans. D. Swenson and L. Marrin Swenson, Princeton: Princeton University Press.

Kohlberg, Lawrence (1969) *Stages in the Development of Moral Thought and Action*, New York; Holt, Rhinehardt & Winston.

Kolb, David (1985) *Experience as the Source of Learning*, London: Prentice Hall.

Krech, D., Crutchfield, R. and Ballachey, E. (1962) *Individual in Society*, London: McGraw-Hill.

Laing, R. D. (1970) *Knots*, London: Tavistock.

Langer, Ellen (1991) *Mindfulness*, London: HarperCollins.

Lawler, Edward (1973) *Motivation in Work Organisations*. Brooks/Cole.

Levi, Primo (1988) *The Drowned and the Saved*, London: Michael Joseph.

Lewin, Kurt (1952) *Field Theory in Social Science*, New York: Harper & Row.

Lindsay, R., Lindsay, L. and Irvine, V. (1996) Instilling ethical behaviour in organisations, *Journal of Business Ethics*, **15**(4): 393–407.

Luft, Joe (1971) *An Introduction to Group Dynamics*, New York: National Press.

Lyon, David (1994) *Postmodernity*, Buckingham: Open University Press.

Manley, Walter (1992) *The Handbook of Good Business Practice*, London: Routledge.

Maslow, Abraham (1954) *Motivation and Personality*, New York: Harper & Row.

McCoy, C. (1985) *Management of Values*, Boston: Pitman.

McDonald, D. and Pak, P. (1996). It's all fair in love, war and business: cognitive philosophies in ethical decision making, *Journal of Business Ethics*, September: 973–96.

Macfarlane, Bruce (1996) Reflections on business ethics, *Economics and Business Education*, Winter: 171–4.

McGregor, Douglas (1960) *The Human Side of Enterprise*, New York: McGraw-Hill.

McLagen, Patrick and Snell, Robin (1994) Some implications for management development of research into managers' moral dilemmas, *British Journal of Management*, **3**: 157 ff.

Miller, Arthur (1997) *The Crucible*, feature film, 20th Century Fox.

Morgan, Gareth (1986) *Images of Organisation*, New York: Sage.

Morgan, Gareth (1988) *Riding the Waves of Change*, London: Jossey-Bass.

Mullins, Laurie (1996) *Management and Organisational Behaviour*, 4th edn, London: Pitman.

Mumford, Alan (1981) What did you learn today?, *Personnel Management*.

Munro, Andrew (1995) Put your hands together one more time for the ipsative debate: a reply to Closs, *Selection and Development Review*, October: 1, 2.

Nagel, Thomas (1970) *The Possibility of Altruism*, Oxford: Oxford University Press.

Nagel, Thomas (1979) *Mortal Questions*, Cambridge: Cambridge University Press.

Nash, Laura (1990) *Good Intentions Aside*, Boston: Harvard University Press.

OED (1984) *Pocket OED*, 7th edn, R. E. Allen (ed.), Oxford: Clarendon.

Parikh, Jagdish (1991) *Managing Your Self*, Oxford: Blackwell.

Pascale, Richard and Athos, Anthony (1981) *The Art of Japanese Management*, New York: Simon & Schuster.

Pearson, Gordon (1995) *Integrity in Organisations*, London: McGraw-Hill.

Peters, Thomas and Waterman, Robert (1982) *In Search of Excellence*, New York: Harper & Row.

Pettinger, Richard (1996) *Introduction to Organisational Behaviour*, London: Macmillan.

Piaget, Jean (1954) *The Origin of intelligence in Children*, London: Routledge & Kegan Paul.

Pompa, V. (1992) Managerial secrecy: an ethical examination, *Journal of Business Ethics*, **11**(2): 147–56.

Popper, Karl (1959) *The Logic of Scientific Discovery*, London: Hutchinson.

Rawls, J. (1971) *A Theory of Justice*, Cambridge, Mass.: Harvard University Press.

Rose, Michael (1988) *Industrial Behaviour*, Harmondsworth: Penguin.

Salaman, M. (1987) *Industrial Relations, Theory and Practice*, London: Prentice Hall.

Sartre, Jean-Paul (1957) *Being and Nothingness*, trans. H.E. Barnes, New York: Methuen.

Scheider, B. (1987) The people make the place, *Personnel Psychology*, **40**: 437–53.

Schein, E. (1980) *Organisational Psychology*, 3rd edn, Englewood Cliffs: Prentice Hall.

Semler, Ricardo (1993) *Maverick*, London: Arrow Books.

Senge, Peter (1992) *The Fifth Discipline*, London: Century Business.

Simon, S. (1974) *Meeting Yourself Halfway: 31 Communication Strategies for Daily Living*, Argus Communications.

Snell, Robin (1993) *Ethical Skills for Managers*, London: Chapman & Hall.

Stark, Andrew (1993) What's the matter with business ethics?, *Harvard Business Review*, May–June: 38–48.

Stewart A, and Stewart, V. (1981) *Business Applications of Repertory Grid*, London: McGraw-Hill.

Storey, David (1991) *Developments in the Management of Human Resources*, Oxford: Blackwell.

Strawson, Peter F. (1962) Freedom and resentment, in *Proceedings of the British Academy*, **xlviii**: 1–25.

Thompson, R. and Hunt, J. (1996) Inside the black box of alpha, beta and gamma change: using a cognitive processing model to assess attitude structure, *Academy of Management Review*, **21**(3): 655–90.

Trevino, Linda and Nelson, Katherine (1995) *Managing Business Ethics*, New York: Wiley.

Trompenaars, Fons (1993) *Riding the Waves of Culture*, London: Economist Books.

Vroom, Victor (1964) *Work and Motivation*, New York: Wiley.

Webley, Simon (1992) *Business Ethics and Company Codes*, London: Institute of Business Ethics.

Webley, Simon (1993) *Codes of Business Ethics*, London: Institute of Business Ethics.

Weller, Steven (1988) The effectiveness of corporate codes of ethics, *Journal of Business Ethics*, May: 389–95.

Welles, Orson and Mankiewich, Herman (1941) *Citizen Kane*, RKO Pictures.

Williams, Bernard (1985) *Ethics and the Limits of Philosophy*, London: Fontana.

Wilson, David and Rosenfeld, Robert (1990) *Managing Organisations*, London: McGraw-Hill .

Winch, Peter (1972) *Ethics and Action*, London: Routledge.

Wittgenstein, Ludwig (1953) *Philosophical Investigations*, Oxford: Blackwell.

Index